INDIA: AN ANTHROPOLOGICAL PERSPECTIVE

INDUS R.
KASHMIR
JHELUM R.
HIMACHAL PRADESH
CHENAB R.
PANJAB
PAKISTAN
STULEJ R.
HARYANA
GANGES R.
NEPAL
INDUS R.
RAJASTHAN
UTTAR PRADESH
JAMUNA R.
GUJARAT
MADHYA PRADESH
NARBADA R.
MAHANADI R.
MAHARASHTRA
GODAVARI R.
ANDHRA PRADESH
KRISHNA R.
MYSORE
CAUVERY R.
KERALA
MADRAS
CEYLON

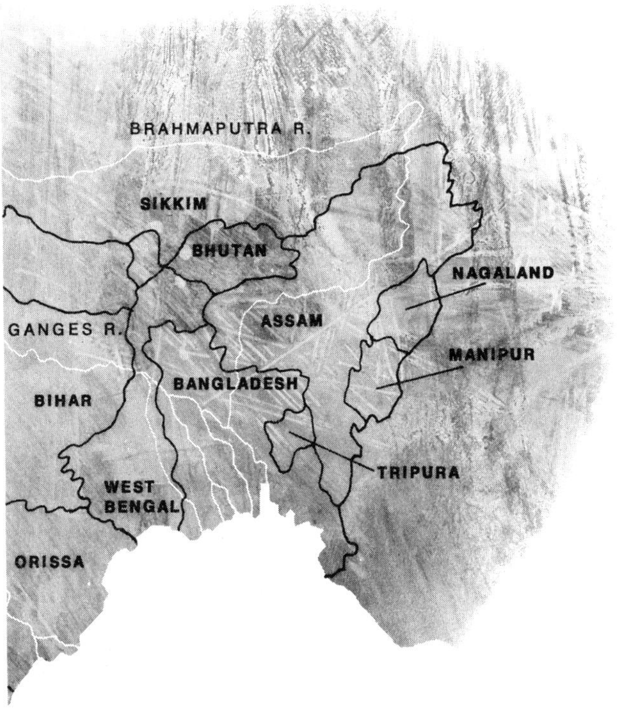
BRAHMAPUTRA R.
SIKKIM
BHUTAN
NAGALAND
ASSAM
GANGES R.
MANIPUR
BANGLADESH
BIHAR
TRIPURA
WEST
BENGAL
ORISSA

GOODYEAR REGIONAL ANTHROPOLOGY SERIES

Edward Norbeck, Editor

ANTHROPOLOGICAL PERSPECTIVES OF:

MODERN EUROPE
Robert T. Anderson

INDIA
Stephen A. Tyler

INDONESIA
James L. Peacock

CIRCUMPOLAR PEOPLES
Nelson H. Graburn and Barry S. Strong

ABORIGINAL NORTH AMERICA
William W. Newcomb, Jr.

Additional Volumes Forthcoming:

Southeast Asia

China

Africa

Philippines

Polynesia and Micronesia

Middle East

Latin America

INDIA: AN ANTHROPOLOGICAL PERSPECTIVE

STEPHEN A. TYLER

Rice University

GOODYEAR PUBLISHING COMPANY, INC.
Pacific Palisades, California

[redacted]

Library of Congress
Catalog Card Number:
72-76937

(Paper) Y-0749-5
(Cloth) Y-0757-8

ISBN: 0-87620-074-9 (Paper)
0-87620-075-7 (Cloth)

Current printing (last digit)

10 9 8 7 6 5 4 3 2 1

Printed in the
United States of America

FOR MARTHA

hṛcchayo vardhate

CONTENTS

PREFACE

There are many Indias—the Sindhu of the ancients, the Āryāvarta of the Āryan invaders, the Bhāratavarṣa of the epic literature, the Jambudvīpa of mythology, the fabulous East of early travelers and adventurers, the Rāj of British Empire, the living, breathing India known to its inhabitants, and the dry, sterile India of geography texts. Each of these is both fictional and real, and each refers to a different entity. So, too, the India of this book is both fictional and real, and refers at times to the India of the ancients, at other times to the India of geographers or to the India as defined by the modern political divisions of India, Pakistan, Ceylon, and Nepal. Needless to say, the India of which I write is the India of scholarly imagination, deriving from the books I happen to have read and my own brief experience of a small, isolated corner of modern India. India as it is known to those who live there remains as fabulous and mysterious to me as it must have to those first Europeans who visited it in the fifteenth century.

ACKNOWLEDGMENTS

Many people have contributed to the writing of this book. Predominant among them are my wife, Martha, and my colleague, Edward Norbeck. Both have provided those vital ingredients—encouragement and criticism. Others have aided me unwittingly. I think first of my teachers and of my friends among the Koyas of India. Too, I owe an intellectual debt to Professors Louis Dumont and Claude Lévi-Strauss—a debt that will be obvious to all who read these pages.

NOTE ON PRONUNCIATION

Vowels marked with a superscript dash (for example, ā, ū) are long. Consonants marked with a subscript dot (for example, ḍ, ṭ, ḍh, ṭh, ḷ, ṇ, ṛ) are pronounced with the tongue curled toward the roof of the mouth. Without the subscript dot, t, d, and n are made with the tongue tip against the back of the upper front teeth. The aspirated sounds dh, gh, and bh are like the combinations sadheart, bigheart, mobheart. Vowels are roughly equivalent to the following English sounds:

a as u in up
ā as a in father
i as i in pin
ī as ee in seek
u as u in bull
ū as oo in moon
e as a in make
ai as ai in aisle
o as o in so
au as ow in cow

Consonants are as follows:

c as ch in chin
ś as sh in shin
ṣ as sh in shin
ṟṟ as tr in patrol
ṛ as ri in rim
ṟ as nder in fender
ṛ̤ as rsh in harsh
ñ as ni in onion
ṅ as ng in thing
ṉ as n in fend
ṁ as m in thump

Other consonants may be pronounced as their approximate English equivalents. In Sanskrit words the accent falls on the next to last syllable when it is long, and otherwise on the nearest long syllable before it. A long syllable contains a long vowel, e, o, ai, au, or a vowel followed by more than one consonant. Aspiration does not count as an additional consonant.

Appendix I contains a detailed discussion of the various language families of India, and Appendix III has a map showing the distribution of language families.

PART 1

On the southern bank of a rocky, unnamed stream in central India, at a place where the cart track from Bastar emerges briefly from the surrounding jungle, there is a small cairn of stones beside the way—the sort of inconspicuous thing one might mistake as the random work of some dusty wayfarers who, whiling away a little time waiting for the oxen to drink their fill, thoughtlessly heaped these stones upon one another. Like so many other travelers, we too paused here in our journey to let the oxen drink and to let the thirsty wood in our cart wheels swell firmly once more against its steel rims. Glad for a moment to look at something besides eternal ruts in a dirt track, I filled my pipe and stared about, looking, but—in the way of all foreigners—failing to see.

Still there must have been something unusual that drew my eye again to that pile of water-smoothed rocks. Perhaps it stayed my glance because its innocent artifice contrasted with the natural tumble of rocks and pebbles surrounding it. Lakṣmayya, seeing what it was that held my interest, reached out his hand and asked for some of my tobacco. I thought he wanted it for himself, but he took the few shreds and scattered them in the crevices of the rocks, uttering the words "mī daya vālē (by your grace)."

At this shrine in the stillness of a hot afternoon, I participated in an ancient rite and thought of all those other peoples, travelers like us, who had paused here, worshiped, and passed on.

ONE

INDIA IN PERSPECTIVE

PERSONAL CHARACTER

Indians are among the world's few truly civilized people. Completely natural and at ease in social situations, they make Westerners look stiff, masked, and uncomfortable both in themselves and with others.

In part, the Indian's competence in social relations derives from the stereotypy of hierarchic relations which enables him to readily identify other actors in a social scene and in general know what to expect from them. The initiatory phases of a conversation quickly establish these identities and expectations with relatively little of the halting ambiguity and uncertainty so characteristic of Western conversational "openers." As between Westerners and Indians, it is the Westerner who is inscrutable. The Indian's social competence is also fostered by two thousand years of life without privacy. Aside from the jungle and the life of a remote ascetic, there is scarcely a place where an Indian can be by himself. From the moment of birth he is constantly surrounded by other people even in his most intimate actions. Privacy and isolated loneliness are not part of the traditional Indian milieu, and one of the world's most pathetic sights is the lone Indian in some large Western city. In a sense, there is no such thing as an intrusion in Indian society. All of one's life is public domain, restricted at times to close kin, but still public. Even one's private business affairs are frequently the object of public scrutiny and there is no more ludicrous sight than the Westerner's obvious discomfiture in his first encounter with an Indian public official who openly and casually discusses the Westerner's private affairs with the coterie of other supplicants and officials surrounding his desk.

The impression of social competence is also part of a deliberate projection of omniscience that is incumbent particularly on high-caste males. Every high-caste man should project an image of total authority and omnicompetence. There is no subject unfamiliar to him and no topic on which he is incapable of pronouncing the authoritative opinion. This, of course, is consistent with the Brāhmaṇ's traditional position in society as the sole repository of all worthwhile knowledge. Authoritative omnicompetence is coupled with what from a Westerner's point of view amounts to an irresponsible disregard for consistency, for yesterday's authoritative opinion is not necessarily today's, nor is it in any way embarrassingly inconsistent with other equally authoritative but, to the Westerner, totally contradictory views on related topics. Indians are eminently expert at "doublethink," entertaining with equal force two totally opposed opinions without feeling mental discomfort. Many Western-educated Indian intellectuals will declare with one breath that the joint family is bad and repressive and should be abolished, only to immediately affirm with the next breath that the values and traditions of joint family life are responsible for the greatness of Indian culture. Or, in the very act of carefully avoiding contact with some poor, untouchable devil in the streets, he will hold forth in rounded phrases on the evils of caste and untouchability. This is not hypocrisy, but it does reveal a fundamental feature of Indian thinking. The moment of dissent or the sense of contradiction is always pushed further and further back, rather than brought to the surface. Here is the mental parallel of the Indian's religious tolerance. Contradictory views are only seemingly contradictory and their opposition is always resolved in a higher, even if unexpressed, synthesis. Just as the competing and seemingly irreconcilable doctrines and deities of different faiths are but chimerical reflections of an underlying unity, so, too, apparently contradictory opinions are mere temporary illusions, poorly refracted reflections of one single, unitary image. This is the mental analogue of the traditional Indian scholastic doctrine of Samanvāya (making different approaches to wisdom accord with one another by referring them to a higher and more inclusive unity). On the whole, Indians are not seriously affected by the kind of cognitive dissonance (the mental discomfort of holding contradictory views) that either paralyzes Westerners or galvanizes them into some action directed at bringing consistency back into their mental lives. Among Indian intellectuals, this disarming of mental dissension promotes a jumbled and uncritical eclecticism. No fact once acquired is too small or insignificant to be carelessly jettisoned and no piece of literature is ever so bad that it can be consigned without qualm to the nether regions of the subconscious. Facts and ideas are indiscriminately garnered and jealously sequestered in whatever mental nook and cranny, and regularly trotted out in irrelevant support of every conceivable doctrine.

In response to a disjointed world dominated by technology, the Westerner is impelled to find refuge in an ever-narrowing fragment of technical competence. Confusing information with knowledge, he substitutes expertise for wisdom. By contrast, the Indian sense of omniscience fuels a jejune dilettantism and the Indian intellectual seeks to project an image of a "renaissance man" equally at home in astrology and astrophysics.

A rigid dogmatist, the Indian intellectual is fond of argument from an axiom. His legalistic turn of mind delights in interminable hair-splitting that scores debate points at the expense of problem-solving. Too, he is subservient to received authority and has a compulsion to quote Sanskrit. Knowledge is primarily knowledge that comes from memory, and rote learning predominates at every level of Indian education. His Western counterpart sins in the opposite direction. Glorifying in problem solutions, he fails to question the validity of the problem. Ever pragmatic, he displaces tradition with novelty.

The Western-educated Indian faces the contemporary scene with something less than equanimity. Taught to value the form of *modernism* or *Westernization*, he also believes that India is the bulwark of *spiritualism* in a world dominated by the *materialism* of the West. Guilty for his concessions to the materialist West, he is driven to search out an identification with the Indian past. Fearful of becoming estranged from his Muslim or Hindu background, he is often filled with nostalgia for the "good" Hindu or Muslim things represented by the old men and women in his family. Questing for this half-forgotten background, he goes to the Pandit or Swāmi who gives him a simple, condensed picture of the old tradition, or he seeks it in the cheap, popularized editions of classical works found in all Indian bookshops. He may even attend Śivānanda's "Forest University" where he receives instruction in English together with generals, high government officials, and wealthy businessmen. Here he is imbued with the notion that he is really acquiring the old tradition despite his inability to use the classical primary sources. What he is searching for is a pattern corresponding with the ascetic tradition—a mode of living in a materialist world without being spiritually contaminated by it. Through it all he is sustained by a belief that even though the West can *do* some things better, the Indian *is* really better. His ambivalence toward the technological achievements of the West is fed by the "*Meru* complex." India is the spiritual core of the world and its mission is to spiritualize the materialist West. This attitude is confirmed and stiffened by the well-publicized antics of such professional Western seekers of spiritual enlightenment as Hollywood stars, rock musicians, and hippies.

The ingrained hierarchy of Indian society creates a set of stereotypic responses to power and authority. Inferiors are expected to be servile and toadying to their masters. Superiors make a great display of authority, ordering their peons about with sharp demands and curt responses. He who approaches a superior must expect to wait in patient and respectful awe until noticed. The same man, humble and deferent before his superiors, becomes a tiger to *his* inferiors, expecting the same quaking submission from them. Down the ladder of hierarchy each in turn plays the role of master and servant, bullying those below and bullied by those above.

The Indian man is a consummate bureaucrat; the pigeonholes and stratified hierarchy of bureaucratic administration suit his hierarchically disposed mind. Too, bureaucracy permits the exercise of power without responsibility. "Unfortunate" decisions are always traceable to higher levels; "fortunate" ones can be made to appear as if they originated from one's own desk. A bureaucratic position is a marvelous fulcrum for power—a place to curry favor with higher-ups, and a solid footing for dispensing favors large and small to allies and potential allies. In a bureaucracy one may appear to make decisions with great reluctance or magnanimity, or refuse to make them with similar reluctance and magnanimity, and in either case the bureaucratic labyrinth facilitates avoidance of all responsibility should that become necessary. Westerners are infuriated by Indian bureaucracy, for they naively believe that bureaucracies are rational instruments designed to fulfill the demands of an official policy. Millennia of experience with bureaucracy have taught the Indian that bureaucracies are instruments of power, designed to be manipulated for one's own ends, not necessarily the ends of official policy.

Power entails a kind of paternalism or *noblesse oblige*. A master is supposed to be like a father to his servants and is expected to come to their aid with loans and assist them in times of distress. So, too, those in authority must conform to a fairly consistent set of cultural ideals. Like the ancient Indian kings who were exhorted to uphold righteousness, an Indian leader should have the object of establishing spirituality. He must be like an *avatāra* (an incarnation of the deity sent to aid mankind) or an ascetic who performs good not for himself but for the benefit of others. He must be deadly serious, dispassionate, and chaste, living in a sort of militant monasticism, his human qualities entirely eschewed. Finally, he should manifest a personal unapproachability and, if possible, wear a uniform of some sort.

Because each caste is in part a separate cultural world with its own distinctive customs and beliefs, it is not surprising that different castes value different personality types, and each caste has a social stereotype. Brāhmaṇs are thought to be pugnaciously intellectual; warrior castes should project an impression of swashbuckling bravado rather similar to the machismo of Latins; Banias are crafty, greedy, miserly, and cowardly; Jats are dense and unrefined; Kunbis are obstinate; Gollas (cowherds) are litigious and full of vice; Kasāis (butchers) are liars, and so on. Whether such stereotypes accurately reflect actual caste personality types is questionable, but the stereotypes do provide a ready-made reference for what may be expected from people of different castes.

Expectations of appropriate behavior and life style vary from caste to caste, but there are some pan-Indian models that all castes are encouraged to honor. Rāma and Sīta, the two principal characters in the *Rāmayana* epic, are held up as ideal personal types for all children to emulate. Little girls identify their appropriate sex role in the submissive, loyal, chaste, and supine Sīta, while little boys see themselves as the dashing, virtuous, domineering, demon-slaying hero, Rāma. Similarly, little girls quickly learn that the only path to glory for a woman runs through men—husbands and sons. Little boys come to know that the strong man always has his faithful allies tied to him by bonds of dependence, and just as mothers buy their children's good behavior with promises of food, a powerful man buys the loyalty of his allies with gifts, loans, and bribes.

Groveling before authority, struggling to extend his scope of power, shifting his alliances, watchfully keeping his own subordinate allies in line, the Indian male is a master politician who seeks power not out of political responsibility or commitment, but for protection and revenge. In a world where the good things of life are strictly limited and the object of constant competitive struggle, a man must enter the arena if for no other reason than self-preservation. Forced from childhood to submit to irrational and capricious authority, a man learns that he can protect and avenge himself only by wresting power from others, and in this *mātsya nyāya* (way of the fishes) world where the stronger devour the weaker, practice of every guile and deceit is not only acceptable but imperative. But one should not give the appearance of coldly calculating advantage. Ready warmth, quick hospitality, open sincerity, depth of feeling, emotional understanding, unsuspicious and easy rapport, open-handed generosity, willing helpfulness, these are the proper appearances. Indians know that someone is not really warm and sincere, or know rather that his openness and emotional understanding are momentary passing responses, but, fleeting though they are, they are somehow as real as anything else. Consequently, Indians see Westerners as calculating, closed, insincere, lacking in warmth, incapable of appreciating the multilayered realities of social life; and Westerners see Indians as guileful, shifting, dishonest, and incapable of holding on to a unified one-dimensional reality.

GEOGRAPHIC BACKGROUND

In Hindu cosmology the universe is shaped like a giant egg (Brahmāṇḍa, "egg of Brahmā") divided into 21 zones. Above the earth are six heavens ranked according to increasing beatitude, below it seven stages of the nether world (Pātāla), and below the nether world are seven zones of purgatory (Naraka) ranked according to increasing misery. The earth itself is a flat disc of vast magnitude. Standing in its center is Mount Meru surrounded by four continents (dvīpa) separated from one another by oceans. Each continent is named for its characteristic tree. The southern continent, inhabited by humans, is named Jambudvīpa for its distinctive rose-apple (jambu) tree. On this continent, the part south of the Himālayas is Bhāratavarṣa, "The Land of the Sons of Bhārata." Other schemes were propounded. The Purāṇas envisioned a concentric system with Mount Meru at the center surrounded by seven concentric continental rings separated from one another by oceans of salt, treacle, wine, ghī, milk, curds, and fresh water (cf. Basham, 1954, 488–489). More naturalistic, even though invented as a poetic or literary device, were the ecological zones of early Tamil literature. The world was divided into five regions or ecological units (tiṇai) consisting of mountains, cultivated plains, desert, a pastoral zone, and a maritime tract. Associated with each region were characteristic fauna, flora, humans, chieftains, deities, settlement patterns, music, musical instruments, occupations, and food.

Regions

Modern geographers less imaginatively divide India (like Gaul) into three major physical regions: The peninsula in the south, the Himālayas in the north, and the Indo-Gangetic plain lying between these two extremes. The peninsular region is roughly defined by a line northward along the Aravalli Hills to below Delhi, then westward paralleling the Ganges-Jamuna rivers to the Rajmahal Hills in Bihār. The Shillong plateau in Assam is an eastward extension of the peninsular block separated from the rest by the convergence of the Ganges, Jamuna, and Brahmaputra rivers. The peninsula is an ancient land form, its mountains worn down by centuries of erosion. The Aravallis attain a maximum height of only 5,650 feet and the western Ghats extending along the west coast are low, broken hills except for the Nilgiri Hills in the south which rise to 8,700 feet. The eastern Ghats along the east coast are even more decayed, and the Vindhya Mountains of the north rarely exceed 2,000 feet. Most of the peninsula consists of a high triangular plateau with a general slope to the east, surrounded by ranges of low hills which slope off to a narrow strip of coastal plain bordering the Arabian Sea in the west and the Bay of Bengal in the east. All the major peninsular rivers (the Mahānadi, Godavari, and Kistna) are monsoon fed, rise in the west and flow eastward cutting narrow gorges through the eastern Ghats on their way to the Bay of Bengal. Siltation at the mouths of these rivers has formed broad, fertile deltas.

Sometimes the whole peninsular region is popularly referred to as the Deccan, but this term more appropriately applies only to the plateau north of the Kistna River. Similarly, the northwest coast is often called the Konkan, and the southwest coast is known as Malabar. The southeast coast in Madras is still sometimes given its ancient name—Coromandel, and the northeast coastal region in Āndhra Pradesh is called the Circars.

Though originally heavily forested, the Deccan Plateau is now practically a savannah characterized by scrub forests and short grass. The Deccan soil derived from ancient lava flows is rich and black, but because of variable rainfall produces relatively low yields. Its physical character also makes it difficult to cultivate. Too dry, it is deeply fissured and as impenetrable as concrete, but too wet it is a sticky mass of black glue. Because it expands massively when wet and contracts when dry, it is constantly churning, cracking foundations, heaving floors, and damaging other human structures. In the southern Deccan, rice and tobacco grown in the bands of alluvial soils along major streams are cash crops but the staple crops of the Deccan are millet and maize with cotton as the chief cash crop.

Most of the coastal plains are intensely cultivated with little natural forest cover. Except for the unproductive lateritic soils of the Konkan, the soil is mostly deltaic or hill-foot alluvium. Much of the land is irrigated and devoted to rice production. Because the monsoons drop much of their moisture when they strike the mountains, high elevations are covered with a subtropical forest of mixed evergreen and deciduous trees. On the lower elevations in the south coffee and tea are grown as plantation crops.

Extending along India's northern border is the vast Himālayan range with peaks of 25,000 feet and above. In contrast to the ancient geologic character of the peninsula, the Himālayas are geologically recent. In the Mesozoic period the Himālayan area was actually a great sea bordered in the south by the peninsular block (Gondwana land). The high altitude and extreme folding of the Himālayan ranges prohibit extensive cultivation except in isolated valley floors, but pastoralism utilizing the pastures at lower elevations is widespread. Also at lower elevations along the sides of narrow valleys, rice, millet, and potatoes are often grown in elaborately terraced fields extending up the mountainsides. Because the high peaks interrupt the northward flow of the monsoon, the mountains are areas of high precipitation, and much of this precipitation feeds the rivers and streams of the Indo-Gangetic plain. Rapid erosion in the mountains has provided rich alluvial soil along the banks of the Indus and Ganges river systems. At higher elevations below the snow line the mountains are covered with evergreen alpine forests, and at lower elevations with mixed deciduous and evergreen forests. At the foot of the Himālayas is a band of dense jungle. Known as the *terai*, it is infamous for its malaria and wild animals.

The Indo-Gangetic plain is a long, crescent-shaped belt of deep alluvium between the mountains and the peninsula. Geologically, it appears to be a filled-in trough traversed by the Indus, Ganges-Jamuna, and Brahmaputra rivers. The flood plains of these rivers comprise a basin 2,000 miles long and 200 miles wide. Although rainfall is highly variable over this vast region, cultivation is less dependent on the monsoons. Water for irrigation is widely available from the rivers whose waters come from the Himālayas. The major subregions are: the Indus, the Panjāb, the Ganges-Jamuna doab (area between two rivers), and the Brahmaputra valley–Ganges-Brahmaputra delta. With the exception of the latter region, this is monotonous country. The dry, dusty plain is unbroken by hills or forests. Punctuated only by an occasional dry riverbed and the trees near settlements, the flat, drab plain extends for miles in every direction. The whole area gives an impression of aridity, but in fact becomes progressively humid from west to east. The dry desert wastes of the west and the lush green vegetation of the Ganges delta are thus the two poles of a continuum.

Though once the site of an ancient civilization, the Indus River now flows through an arid land. Intensive cultivation is primarily limited to a band of irrigated alluvial soil adjacent to the river. Wheat is the staple crop of the region, and rice is grown under irrigation. In the hilly uplands beyond the river valley, agriculture is characterized by marginal dry farming. In much of the area to the west of the valley, pastoralism or pastoralism combined with dry farming is the prevalent mode of production. The thin grass and limited water sources of this area will support only a small population of semi-nomadic peoples.

The Panjāb is the land between the five rivers—Jhelum, Chenab, Ravi, Beas, and Sutlej. This was the heartland, the *Āryāvarta* of the early Āryan invaders. Once endowed with more adequate rainfall, the Panjāb is now semiarid, almost entirely dependent on irrigation. Extensive irrigation projects combined with the fertile sandy loam have made the semiarid Panjāb one of the chief agricultural producers in India. Wheat is the predominant food crop, and cotton and sugarcane are the important cash crops.

East of the Panjāb lies the heartland of India, the *Bhāratavarṣa* of the epics. Here in the middle reaches of the Ganges River is a densely populated agricultural tract. Higher rainfall results in increased cultivation of rice in the eastern portions of the region. Rice, wheat, barley, millet, and maize are the principal food crops. Sugar cane is the premier cash crop. Nearly the whole of the Brahmaputra valley and Ganges-Brahmaputra delta region is a vast, green, wet, low-lying, deltaic plain. With 40–80 inches of rain per year and flat, level land, it is a region well suited to the production of rice. Practically the whole area is given over to production of rice and jute. With the Malabar coast this deltaic region is more densely populated than any other area in India.

Climate and Monsoon

Indians recognize three major seasons: the hot weather, the rains, and the cold weather. Beginning in March the daytime temperature gradually rises from the high 80s to well over 100 in late May. In the Deccan, temperatures of 120 are common. Nighttime temperatures are cool only by comparison, often staying in the high 90s. Discomfort is increased by the hot, dry winds and blowing clouds of dust. Wells run dry, limp vegetation turns gray with dust, and the brown earth cracks and heaves under the merciless sun. Villages and fields bake in a hot silence broken only by the incessant cries of the "brain-fever" bird or the weary creak of a windlass drawing tepid water from the village well. The somnolent villages stir into activity only for weddings—the major diversion of the hot season. These months of unremitting heat are broken only by the "mango showers" of late April. In late May and early June giant thunderclouds begin to appear, soon followed by violent squalls and cyclonic winds. Eventually, the violence subsides and each day brings intermittent showers. With the onset of the rains the land is transformed. The dry, dusty plains turn light green and the formerly quiet villages bustle with activity. As if by spontaneous combustion, the air, clothing, and bedding are filled with hordes of insects, while shoes, books, and clothing are covered with mold and mildew. With the preparation of nursery beds for rice during the first rains, a new agricultural season begins. As the rains slacken off in September, fields are prepared for the dry-season crop, and as the temperature cools through October and November the crops sown with the rains are harvested. By December the daytime temperature seldom exceeds the high 80s and nights are in the cool 40s with an occasional frost in the north. January, like early September, is a period of food shortage when supplies from the previous harvest begin to run low. In February, the crops sown in September and October begin to be harvested and by the end of the month temperatures once again commence their annual climb.

Clearly, it is the monsoon that animates the seasonal cycle. In late May the southeast trade winds gradually push an equatorial low-pressure area northward into the Arabian Sea and Bay of Bengal where it is deflected inland. This moisture-laden air strikes the west coast in early June and slowly moves inland until it hits the Himālayan Mountains and retreats, bringing a second monsoon to much of the southeast coast in October and November. In many areas as much as 80 to 90 percent of the annual rainfall is contributed by the monsoon. The distribution of this moisture is markedly uneven. Some areas, like Cherrapunji in Assam, may receive as much as 500 inches of rain while others like Sindh may receive none. The west coast, the Himālayas, much of Assam, and the Ganges delta receive more than 80 inches of rain per year. Most of the Indus valley and what is now West Pakistan receive less than 20 inches. Except for the coasts, the peninsula receives between 20 and 40 inches per year. Parts of the northern peninsula and most of the Ganges valley receive between 40 and 80 inches per year. Western Panjāb receives between 20 and 40 inches. In those areas receiving 20–40 inches or less, yearly fluctuations in rainfall are critical. Farmers look daily at the gathering clouds of the coming monsoon estimating the possibility of good rains, for when the rains fail or are late the farmers' crop is seriously damaged or obliterated and famine stalks the land. The mournful plaint, "The rains did not come," is heard in every village street and bazaar. As the monsoon comes closer the hope of good rains and the prospect of an end to the debilitating heat charges the air with anticipation. At the first hesitant drops of rain, men stop work, children cease their play, and women appear in doorways, each waiting in hushed expectation to see if the drops will come faster. When the hoped-for deluge comes, men stand in the rain laughing and chatting with one another, and the children run through the rain, heads tilted back to catch the rain in their open mouths. But when the rain fails to materialize, leaving only a few damp pockmarks in the dust, the men grumble and return to their tasks with bowed heads. Women and children limply resume their chores, feeling they have witnessed an evil portent.

Cultural Response to Geographic Conditions

Surrounded by water and a high mountain chain, India has historically been isolated from the rest of the world. This isolation, however, has only been relative. At all times these barriers have been penetrated by folk migrations and invasions, but the facts of geography have conditioned the pattern of these penetrations. Thus, in the earliest periods, the principal access was through passes in the mountains of the north, and traditionally this has been the chief point of ingress from the Eurasian land mass. Here, too, have been the major trade routes linking India with other ancient trading centers. It is not surprising then that the earliest urban civilization developed in the northwest. When Arab traders learned to use the prevailing winds to sail between Arabia and the west coast of India, other trading centers developed along the west coast. Similarly, all the premodern cities developed in riverine and deltaic areas capable of producing an agricultural surplus. Within India these ancient cities were linked to one another by long-established overland trade routes. Often these routes paralleled the great river systems, but the north-south routes either followed the relatively accessible coasts or utilized passes through the hills of the northern peninsula. In all, the easiest route both for trade and political expansion has been over the featureless Indo-Gangetic plain. This is reflected in the predominantly eastward expansion of the Āryan invaders and later political unification of the region under the Mauryan emperors. Extension of empire southward was conditional on political unification or conquest of the Indo-Gangetic plain. Islamic invaders repeated this pattern, only gradually and incompletely extending their control over the south. In general, then, the north, and particularly the Indo-Gangetic plain, has always been more open to the influence of foreign peoples than the rest of the subcontinent. Significantly, the major urban centers of the south were oriented to the coast and deltas. This coastal orientation of the Dravidian cities and kingdoms not only reflects the maritime conditions of foreign contact, but promoted the exportation of Indian culture throughout southeast Asia. Finally, the relatively inaccessible jungles and hills are refuge areas, places to which conquered tribes could flee and maintain themselves in relative isolation and safety from the imperialist urban civilizations of the rivers, coasts, and plains.

Just as geographic features have influenced ancient patterns of contact between peoples and the development of urban centers and political divisions, climatic factors have been responsible for some novel aspects of Indian life. Perhaps the most interesting climatic adaptation was the hill station. During the hot weather the whole apparatus of the British Rāj moved from its headquarters in lowland cities to rather elaborate temporary quarters established in various hill towns where the weather was cool. Those who were forced to endure the extreme heat and humidity of the plains coped as best they could with punkahs and with screens woven of roots which when sprinkled with water gave off an aromatic odor and cooled the hot breezes. Patterns of house construction were similarly adapted to the hot climate. Thin wattle walls permitted air circulation, and thick masonry walls or mud walls of other house styles insulated the interiors from the heat. Ubiquitous clay pots held drinking water cooled by evaporation through porous clay walls. The light, loose-fitting garments worn by Indians were much better adapted to the heat than the heavy, tight-fitting clothes of Europeans.

Both climate and culture contribute to the incidence of disease. The heat and incessant dust of the hot season promote various pulmonary infections and eye irritations. Constant exposure to dampness during the rainy season brings on colds, malarial seizures, and rheumatic attacks. Epidemic diseases like cholera and typhus take a heavy toll. Work in flooded paddy fields brings on swollen joints, aches, fevers, and skin irritation. The flooded fields and general lack of drainage during the rainy season provide optimum conditions for mosquito breeding and the consequent high incidence of malaria. During the cold season many Indians are inadequately provided with warm clothing and blankets, and since houses are not heated, chills and fevers result. Inadequate facilities for storing grain encourage rats, and the rats attract snakes. House construction is not predicated on pest exclusion, and diseases borne by rats, flies, mosquitos, and other insects have a ready entrance. Lack of sanitary facilities and inadequate isolation of the diseased promote the rapid spread of contagious diseases. The popularity of pilgrimages to temples and religious festivals similarly increases the spread of contagious diseases. Among the widely distributed diseases are malaria, tuberculosis, several forms of dysentery, typhus, cholera, plague, dengue and blackwater fever, filariasis, and yaws. Less widely distributed are smallpox, typhoid fever, leprosy, trachoma, syphilis, various skin infections, and *Kala Azar*. Here, too, belong the diseases of malnutrition, beriberi and protein deficiency. The incidence of beriberi is encouraged by the practice of eating milled rice, white flour, and polished rice in which the nutritional value of the whole grain is lost. Curiously, eating polished rice is associated with wealth. Only the more affluent can afford polished rice. Poorer people must make do with unmilled rice or millet. The practice of vegetarianism, where it is not adequately supplemented with dairy products, contributes to protein deficiencies. The Indian diet receives most of its proteins from various legumes, but since these lack one of the essential amino acids, they cannot entirely replace animal protein. Finally, the incidence of disease is directly related to the general lack of medical services. Qualified doctors are scarce, hospitals are generally found only in larger cities, health teams and the few clinics cannot begin to handle all the outpatient cases to say nothing of the millions of essential inoculations. Attitudes toward disease also complicate matters. Illnesses frequently are not attended to before they become serious, and there is no widespread belief in the efficacy of preventive medicine—even if it were available. Patients, even with the most highly communicable diseases, are not isolated or quarantined, and other antiseptic procedures are absent. Recently expanded government health services have alleviated this situation somewhat, but they are actually barely able to keep pace with the expanding population.

Climate and disease also influence patterns of work. During the hot weather outdoor physical labor is practically impossible. From noon to evening the pace of activity slows to a standstill as everyone seeks the shade. High temperatures combined with hot enervating winds and constant dust make people irritable, and as the hot season wears on tempers flare. Fortunately, the busiest agricultural seasons occur during the rains and cold weather. The hot weather is a slack time in the fields, but pity the poor office worker who must contend with the searing heat and contentious colleagues. The constant low-hanging clouds, intermittent daily showers, and constant wetness during the wet season can be depressing, and extra time and care must be given to the storage of household items in a constant battle against the encroaching green mold and mildew that flourishes in the rainy season. Malnutrition and incessant exposure to disease contribute to a generalized syndrome known in India as "weakness." People excuse themselves from labor because they feel too "weak" to carry on. It should be noted that this syndrome is most frequent among the wealthy and educated. Laborers more often absent themselves from work owing to "fever" or intestinal troubles.

Demography

In 1961 the population of India totaled 439,235,000 people with a density of approximately 358 persons per square mile. Roughly 82 percent of the population was classified as rural in the 1961 census. In 1901 India had a population of 236 million; in 1921, 251 million; in 1941, 319 million. Since 1941 the population has increased at the rate of 1.7 percent per year. Here it is significant to note that not only has the total population increased in every census, but the rate of increase has been greater. Despite these vast increases, the population is still predominantly rural, though the percentage increase in urban population has been higher in the last two censuses. Experts may disagree about the magnitude of the population problem in India, but it is self-evident that the population cannot continue to increase at the current rate. It may be that the only significant measure of overpopulation is the relation between population size and available food resources, but this equation is rather meaningless when we already know that a large proportion of the Indian population now exists at a subsistence level. Increases in agricultural and industrial production have offset some of the effects of population growth between 1941 and 1961, but in order for India to merely stand still there must be an 11- to 12-percent increase in productivity to keep pace with the current rate of population growth, and the majority of this increase will have to be in basic food supplies. This seems unlikely, and the only alternative is an effective program of population control.

RACES OF INDIA

Even the most casual visitor in India is immediately impressed with the apparent physical diversity of the Indian populace. Differences in stature, skin color, eye color, head shape, hair, and facial features all contribute to the seemingly inescapable conclusion that the present populace of India is a distillate of numerous distinct "racial" types. It is but a short step from this impressionistic conclusion to the notion that these differences should be measurable and that the results of such measurement should provide an objective classification of racial types. Constellations of numerical indices for facial features, head size, stature, skin color, and the like should represent a measure of racial similarity. Those who share constellations of these indices within defined ranges of variation should then be classed as members of the same distinct "race."

Such phenotypical classification is based on the assumption that physical features are both hereditary and immune from environmental influence. Except for changes resulting from racial interbreeding (racial mixture), races remain stable through time. As a consequence of this presumed stability through time, racial classifications assumed an historical function. They could be used to trace out the migrations and mixtures of different races and thereby provide valuable chronological insights.

In the working out of this program of investigation, it was only necessary to add that each race was inherently associated with a specific set of mental or characterological features or with a particular cultural tradition. Characterological features (acquisitiveness, aggressiveness, and the like) or specific items of culture (house types, weapon and tool types, languages, means of subsistence) could then be attributed to one or another of the races constituting the population of any country. Physical anthropologists thus shifted from answering the comparatively simple question of "What physically different kinds of people are there?" to the more complex questions of "Where did they come from?" "How did they get here?" "What specific cultural traditions did they bring with them?"

This grand scheme of inquiry was momentarily impeded by the discovery that phenotypical features were subject to environmental influence. Head form could be changed by cradling practices, stature could be increased by dietary changes, and, in general, differences in the conditions of growth clearly indicated that physical types were unstable. Hence the whole intricate structure of investigation was threatened by the collapse of its foundation—the invariance of physical types.

Even earlier the supposed correlations between race, language, and culture were shown to be erroneous. Peoples of supposedly different "races" used the same language, and often peoples of the same "race" used different languages and had dissimilar cultures. To be sure, some of these correlational failures could be explained away, but the explanations were frequently characterized by specious reasoning and general lack of agreement. No two investigators could arrive at even roughly similar conclusions from the same set of data.

In recent times there has been a brief revival of racial classification based on *genotypical* rather than phenotypical features. Genotypical characteristics are gene-linked, transmitted genetically, and within certain limits are invariant. They are transmitted from one generation to the next within an interbreeding population having a definable "gene pool" or statistically characteristic genetic makeup. For India the most important attempts at genotypical classification are based on serology—that is, the distribution of A, B, O, AB, M, N, MN, and Rh factors in the blood groups of a population. A race, then, should be characterized by its percentage distribution of A, B, O, AB, M, N, MN, and Rh factors or, more precisely, the genetic factors that produce these blood groups. Thus one group might be described as having 34 percent type O, 23 percent type A, 33 percent type B, and 10 percent type AB, while another might have 47 percent type O, 24 percent type A, 24 percent type B, and 5 percent type AB.

The initial enthusiasm for racial classification based on serology has been dissipated by the discovery that serological factors are not entirely invariant and by the fact that the mere percentage distributions by themselves frequently do not sufficiently discriminate populations. Thus, like most genetic factors, blood types are subject to mutation and in some cases environmental selection. Similarly, the standard statistical assumption of population genetics to the effect that human populations have random mating practices is directly controverted by the contrary evidence of cultural anthropology. Finally, much of the blood-group data is suspect. In most cases, proper statistical sampling procedures were not carried out; in other cases, the serum samples were contaminated by improper handling. Consequently, genotypical racial classification failed for precisely the same reason that phenotypical racial classifications failed—the basis of the classification system was not invariant.

Phenotypical Classificatory Schemes

Many early anthropologists and travelers speculated rather haphazardly about Indian physical types, but systematic speculation begins with H. H. Risley (1915, 1–61). Basing his conclusions on anthropometric measurements, Risley recognized three principal racial types: Dravidian, Aryan, and Mongoloid. Mixtures with other races produced a total of seven types: Turko-Iranian, Indo-Aryan, Scytho-Dravidian, Aryo-Dravidian, Mongolo-Dravidian, Mongoloid, and Dravidian. Localized in the extreme northwest, the Turko-Iranians were tall, fair, broad-headed and narrow-nosed. Typical of western Indians were the broad-headed, moderately fine-nosed, fair, medium-statured Scytho-Dravidians. In the central portions of northern India were the Aryo-Dravidians with long heads, light brown to black complexion, medium to broad noses, and slightly less than medium stature. The Mongolo-Dravidians were located in lower Bengāl and Orissa. Their heads were broad, complexion dark, stature medium, nose medium to broad. In the Himālayas, Nepal, Assam, and Burma the predominant type was the broad-headed, yellowish-skinned, short, fine- to broad-nosed, flat-faced, oblique-eyed Mongoloids. Finally, inhabiting the entire southern part of the subcontinent were the short, dark- to black-skinned, broad-nosed, long-headed Dravidians.

Risley opined that the Dravidians were the oldest of the seven types and possibly related to the Australian aborigines. They were associated with a distinctive language (Dravidian), stone monuments, and a primitive system of totemism. The Indo-Aryans entered India from the northwest and, since they brought their own women with them, were not forced to mix with the indigenous Dravidians. This factor accounts both for the "purity" of the type and for the fact that caste distinctions are much less rigid among the Indo-Aryans. The first wave of Indo-Aryans was followed in time by subsequent Indo-Aryan migrations, but the latecomers were unable to bring their women and thus lost racial purity. They intermarried with Dravidians and by the "stress of the contact" between Dravidians and invaders there arose the caste system, the structure of Hindu ritual and usage, and the Aryo-Dravidian racial type. The Mongolo-Dravidian type similarly resulted from intermarriage between Mongoloids invading from the east and the autochthonous Dravidians. The "physical degeneration" apparent in the type was partly due to the "relaxing climate" and "enervating diet," but still more the consequence of the "practice of marrying immature children." A third foreign invader, the Scythians, forced their way into India from the west only to meet a fate similar to that of other invaders—intermarriage with Dravidians and subsequent development of the Scytho-Dravidian type. This intermarriage produced the Marāthās and left a bequest of techniques of guerrilla warfare, "unscrupulous dealings," and "genius for intrigue."

The most recent attempt to found a system of racial classification is that of B. S. Guha (1938). In Guha's system there are six main races with nine subtypes:

1. Negrito
2. Proto-Australoid
3. Mongoloid
   a. Paleo-Mongoloid
      (1) long-headed
      (2) broad-headed
   b. Tibeto-Mongoloid
4. Mediterranean
   a. Paleo-Mediterranean
   b. Mediterranean
   c. Oriental Mediterranean
5. Western Brachycephals
   a. Alpinoid
   b. Dinaric
   c. Armenoid
6. Nordic

The Negrito survives in India among the Andamanese, the Kadaṉs and Palayaṉs of Kerala, the Irulas of Wynad, and the Angami Nagas of Assam and the

Rajmahal Hills of eastern Bihār. The Negritos were largely absorbed by the Proto-Australoids. Originating in the west, the Proto-Australoids survive in Dravidian tribal populations and are connected with the tribes of Australia. Long-headed Mongoloids represent a more ancient stratum of the population and prevail among the Assam tribes. The round-headed Mongoloids are found in Burma and the Chittagong Hills. Tibeto-Mongoloids are found in Sikkim and Bhutan and appear to be recent arrivals from Tibet. The Paleo-Mediterranean type of medium stature, dark skin, and slight build is found largely in Mysore, Āndhra, Madras, and Kerala. The "true" Mediterranean type is taller and fairer than the Paleo-Mediterranean and occurs in the Panjāb and upper Gangetic valley. This group represents the civilized Dravidian people of north India who became Aryanized. The Oriental Mediterranean type characterized by a long nose and fair skin is found in the Panjāb, Sind, Rājputāna, and western Uttar Pradesh. The brachycephal groups are widely scattered throughout India. Dinaric types occur in Bengāl, Orissa, Mysore, and Madras. Alpinoids predominate in Gujarāt. Armenoids occur in dispersed groups along the west coast, in central India, along the Himālayas, in western Uttar Pradesh, and Bihār. The Nordic types descend from the ancient Aryan invaders and are strongly represented in the northwest frontier, the Panjāb, Rājputāna, and the upper Gangetic valley. They are also represented among high-caste groups scattered throughout the country.

Although Guha's system has not been universally accepted, it does represent a generally consistent picture of the facts based on physical measurements.

Serological Studies

Available serological data neither confirm nor disconfirm earlier phenotypical classifications except in the sense that the distribution of gene frequencies for blood groups does not correspond to the distribution of phenotypical features. There is, for example, no specific configuration of blood groups that can be associated with a Negrito race in India. What emerges from the serological data is a much less differentiated classification.

To overgeneralize, the picture which seems to emerge from blood-group distributions is that high castes have higher frequencies for A, intermediate and mixed castes have a preponderance of B, and unmixed tribal groups have high O frequencies. The preponderance of B may be the result of interbreeding and environmental selection. Alternatively, the high incidence of B could result from its presence in an aboriginal population deriving from central Asia. Since contemporary blood distributions indicate a high frequency of A in Europe, this is presumably the external source of the high A frequencies found in the higher castes. Evidence would seem to point, then, to the unmixed tribal groups with high O frequencies as the original Indians.

LANGUAGE

India's languages are as diverse as her peoples. Not only do different groups speak unrelated languages, they often speak widely divergent regional dialects of the same language, and utilize a bewildering variety of literary and colloquial styles in appropriate contextual situations. Because a common language is a major source of group identification, it is not surprising that this linguistic diversity should parallel the segmentary character of Indian society. Yet, despite these tendencies to separation and distinctiveness, the long history of contact between speakers of different languages has produced common features in all the languages.

The spread of Āryan doctrine encouraged large-scale borrowing of Sanskrit words and semantic categories, and Sanskrit itself provided the grammatical and literary model for the subsequent development of regional literary traditions. In later times the political domination of the Moghuls promoted wide adoption of Persian legal and revenue terminology, and contributed to the growth of a universal administrative vocabulary and courtly literature.

On the other hand, the vagaries of history have also been responsible for many of the features that reflect diversity. Thus the incomplete political unification of India until recent times is reflected in the absence of an official *lingua franca,* the continued agitation over the language question, and the formation of states corresponding to linguistic rather than economic, political, or geographical regions. Here, too, one can see the development of separate literary traditions in the service of dissident religious movements or under the patronage of rebellious local rulers as ancient applications of the divisive power of language.

Language Families

The many languages of India are divided into four separate families: Indo-European, Dravidian, Austro-Asiatic (Austric), and Tibeto-Burman. Belonging to the same linguistic stock as French, English, Greek, and other European languages, speakers of Indo-European languages comprise 73.3 percent of the Indian population. Largely resident in the northern and central portions of the subcontinent, their distribution corresponds to the facts of their external origin.

The Dravidian languages, spoken by 24.5 percent of the population, are located in the south with isolated pockets in central and northwest India. These remnant populations clearly reflect displacement of Dravidian peoples by the invading Indo-Europeans. Although scholars are not in full agreement, preponderating evidence supports an ancient relationship between the Dravidian family of languages and the Ural-Altaic language family. Similar disagreement surrounds the relation of Dravidian to the as yet untranslated language of the early urban civilizations of the Indus valley, but here, too, the most convincing evidence points to the Dravidians as the founders of the Indus civilization and authors of the enigmatic Indus inscriptions.

Dispersed throughout the highlands of central and eastern India, speakers of Austro-Asiatic languages are remnants of a people once widespread in India and southeast Asia. Their presence in relatively isolated mountain and jungle areas reflects a long history of retreat in the face of invaders. They now comprise only 1.5 percent of the population.

Along the Himālayan borderlands from Ladakh to Assam are speakers of Tibeto-Burman languages whose linguistic and ethnological affinities are with peoples of Tibet and Southeast Asia. Comprising only 0.7 percent of the population, their small number and marginal location correspond to their relatively unimportant role in the formation of Indian culture.

Language and Culture

This picture of structurally separate, independent language families, though correct from the point of view of comparative and historical linguistics, unfortunately disguises an historical process that has worked to decrease the differences between languages. Although long-term historical processes have contributed to the differentiation of languages within the same family, these same processes have also tended to reduce the differences between languages of different families. This latter tendency is reflected by the fact that most of the languages of India share certain common features which serve to differentiate them from the languages of other geographic areas. This is particularly true of Indo-Aryan, Dravidian, and Munda. Borrowing of lexical items between these language families constitutes one of the characteristics of this process. To a limited extent, the languages of each family possess a common vocabulary. Phonologically, the reduction to common features is most evident in the universal presence of a series of retroflex consonants and a common process of vocalic assimilation. Syntactically, the most important common feature is the high frequency of noun predications. Less universal is the use of specialized numeral classifiers for enumerating people as opposed to animals or things. Although each language handles the matter in its own way, there is also a common emphasis on the use of structural features to indicate those differences in social status entailed by the caste system. India is thus a "convergence area" or a "linguistic area" defined by a common set of linguistic features or processes (cf. Emeneau, 1956). This convergence of languages from different families has created a situation in which the modern Indo-Aryan languages are more similar to Dravidian languages than they are to other Indo-European languages. One scholar (Andronov, 1964) has recently contended that this convergence between Dravidian and Indo-Aryan is the initial step in the formation of a new language family which will be neither Indo-Aryan nor Dravidian. Evidence indicates that this has already occurred in limited geographic areas. Gumperz (1969), for example, has demonstrated that code-switching among bilingual speakers of Marāthi (Indo-Aryan) and Kannaḍa (Dravidian) involves only the simplest word-for-word translation. The syntactic transformation rules necessary for translating one language into the other are minimal. This is clear evidence of structural convergence in which long and intimate contact between speakers of languages originally belonging to different families has gradually eliminated the structural differences between languages. In this geographic region the use of Marāthi or Kannaḍa differs but little from the stylistic or contextual use of variant features in the same code.

Convergence, or more properly consensus, is also reflected in the development of modern regional standard dialects. In this process one variety or dialect of a regional language comes to be elaborated, accepted, and taught as the standard form of the language. Contributing to this development were the introduction of printing presses and the publication of books and newspapers. In most cases this modern literary form conflicted with an earlier literary tradition. The archaic and often highly ornamented forms of earlier literature were usually far removed from the forms of common or colloquial speech. The distance between the literary form and ordinary speech was often so great that literacy involved almost as much effort as the learning of a totally foreign language. The new regional standards are almost always a compromise between this older literary form and colloquial speech. Elements of each were incorporated and an entirely new language form was created. Coexisting with this new standard are other regional and local dialects and the earlier literary form. To further complicate the picture, the new standard dialect often developed two distinct forms, a more formal variety used in writing, formal speeches, radio broadcasts, and classroom lectures, and an informal variety used in conversation. Many areas also have further dialectical subdivisions along caste lines. Thus in the south there is a difference between Brāhmaṇ and non-Brāhmaṇ speech, and in other areas a distinction between high caste and low caste or between educated and illiterate speech.

A speaker of Telugu in Āndhra Pradesh, for example, has a choice between standard (that is, Circars dialect) or nonstandard Telugu, literary or nonliterary Telugu, modern literary forms or older literary forms, formal or informal modes, Brāhmaṇ or non-Brāhmaṇ (in some areas educated or noneducated replaces the Brāhmaṇ, non-Brāhmaṇ contrast) dialects, and finally between Rāyalasīma and Telangāna, regional dialects. These possibilities are outlined in Figure 1.

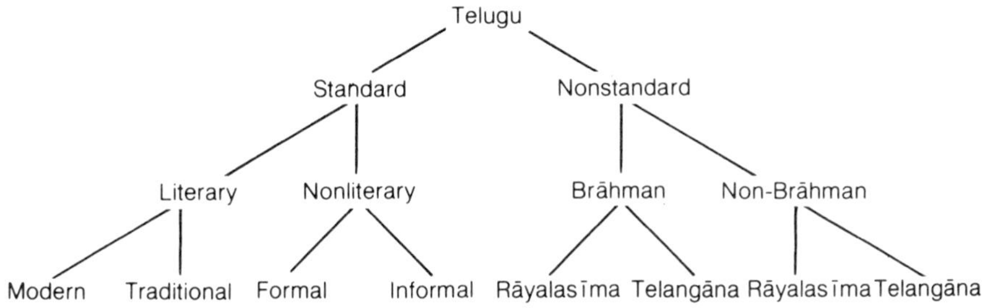

Figure 1. Telugu speech varieties.

Each of these speech varieties is marked by differences in phonology, morphology, syntax, and vocabulary. In addition, most Telugu-speaking residents of Telangāna would have a choice between Telugu and Urdu while those in southern Rāyalasīma and Circars would have a choice of Telugu or Tamil. Residents in the eastern parts of the state would have a choice between Telugu and Kannaḍa, and those on the northern boundaries would have to choose between Telugu and Marāthi. Finally, every educated speaker would have the option of using English. A speaker's use of one or another of these codes is constrained by various contextual factors. In order to choose the appropriate speech variant, he must, for example, know something about the social identity of those being spoken to, and he must evaluate the social situation in order to decide if it is formal or informal. These are only two of the numerous contextual features that any Telugu speaker would take into account in his choice of the appropriate speech form.

Surmounting all this diversification is the use of English as a *lingua franca*. English is still the only language that can be relied upon as a standard means of communication among educated Indians from widely separated areas. Here, too, we may note the emergence of a new English dialect. Indian English differs more from American English than the latter does from the variety of English spoken by the upper class in the British Isles. Thus in any given day an educated Indian may find himself speaking Indian English to some colleagues at the office, a formal standard dialect to others, a colloquial standard or caste or regional dialect at home, and a purely local village dialect in his natal village.

The diversity of languages and the persistence of competing regional standards has created a situation in which India has no national language, despite chauvinistic attempts to foist off Hindī as the official government language. In the south, particularly in Tamilnad, these attempts to enforce the favored position of Hindī have been met with riots, demonstrations, and noncooperation. Because of the severity of the reaction, the central government was forced to withdraw from its avowed purpose of imposing Hindī as the official national language. Here we may note that this is consistent with previous government policy. Beginning with the formation of Āndhra Pradesh as a political unit whose boundaries corresponded to the geographical distribution of Telugu, the boundaries of nearly every Indian state have been redrawn in conformance with linguistic boundaries. Within each of these politico-linguistic entities the local regional standard has been promoted as the major means of communication even though lip service was paid to the encouragement of Hindī. After establishing a pattern of acquiescence in the face of linguistic "nationalism," it is hardly surprising that efforts to reverse this pattern have met with defeat. It is now doubtful that any one of the regional languages will be acceptable as the official Indian language in the foreseeable future, and even though most would argue that absence of a common medium of communication is detrimental to implementation of national policies, I believe the prejudice in favor of monolingualism should be recognized for what it is—a prejudice. After all, Indian kingdoms for centuries were able to function effectively despite the diversity of languages. Again, it can be argued that the nature of modern technology and the complex demands of modern government are better served by a common language, but only if the tolerance and innovativeness fed by diversity are less desirable than a rigid and sterile conformity. What we should expect from India is not the popular solution of a single national language and all the repressive trappings of centralized authority, but rather a creative response that taps the potentialities of multilingualism and diversity.

Writing

Writing has been known in India since approximately the third millennium B.C. when it was extensively used by the peoples of the Indus civilization. After the downfall of the Indus civilization (ca. 1500 B.C.), there is no clear evidence of writing until the third century B.C. References to writing occur in literature deriving from a date prior to the third century B.C., and the appearance of a fully developed script suggests that some form of writing probably existed as early as the fifth or sixth centuries B.C., but the earliest direct evidence of writing in India after the Indus script consists of the edicts of King Aśoka inscribed on rock pillars. The Aśokan edicts employ two scripts, Brāhmī and Kharoṣṭhī. Some authorities trace the origin of the Brāhmī script to the Indus script, but others derive it from early North Semitic scripts. Many of the signs of the Brāhmī script resemble those of the Indus script and although there are also similarities between the Brāhmī signs and those of North Semitic, the latter has no consistent method of marking vowel signs. In the Brāhmī script vowel signs are indicated by adding diacritic marks to the basic consonant sign. Ultimately, the relation of Brāhmī to the Indus script will be resolved only when the Indus script has been translated.

The Kharoṣṭhī script derives from the Aramaic alphabet and is read from right to left. It appears to have been altogether contemporaneous with the Brāhmī script, but there is a possibility that it may have been devised under the influence of the Brāhmī script. Kharoṣṭhī was used in India and for many years in central Asia. In central Asia it was displaced by the Gupta alphabet and it is from this latter alphabet that the Tibetan script is derived. All the other Indian scripts derive from Brāhmī. The most famous of these is Devanāgarī ("Script of the City of the Gods") in which Sanskrit, Prākṛts, and (with slight modifications) the modern Indo-Aryan languages are written. With the exception of Tamil, the Dravidian languages evolved circular rather than angular scripts.

In addition to inscriptions on stone and copper plates, early literature was written on palm leaves. In the north writing was done with a reed pen and ink made from lampblack or charcoal, but in the south letters were inscribed with a stylus and ink was rubbed into the scratch marks.

PART 2

FORMATION OF INDIAN CULTURE

For five thousand years Indian consciousness has assumed a correspondence between cosmic order and mundane human experience, between the macrocosm and the microcosm. The ancient Indian texts express varying and sometimes contradictory accounts of cosmic order, but the dominant interpretation represents the macrocosm as that which is undifferentiated, immutable, timeless, beyond history. Itself uncreated, it is that which creates. By contrast, the microcosm as a product of creation is in constant flux, is maximally differentiated, and at the mercy of time. The microcosm and macrocosm are mirror images of one another, but because the microcosm is a part of cosmic order the macrocosm must have a dualistic character. It must represent both the prior ground from which the created world emerges in all its variety, and it must contain all the processes necessary to bring about creation. Consequently, the most general notion of the macrocosm is that it consists of two states: active and potential, and most Indian creation myths stress the agency of the macrocosm as acting upon itself in the process of creation. The macrocosm creates out of itself by its own power. Since the active state accounts for creation and is also timeless, the Indian notion of creation is necessarily one of repetitive creations. Creation is not a singular, one-time event in the ancient past, but a continuous, eternal process, and the aim of all Indian religious thought is to yoke this process of continuous creation either in the service of the social order or of individual freedom. The orthodox Sanskritic tradition has always sought to harness it to the social order, and all unorthodox traditions have originally attempted to make it serve as a means to individual freedom, to use it as a means to escape from the mutable to the immutable.

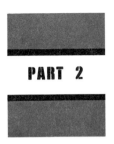

In the realm of human experience represented by the microcosm, Indian thought has allowed only two opposed possibilities: the correspondence between cosmic order and human experience is mediated through the social order, or it is expressed directly as a relation between the individual and the cosmos. This opposition has far-reaching consequences. *If the correspondence is mediated through the social order, then the individual is not a datum of society* (cf. Dumont, 1970*a*, 133–151), *but if the correspondence is between the individual and the cosmos, then society is not a datum of individual experience.* Indian thought thus establishes two mutually exclusive categories: the individual is either totally subject to society, or he is totally free of it. There is no middle way. The microcosm, like the macrocosm, is dualistically conceived, and its categories correspond to those of the macrocosm. Thus the social order corresponds to the active state of the macrocosm while the individual corresponds to the potential state of the macrocosm.

Just as the categories of the microcosm are opposed, so too are their correspondence relations. The individual corresponds to the potential state via an identity relation. The individual becomes the same as the potential state. The social order is never identical to the active state; it corresponds to it by means of an equivalence relation. They are essentially alike, but separate and distinct.

Axiomatic in Indian thought is the notion that ritual is *the* connection between the cosmos and the social order. To perform a rite correctly is to participate directly in cosmic process. What follows from this axiom is an identification between the social order and the order of ritual. Society becomes a ritual organization. Here we may express these relations as a set of equivalencies: social order = ritual order = cosmic activity. This ritual order presupposes hierarchic differentiation. Someone must perform the rite, someone else must commission it, and someone else must provide the goods and services necessary for it. Those who perform the ritual are higher than those who commission it, and those who commission it are higher than those who provide the goods and services for it. Because the ritual order entails hierarchic differentiation, the social order must necessarily be hierarchic.

In contrast to this necessarily hierarchic structure of society is the maximal freedom and egalitarianism entailed by the view that the individual is the locus of the correspondence between macrocosm and microcosm. Just as the very notion of society implies hierarchy, the notion of free individuals implies total egalitarianism. Where there are only free individuals there is no society. Consequently, the notion of freedom in India has always had an extra mundane reference and has always involved a denigration of ritual. Ritual as the expression of the relation between macrocosm and microcosm is replaced by asceticism, devotionalism, and other mystical processes which characteristically express an identity between the individual and the potential state of the cosmos. Doubtless this opposition between hierarchic social order on the one hand and egalitarian individualism on the other represents an archaic mythological opposition between man in society and man in a state of nature, or more succinctly between culture and nature (cf. Lévi-Strauss, 1969, 3–11). The origin of society entails the death of freedom and the subjugation of the individual. Just so, the Puruṣasūkta, one of the Vedic creation myths, describes the whole creation itself and the creation of hierarchic society as a primeval human sacrifice.

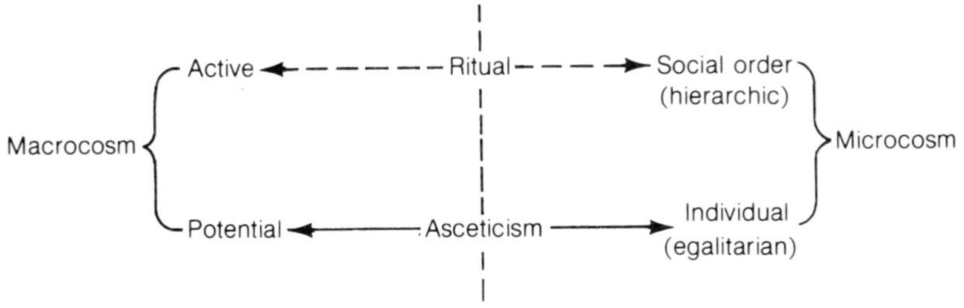

Figure 2. Conceptual paradigm of Indian culture. Broken arrow indicates equivalence relation; solid arrow indicates identity relation.

These basic categories of Indian thought constitute the fundamental conceptual paradigm of Indian culture, as represented in Figure 2. This essential paradigm of Indian culture was first articulated in the cities and fields of the Indus civilization. Here, on the fertile alluvial plain of the Indus River, its emergence was contemporaneous with an agricultural revolution. Settled agriculture based on exploitation of the alluvial plain and the annual inundations of the Indus River made possible a sedentary population capable of producing a surplus grain crop. This mode of production was predicated on a division of labor that expressed a hierarchy of rights of access to the produce of land. With relatively simple technology the Indian cultivator for centuries has produced a yearly harvest more than sufficient to satisfy his needs, but in the Indian scheme of things this harvest was not merely the product of the cultivator's labor, it was made possible by the cooperative effort of a dominant group of warrior-cultivators, artisan-priests, and laborers. Each, through the medium of his occupational specialty, contributed to the harvest and each consequently earned a share of it. Though each received a share of the grain heap produced in the cultivator's fields, these shares were never equal. Some have always had more rights than others. At all times rights in the grain heap have been hierarchical, and though the actual hierarchy has been in constant flux as different groups acquired dominant access to the grain heap, the idea of hierarchic distribution remained constant, the unvarying form behind the illusory changes wrought by ceaseless struggles for power, supremacy, and empire.

Here we sense most clearly the dreary futility of the historian's catechism. Chronicles of kings, the mayhem of armies, and the pettiness of human deeds fade into insignificance within this immutable paradigm. In India we are searching for history in a land that has expunged history, in a world where prophets are not merely without honor, they are unnecessary. If there is then no dialectical movement in the tracery of time from 3000 B.C. to the present, then the whole tale of India can be told in the crumbling bricks of the Indus civilization, and we need not concern ourselves with the subsequent doings of men, with the subtle but nonetheless meaningless flux of human events.

Here we must equivocate, for though the archaic paradigm continues unchanged into the present, it is clear that it has been painstakingly reconstituted rather in the manner of some grand and colorful jigsaw puzzle laboriously put together then violently and heedlessly ripped apart only to be reassembled. When the barbaric Āryan tribals destroyed the Indus cities, wrenching apart what had first been pieced together by tribal cultivators, they brought to completion a cycle of growth and dissolution. But slowly through succeeding years the past was recaptured, the paradigm reassembled. What had been destroyed was reconstituted in the confrontation between conquerors and conquered. In the final Hindu synthesis, the conquered prevailed over their conquerors, completing the first stage in a new cycle of growth and dissolution.

Now we are witness to another age of destruction. To be sure the new barbarians with their engines of war come disguised as emissaries of peace, but let there be no doubt that an ancient civilization is being destroyed even more completely and totally than before, for now the attack is skillfully directed at the very structure of the paradigm. The preeminence of the land with its necessarily fixed hierarchy of rights to finite means has been challenged by the myth of egalitarian access to infinitely expanding means. Too, the contemporary Indian is encouraged to believe that hierarchy can be excluded from society, that freedom can be realized in the mundane realm, and that neither ritual nor asceticism is necessary.

Perhaps this assessment is hasty. With our attention diverted by epiphenomenal movement we are searching for auguries of order, seeing portents of change and signs of incipient decay where none exist. Thinking that at last we have reached the coda of some tiresomely repetitious theme, that the triumph of egalitarianism is assured and the cycle finally broken, we have failed to see that all this is but another aspect of the ancient confrontation between egalitarianism and hierarchy. In fact, it has been the conflict between these two notions that has characterized all Indian speculation, and it was the unique contribution of Hinduism that established a successful equilibrium between them, transforming them from mutually contradictory ends to complementary orientations. What we now seem to see in modern India is the development of a new disequilibrium, the renewal of the ancient conflict; and though the actual terms of the contemporary struggle are different, a genuine difference in their implications remains to be demonstrated.

TWO

PREHISTORICAL CULTURES

From about 400,000 to 3500 B.C. the Indian subcontinent was inhabited by various Stone Age peoples. Except for their ubiquitous stone implements, these early inhabitants are shadowy, insubstantial figures. No skeletal remains have been satisfactorily attributed to any of their characteristic industries, nor is there direct evidence of their manner of life. It can only be surmised that they were fully human and that they survived by means of a rude form of hunting and gathering. Sometime in the third millennium B.C. these Stone Age peoples were displaced in the northwest by pastoralists and settled agriculturalists living in small, permanent settlements. Somewhat later in the central and southern parts of the subcontinent they were followed by nomadic pastoralists and seminomadic swidden farmers. The farmers of the northwest were replaced during the latter part of the third millennium B.C. by a distinctive civilization characterized by large urban centers based on the production of an agricultural surplus and extensive mercantile operations. This transition from hunting and gathering to urban life was not everywhere an orderly sequence. Many areas lagged behind in these developments, and traditions characteristic of earlier periods not only coexisted with later traditions but in some cases even survived them. In the northwest the course of urban development was interrupted about 1500 B.C. by barbarian pastoralists from Iran. Some of the early cities survived the barbarian onslaught and persisted in attenuated form for some centuries, but it was not until 800–600 B.C. that new forms of urban life reappeared, this time in the fertile valleys of the great northern rivers.

THE STONE AGE

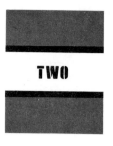

The Stone Age cultures of India are divided into three somewhat overlapping periods which seem to follow one another in a more or less orderly stratigraphic sequence. The periods are: Early Stone Age, Middle Stone Age, and Late Stone Age. Except for occasional regional variations and instances of local stagnation, sites representative of these three groups are found throughout the subcontinent, and appear to indicate a continuous line of development.

The Early Stone Age is characterized by a hand-ax industry similar in many respects to those of western Asia, Europe, and Africa. Quartzite hand axes, cleavers, chopping tools, and flakes are the principal implements. The major regional variation is a higher proportion of chopping tools in some of the northern sites which may indicate an affinity with the chopper-chopping tool industries of eastern Asia. During the later years of the Early Stone Age the flake tools show a progressive refinement with more delicate and regular flaking.

By the time of the Middle Stone Age this flaking technique had become the principal form of tool-making. Predominantly flake industries consisting of agate, jasper, or chalcedony scrapers are the hallmark of the Middle Stone Age. A few sites contain pointed flakes that might have been used as knives, awls, or borers. These flakes were probably struck off a prepared parent core with a stone or wooden hammer. Some assemblages near the end of the Middle Stone Age contain burins and tanged and shouldered points which were probably used as knives and scrapers. There is a general reduction in size and greater technical refinement in these tools from the end of the Middle Stone Age.

In the Late Stone Age the development toward more delicate and refined tools culminates in a distinctive microlithic tradition. Small blades were removed from a carefully prepared core by indirect percussion, probably by a bone or wooden chisel struck with a hammer. Many of these small tools were intended for hafting. More important than this evidence of advancing technical skill in the manufacture of stone tools are the indications of cultural practices which can be inferred from other artifacts found in association with the tools. In some of the caves and rock shelters which were among the habitations of Late Stone Age peoples, numerous bones of both domestic and wild animals have been found. Many of these caves and rock shelters in central India are decorated with colored wall and ceiling paintings mainly representing various wild animals and a few possibly domestic cattle. It is improbable that these men of the Late Stone Age were actually cattle-keepers. More than likely, the domestic cattle represented in the paintings were stolen from more advanced peoples with whom these cave dwellers were in contact at the close of the Late Stone Age. A number of scenes in the paintings depict just such cattle raids. Other scenes illustrate figures engaged in hunting, and it seems clear that this occupation was more characteristic of Late Stone Age man. Another panel clearly reveals groups hunting with bows, arrows, and spears. Other sites excavated along sea coasts provide evidence that these primitive peoples also included fisher folk who may have had boats of some kind. Even in the absence of absolute dating it is clear that peoples living in this Late Stone Age hunting-and-gathering mode of life persisted into periods which were characterized in other areas by more advanced technologies. In this respect they were probably no different from many contemporary Indian tribal groups who in their remote villages persist in a way of life significantly different from that of their more "civilized" neighbors.

PEASANT VILLAGES AND PROTO-CITIES

In contrast to the impermanent settlements selected by Stone Age men for their proximity to water, game, and workable stone, the early pastoralists and agriculturalists of Baluchistan established permanent villages along low mountain streams and valleys where land and water for crops and animals were plentiful. Here in the northwest the convenient rock shelter, sand dune, or rude thatched hut of Stone Age man gave way to more comfortable and permanent dwellings constructed of packed mud or sun-dried brick. These permanent settlements were probably originally campsites of seminomadic pastoralists who appear to have preceded the agriculturalists in time. With the steady development of agricultural technology the nomadic pastoralists gradually settled permanently on their former campsites or were replaced by intruders. The inhabitants of these early Baluchistan villages had domestic sheep, goats, and oxen. In some sites a crude handmade basket-marked pottery is present and in others a more sophisticated wheel-thrown painted ware makes its appearance along with copper objects. Direct evidence of agriculture is found only in the later phases of these early sites. Wheat was evidently the main crop and the presence of primitive irrigation bunds may indicate some degree of control over water resources which must always have been scarce in this generally arid area.

Beginning sometime early in the third millennium B.C., a cultural complex appears in the piedmont zone adjacent to the Indus plain. Named for the typesite Amri, this complex consists of several probably related cultures. All of these sites share a common settlement pattern and are characterized by similar pottery traditions. Typically these settlements were located above the flood plain in the tributary valleys of the Indus. Many of the settlements were fortified with walls of irregular mud brick and stone. Although the Amri pottery traditions are distinct from those of the Indus civilization, it is still possible to see in them the beginnings of the distinctive motifs of the Indus pottery. On the whole, the Amri culture seems to have been a direct predecessor of the Indus civilization. Because so many of the Amri settlements were destroyed by fire at a time coinciding with the emergence of the Indus cities, it has been speculated that the cities arose in the Indus valley in part as a response to external threat. People fled from the smaller isolated communities and congregated in larger settlements where they would be safe from attack. Attractive as this notion is, there is the possibility that the Indus cities were themselves formed by peoples who conquered the Amrians. The forging of the Indus empire could thus be read as a record of imperial conquest. Even if the Amri and Indus cultures prove to be directly related, it is still not easy to rule out the possibility that the destruction of the Amri settlements resulted from internal imperial expansion rather than attacks from foreign invaders.

Sometime around 2500 B.C. these proto-cities in the piedmont were superseded by the Indus culture, a fully developed urban civilization centering on the rich alluvial flood plain of the Indus River.

Covering an immense territory of nearly half a million square miles, the Indus civilization was the world's first great empire. Its north-south axis ran from the Arabian Sea to the foot of the Simla Hills, and recent excavations have extended its reach eastward to the Jamuna River basin and southward to the estuaries of the Narbada and Tapti rivers on the Gulf of Cambay. In contrast to most other early civilizations, the Indus civilization was relatively isolated and protected from invasion by high mountains. There are, however, numerous penetrable gaps in this northwestern mountain chain, and through these India's invaders and conquerors have found their way to the lush plains of the Indus and Ganges rivers. For this reason, the northwest has historically been a schizoid region—looking both east and west. Not only was this the prevailing tendency in the third millennium B.C., it is reflected in the present-day partition of the subcontinent into the nations of India and Pakistan. Although there have been numerous speculations on the relationship between the Indus valley and Sumerian civilizations, the evidence indicates that this was essentially a relationship based on trade. In fact, it is owing to this trading relationship that we were first able to date the Indus civilization. Numerous seals characteristic of the Indus civilization found at datable levels in Sumer constituted the most conclusive evidence for ascribing an approximate date to the Indus civilization. More recently radiocarbon tests have indicated an approximate date of 2150 to 1750 B.C. as the time span of the Indus civilization.

Thus far, the Indus civilization has been referred to as though it were one homogeneous culture. This is not the case, however, for there were at least four distinct, but probably related, urban civilizations in the Indus valley. The first of these was the Amri culture (p. 30), located on the lower reaches of the Indus River. The Indus culture followed the Amri by several hundred years. Following the Indus culture was the Jhukar culture, with a distinctive architecture, pottery, and seal style. The fourth and last pre-Āryan culture in this region was the Jhangar culture, known only from its pottery remains.

Archeological Evidence

The Indus civilization is known largely from three archeological sites: Harappā, Mohenjo-daro, and Chanu-daro. That these were all part of the same civilization is an inescapable conclusion derived from their numerous similarities. The general features of these urban centers are so strikingly homogeneous that all of them must have been deliberately built according to the same plan. In each, there are two principal streets oriented to the cardinal points of the compass. Radiating from these central streets are numerous side-alleys and thoroughfares. Each city had an extensive drainage system, in many ways far surpassing the sewage-disposal systems of contemporary Indian cities. Both Harappā and Mohenjo-daro are dominated by an acropolis or citadel built with mud and mud brick to a height of 40–50 feet above the plain. Located on this acropolis were ritual buildings and places of assembly. At Mohenjo-daro the state granary was located on this acropolis while at Harappā the granaries were built between the acropolis and the river.

The Indus people built with burnt brick—all of a standard size. The larger houses had side-street entrances leading into a courtyard where animals were kept and cooking was done. The water supply for each home came from wells often located in the courtyard. Inside, houses were partitioned into several rooms, one of which was a bathroom. Unbroken by windows, the featureless outside walls of the houses impart a forbidding air to the excavated streets.

Contrasting with these large houses, which must have been the residences of the wealthy urban merchants, are much smaller houses in a segregated quarter localized around a special well. There, workers' quarters are arranged in two parallel rows with a narrow street in between. Identical in size and plan, the workers' quarters suggest a military establishment or a modern factory town, and attest to the regimentation and uniformity of this civilization. Behind the workers' quarters at Harappā are orderly rows of circular floors built of baked brick and containing a huge wooden mortar in which grain could be ground. Near the mortars are the massive state granaries, and not far away are the furnaces used by the metalworkers.

The metals worked by the Indus people were copper, bronze, and tin. Tin came from the west, but the source of copper must have been relatively near, as the arsenic content in the Indus copper is higher than that of Sumer. Metallurgical techniques included both casting and forging.

The Indus valley people had an extensive system of weights based on a binomial coupled with a decimal system. The entire system was factorable by 16. This usage prevails to the present day, showing itself in such idiomatic expressions as "8 anna crop," and in the monetary system, which before recent revision consisted of 16 annas to a rupee. Almost all the scales and weights found were accurate.

The agricultural surplus which presumably filled the huge central granaries of Mohenjo-daro and Harappā was produced by peasants residing in numerous satellite agricultural communities surrounding the large urban centers. The major crops were barley, wheat, sesamum, field peas, and cotton. Cotton was spun and woven, and cloth may have been an important export product. Domesticated animals included the humped bull, the domestic buffalo, goats, sheep, pigs, dogs, cats, elephants, camels, horses, asses, and fowl. Aside from navigation and pack caravans, the major means of transport was the ox cart, differing but little from its contemporary Indian counterpart.

Despite this extensive evidence of agricultural economy, there are few clues suggesting the actual technology and agricultural practices of the Indus people. There is no evidence of extensive irrigation nor are there any remains of agricultural implements. Apparently the plow was unknown for it never appears on seals or pottery, although one of the ideograms of the Indus script may depict a rake or harrow. In all likelihood the Indus peasants exploited the alluvial plain in a manner exactly like that of the modern Indian peasant. Wheat and barley, the principal food grains, would have been sown after the floods had subsided and harvested in the spring (the rabī crop of modern India). Such crops as cotton and sesamum (the kharif crop) would have been sown at the beginning of the inundation period and harvested at its close in the autumn. Control of water resources for the autumn crop would have been effected by low earthen embankments surrounding the fields. Both modes of production exploit the fertility of the annually renewed alluvium and take advantage of natural sources of water supply with relatively simple technology and a minimum of skill and labor. Neither method would have left surviving evidence for the archeologist.

The Indus people were engaged in far-flung trading enterprises. From Persia they acquired gold, silver, and tin; turquoise and lapis lazuli came from Afghanistan; red ochre came from the islands of the Persian gulf; amethysts and amazonite came from southern India; and deodar wood came from Kashmir. That they engaged in overseas trade with Sumer is known from the characteristic Indus seals excavated there. In addition textual references from Mesopotamia describe objects imported from Meluhha (the Indus valley) including ebony, carnelian, copper, and ivory. Although no remains of sailing craft have been found, the Mesopotamian sources refer to the "ships of Meluhha" and several representations of ships have been found on seals and pottery. The most important evidence for seafaring trade comes from a recently excavated site at Lothal near the Bay of Cambay. Here was found a great brick dockyard with channels to the sea. Near the dockyard were several heavy pierced stones similar in design to anchors used in Indian shipping in the recent past. Long-distance inland trade was probably conducted in caravans of pack animals. It is quite obvious that all this trade must have required a large and influential merchant class, and the regulation of exchange.

Religious Artifacts

There are no definitely religious shrines or temples in any of the Indus cities, with the possible exception of Mohenjo-daro. A large mound at that site under a recent Buddhist stūpa might be a temple. Whether there was an established priesthood is unknown, although the different forms of male attire depicted on seals and statuary is often interpreted as indicating the existence of a priestly class. Similarly, the small cell-like apartments surrounding the great bath at Mohenjo-daro are often identified as quarters for priests. The great bath itself probably indicates that ritual lustrations were as important to the Indus valley people as they are to contemporary Indians. Considered as a total unit, the entire citadel area in both Mohenjo-daro and Harappā appear to have had some important ceremonial function. Approached by terraces with large gateways and guard rooms, and surmounted by a large pillared hall, the great bath, and the priests' cells, these elevated citadels were evidently the center of religious and ceremonial rites in which vast processionals seem to have figured.

There are numerous mother-goddess figurines, probably indicating that there was a popular fertility cult. This feature reappears in later Hinduism in the form of a feminine principle represented in Śakti worship, and the worship of Pārvatī, wife of Śiva. There are numerous male figures, also probably part of a fertility cult, since many of the figures are phallic symbols. Representations of plants and trees probably stand for vegetation deities. Animal deities are represented most frequently by a horned creature, often with a basket around its neck, as though it were feeding. There are many other such "hybrid" animals represented on seals in addition to such nonhybrid animals as the humped bull, ox, and elephant. There is one figure of a three-faced deity sitting in a yoga posture, surrounded by animals. This deity is sometimes referred to as Proto-Śiva, indicating its probable relationship to the contemporary Śiva Paśupati (lord of beasts). This same deity is also shown holding Śiva's trisu (three-pronged fork). Another figure is seated in a yoga posture surrounded by serpents, just as the present Śiva is often depicted. Among religious symbols, the swastika appears frequently. Figurines of dancing girls are assumed to represent religious dancers.

Pottery and Sculpture

Indus pottery differs from that of the Amri culture in its thickness, decorative design, and color. Amri pottery is thin-walled, decorated with a geometric design, wheel-turned, porous, and shows attempts to use polychrome with a pink, gray, brown, or reddish band at the neck. The Indus pottery is thick-walled, wheel-turned, kiln-fired, and red, with a design usually painted on in clay. The Indus people used a slip of red ochre, painted a black design over the slip and then fired the pot. The patterns most frequently used were intersecting circles and tree patterns in panels alternating with other designs. Animal figures and cross-hatchings were common. There were few human figures, and polychrome was not usual. This latter feature distinguishes the Indus from the later Jhukar culture which made extensive use of polychrome. In addition to pottery, small figures of clay were common. Most of these were probably made as toys or dolls for children. There was relatively little stone work in the Indus culture. The only representations of this art medium are two small torsos which display a technical ability and feeling for form that might possibly indicate a more intimate acquaintance with sculpture than finds indicate. In addition to these artifacts are numerous beads, jewelry, bronze figurines of dancing girls, and steatite seals. The latter are the most characteristic product of the Indus culture. Usually square or rectangular, they have a perforated bos, indicating that they were probably worn around the neck. There is a difference in the male costume represented on the seals and that found on sculpture. The seals show men wearing a robe fastened over the right shoulder in the manner of the modern sari. Sculpture, on the other hand, shows men clad in loincloths.

Economic Centralization

Separated by more than 400 miles and located at the upper and lower reaches of the Indus River, the two major cities, Mohenjo-daro and Harappā, give the appearance of being twin capitals of an extensive empire supported by a state-controlled agriculture and commerce. While we may marvel at this early feat of political and economic centralization, it must not be forgotten that it was achieved at the cost of unvarying cultural uniformity and an incredible conservatism which eventually became stagnation. Much of this conservatism and uniformity must be attributable to autocratic rulers and a rigorously enforced set of laws. How else are we to explain the standardized techniques of production, the unvarying size of bricks, uniform pottery types, invariant art styles, the system of weights and measures, strict control of street frontages, the repetitious city plans, and the unchanging script? It is as if all these things once established were decreed to be unchanging. Over the centuries one would expect to find changes reflected in building style, pottery, street layout, and so on, but these features remain virtually unchanged through the whole life span of the culture. Even relatively primitive features which one might expect to change under the influence of new techniques and ideas imported along with the trade goods from Mesopotamia are unaffected. By inhibiting its response to changing circumstances it may well be that the rigid uniformity and ingrained conservatism of the Indus culture were in no small measure responsible for its downfall. Unable to adapt to the threat of new invasions which ruptured the tentacles of empire, it eventually collapsed under the unresponsive weight of its own sterile traditions.

Later Cultures

The Jhukar culture, although found on the same sites as the Indus culture, is much later and is generally inferior to the Indus culture. They had no writing, their round seals were less elaborate, and, although the Jhukar people used many of the building techniques of the Indus culture, their ability as builders was not well developed. Their lack of competence is evident in the irregular size of bricks and the uneven construction of walls. The distinctive Jhukar pottery has black painted designs on a buff background with a red or cream slip in bands. Much of the Jhukar pottery was finsihed by beating—a technique still typical of Indian pottery. In general the Jhukar remains give the impression of a tradition continuous with that of the Indus civilization, but definitely degraded. Apparently the Jhukar people were the remnants of a population partially destroyed by invaders.

Following the Jhukar phase on some Indus sites was a wholly different cultural tradition known as Jhangar. Characterized by a low-quality, gray-black burnished pottery with incised decoration, there is no apparent connection between this Jhangar tradition and those preceding it. This suggests that the original Indus sites, by roughly 1000 B.C., were partially occupied by foreign intruders. In other areas there is no distinctive Jhangar phase. The evidence suggests instead a fusion of Indus traditions and those of several possibly different intrusive peoples. The highly variable evidence from the upper levels of the Indus sites taken together with contemporaneous evidence from the Indus borderlands suggests a series of waves of immigration from Iran in the second millennium.

Fundamental Questions

The Indus civilization poses four fundamental questions: (1) What was its origin? (2) What was the means of its downfall? (3) What is the nature and meaning of its inscriptions? (4) What was its relation to later Indian civilization?

In other parts of the old world it has been possible to demonstrate that the rise of cities was a gradual process, proceeding step by step from the foundations of earlier nonurban agricultural societies. In India it has not yet been possible to discern the clear outlines of a similar process of evolutionary change. It is true that the Indus civilization is preceded in time by small agricultural communities occupying areas adjacent to the great urban centers, but there is no clear record of a cultural connection or developmental sequence linking them in a continuous tradition with the Indus cities. Nor do the earlier levels of occupation in the urban sites themselves yet provide evidence of such a developmental sequence. This absence of a local developing urban tradition suggests that the founders of the Indus civilization were either themselves intruders who brought the idea of cities with them or were indigenes who hit upon the idea of urban centers as a means of protection from intruders. Neither possibility is entirely credible. If they were intruders, where did they come from? Presumably they would have come from some earlier urban civilization and there would be some direct parallel between the form of the Indus civilization and other urban civilizations in the Near East. Yet the evidence points instead to only very indirect parallels. In short, the Indus civilization appears to be an indigenous development which is not derivable *in toto* from extraneous sources. But if the Indus civilization stems from local sources then it seems unlikely that the whole panoply of attributes associated with urban life can so easily be derived merely from a need for defense. Urban centers require an economic base capable of supporting a diversified population. Here the location of the major Indus cities on alluvial plains in contrast to the isolated upland and montane villages of the earlier Indian agricultural communities suggests some kind of agricultural revolution which made possible the exploitation of the rich alluvial soils adjacent to the Indus River and its tributaries. The production of an agricultural surplus could then be attributable to the richer soil and dependable water supply from seasonal inundations. Such an agricultural revolution combined with a presumed need for defense may well have set the stage for the rise of cities in the Indus valley.

From records of trade relations with Near Eastern cities, it is evident that in their declining years the still-existing centers of the Indus civilization had lost contact with the Near East. This loss of contact suggests a gradual cultural deterioration, partially reflected in the sites themselves. The death of the Indus civilization thus was prolonged rather than catastrophic. The causes of its demise have been variously attributed to barbarian invaders and to ecological change. Evidence for the latter is only partial and inconclusive. It is known that the cities were occasionally subject to floods, but the record insists that the cities persisted in spite of these disasters. Only if such flooding could have been persistent or could have in some way prohibited cultivation of significantly large portions of the alluvial plain for a number of seasons would it account for the decline of the whole civilization. It has been speculated that the tons of firewood that must have been consumed in baking the millions of bricks that went into the building of the Indus cities must have eventually denuded the surrounding countryside. This extensive deforestation would have altered the transpiration of moisture and reduced the rainfall. Eventually the desert would have begun to encroach upon the cultivated fields, gradually making them unfit for agriculture. Despite its initial plausibility, this argument cannot be accepted. In the first place, it is doubtful that deforestation was systematic over a large enough area to have affected rainfall appreciably. In the second place, it seems clear that the Indus farmers were not dependent on the even then variable rainfall of the Indus basin. At all times they took advantage of the natural supply of moisture provided by the seasonal inundations of the Indus River. The second argument also invalidates those cases for ecological change which have been built upon the basis of purely fictional southward deflections of the monsoons. It is possible that soil salinity resulting either from the rising water table created by the increasingly silt-elevated riverbed or from heavy irrigation may have contributed to ecological disaster, but this is pure speculation unsupported by evidence of any kind.

Lacking conclusive evidence of dramatic and catastrophic ecological changes, it seems reasonable to assume that the Indus civilization was destroyed by human agents. It is usual to identify these agents as barbarian hordes of Indo-European-speaking invaders known as Āryans. The evidence adduced in favor of this identification consists of various strands. First, the Āryans are thought to have arrived in India at a date corresponding to the downfall of the Indus civilization (1500–1700 B.C.). Second, the sacred books of the Āryans record their conflict with indigenes occupying an area corresponding with that of the Indus civilization. These indigenes were rich in cattle and lived in fortified strongholds. In their hymns the Āryans proudly celebrated the destruction of these strongholds and the expulsion of their dark-skinned inhabitants. The archeological record agrees that some of the cities were destroyed by human violence. Smoke-blackened walls and unburied skeletons haphazardly scattered through the streets testify to these ancient acts of violent destruction. It is difficult to believe, however, that the destruction of such a vast civilization could be the work of small wandering bands of barbarians, and it is also difficult to believe that the invading Āryans arrived in India as a vast military horde debouching suddenly onto the plain and arraying themselves in siege before the strongholds of the Indus people. More probably the Indus civilization was gradually disrupted and eventually beaten down not only by the constant threat posed by the invaders but partially at the connivance of its own people. This at least would be in keeping with the facts of historical invasions of later times. The picture that emerges then is one of a constant and long drawn-out series of minor raids and confrontations, of a gradual loss of security and disruption of farming and trade, of the destruction of outlying agricultural villages, and finally of local segments of the population independently suing for peace with the barbarians. The end result was that the bonds of empire were weakened, the cities were cut off from reliable sources of food, until finally each in turn eventually succumbed.

There have been many attempts to translate the Indus script, but not one has been successful. Some of these ventures have been wild guesses unsupported by evidence or reason, but others have been serious scholarly efforts. The major impediments to translation have been the absence of bilingual texts and the brevity of the inscriptions. Aside from a few inscriptions incised on pottery and copper tablets, the majority of the available inscriptions consists of short passages (the longest of about twenty characters) engraved on stamp seals with accompanying figures of animals, plants, and gods. It is generally supposed that the seals were used as a means of identifying property and that they were an important feature of the extensive system of Indus trade. Although the precise number of characters in the script is a matter of debate, there are too many characters for an alphabetic or syllabic writing system and too few for an ideographic or purely pictographic system. A reasonable assumption recently put forward by a group of Finnish scholars is that the writing is logographic and based on a rebus system. The writing is generally from right to left with occasional boustrophedon (right-left, left-right) passages on inscriptions of two or more lines. Until the script is translated there can be no definitive statement of the linguistic affiliation of the Indus language or of the origin of the writing system itself. Many candidates for linguistic relationship have been put forward, but the most reasonable is that the Indus language was related to the Dravidian family of languages. Because the Mesopotamian script antedates all other writing systems, it seems likely that the Indus script, like that of ancient Egypt, was in some indirect way derived from the Mesopotamian but acquired a purely local and unique character.

Many of the themes and motifs of later Indian civilization are already present in the Indus civilization. Phallic worship, mother-goddess cults, ritual lustration, sacred plants such as the pipal, hieratic symbols like the swastika, and theriomorphic deities all attest to a set of religious themes and motifs as characteristic of contemporary Hinduism as of the Indus civilization itself. Similarly, such contemporary items of technology as the system of weights and measures, bullock carts, and grinding floors are clearly descendants of the Indus civilization. In social organization, it is not difficult to suppose the elements of a rigidly stratified society in the evidence of segregated laborers' quarters, extensive specialized crafts, peasant cultivators, and the guild of wealthy merchants. There is little direct evidence of either a separate warrior or priestly class, yet if the cities were defensive strongholds then it is not unlikely that they were defended by a specialized warrior class. Similarly, the exaction of grain tribute from outlying villages and the imposition of centralized authority in general presuppose some form of legitimate force. Nor can it be doubted that the elaboration of religious forms so eloquently attested by various artifacts indicates other than a class of religious specialists. Yet, despite this evidence there is such a sense of heavy-handed mercantile and bureaucratic ideology in the conservatism and utilitarian sameness of the whole Indus civilization that one is reluctant to postulate the existence of warrior-kings or priest-kings. On the whole it is a civilization more consistent with the ethos of IBM than of the flamboyance of oriental despotism. Even so, it is difficult to believe that a bureaucratic merchant class could easily build and maintain such an extensive empire without the use of force or in the absence of sacred authority. What, other than profit, force, or religious sanction, could have persuaded the peasant to relinquish his harvest, the potter his pots, the jeweler his gems, or the merchant his goods? How are we to understand a society which lacks clear evidence of the persuasiveness of market orientations, or of overwhelming subjugation to military or religious authority?

We are necessarily in the realm of conjecture, but I believe the Indus civilization appears so enigmatic not only because of missing bits of evidence, but primarily because we attempt to interpret it through our own familiar but inappropriate paradigm of religion, economy, and polity as separate though vaguely interconnected institutions whose inherent structures account for human motivation. Instead, I believe we should see the Indus civilization as one of the earliest expressions of a "totalizing" society in which each part is not simply a relation to some other part but in itself expresses a relation homologous to that of every other part. The social macrocosm is not simply the interdependent sum of its constituent parts, but is totally replicated in each microcosmic unit. Such a society is equivalent to a ritual, and the organization of society is a ritual organization. Thus, *the Indus civilization with its fertility cults, castelike subdivisions of society, and centralized agricultural economy represents in its earliest form the essential paradigm of all subsequent Indian civilization*, and behind the diversity of modern India it is still possible to discern this ancient form, elaborated but never destroyed in the turmoil of Indian history. Here, then, in the northwest there developed a perduring form of civilization founded on a changeless mode of agricultural production and a ritual system of economic distribution. The great granaries at Mohenjo-daro and Harappā are the enduring symbols of a civilization whose essential characteristics have always centered on the grain heap. From ancient times this grain heap produced by the yearly toil of peasants was garnered from the villages by a central government and redistributed by fixed mode of payment to all those who participated in its formation. Each step in the process was watched over and carefully nurtured by religious functionaries whose special access to the supernatural founts of fertility guaranteed a rich harvest. In both symbol and substance the grain heap expressed the ritual interdependence implicit in the division of labor. Each division of society played an essential role in the formation of the heap and each received a share of it in return. But there is more here than mere economic interdependence. Because the society is itself a ritual system, one's occupational specialty is a ritual specialty. The peasant, the potter, the metalworker, the merchant, the warrior, the priest, each is master of a ritual, each is part of the total ritual, and the total ritual is the society itself. Participation in this system of production transforms the peasant from agricultural laborer to ritual specialist. Each division of labor shares in a ritual system, each is necessary, and each depends on the other. The whole system is thus transformed from a mere "mode of production" to a gigantic ritual geared to the rhythms and necessities of life itself. The "state," "economy," "religion" are organizations of ritual, not just forms of polity, production, and piety. When we come to the realization that the Indus civilization was organized around the notion of society as a ritual organization, then we can understand why it was so uniform and conservative, and possibly why it disappeared only to live on.

THE REBIRTH OF CITIES

After a brief interregnum beginning with the destruction of the Indus cities, the course toward urban life begun in the hills and valleys of Baluchistan was resumed, but this time in an area farther to the east on the fertile alluvial plain between the Ganges and Jamuna rivers. Here there eventually developed an urban civilization which was to set the pattern of Indian life for succeeding centuries. The cities that arose in the *doab* (area between two rivers) are associated with the eastward movement of the Āryan invaders, and many of the excavated sites correspond to towns and cities recognized as having provided the milieu and general urban background of Āryan epic literature.

The gradual eastward expansion of Āryan occupance and subsequent cultural unification of the north is reflected in the character of archeological remains. The sites display progressive uniformity in their upper strata and marked variability in their lower strata. The Panjāb sites closest to the Indus cities indicate a hiatus between the late Indus remains and an intrusive painted gray pottery found in association with iron and dating from 1400 to 1000 B.C. Further to the east in the Ganges-Jamuna *doab*, the lowest strata, dated at approximately 1400 B.C., begin with an ochre-colored pottery which is followed by painted gray pottery and iron around 1000 B.C. Beyond the *doab* to the eastern reaches of the middle Ganges, the lowest levels, dating from 1100 B.C., are characterized by the presence of a black-and-red painted ware and the absence of painted gray ware in upper strata. Extending from 500 to 200 B.C., the upper strata of sites in all these areas contain a fine black polished ware. In the universal incidence of this black polished ware it is possible to read a record of gradual cultural unification which corresponds with the political unification of the area wrought by the Mauryan emperors in the fourth and third centuries B.C.

As for the character of the settlements represented by these sites, a similarly progressive trend from village to city emerges. In the west it is possible that the ochre-ware culture is an outlying remnant of the Indus civilization, and the presence of mud or mud-brick walls tends to confirm this possibility. By contrast, the settlements associated with the painted gray ware were probably small villages or rude market towns consisting of wooden structures. The absence of defensive walls and substantial masonry structures corresponds to what is known of early Āryan building traditions and is consistent with the Āryan pattern of loosely knit tribal organizations. With the rise of petty kingdoms and local empires it became necessary to protect these settlements with brick ramparts and moats, and this is the pattern characteristic of the black-polished-ware sites. In the protected environs of these settlements, kings held their courts, merchants plied their trade, and artisans fashioned items of household and courtly use, while builders and masons extended the defensive walls and embellished the royal buildings. In short, all the elements of urban civilization, save writing and coinage, were undeniably present in these sixth-century settlements. And although writing is not attested until the rock-cut pillar edicts of the emperor Aśoka in the second century B.C., we can be certain that it underwent a period of development prior to this time.

NEOLITHIC CULTURES

The outlying borderlands of the east and the peninsula south of the Vindhya Mountains did not participate in these formative developments. Outside the seminal riverine areas of northwest and north-central India, there is no evidence of cities before the fifth century, and those that occur after that date were almost certainly emulations of the northern example if not the direct result of northern colonization.

Roughly contemporaneous with the urban civilization of the Indus valley, a neolithic culture marked by polished or ground stone axes had developed in the south. This neolithic tradition continued until about 1000 B.C. when it was replaced almost overnight by the use of iron and in some areas by an iron-using megalithic culture. These neolithic peoples were seminomadic cattle-keepers and agriculturalists who lived in small, scattered hill settlements consisting of circular huts of wattle plastered with mud and cow dung. On the hillsides they built small terraces with stone retaining walls behind which they cultivated various grains and millet. In addition to these permanent settlements near their terraced fields, they also built cattle stations to facilitate seasonal pasturage. These cattle stations were large timber-stockaded cattle pens located in the forest at considerable distance from their permanent settlements. In all, these neolithic settlements evoke a way of life not too different from the hill cultures so poetically described in the Tamil literature of much later date. In fact, with the addition of a few modern trappings, it is very similar to the life followed by many contemporary Indian cattle-herding tribes and castes.

In the western littoral and central portions of the upper peninsula, neolithic cultures are followed by a black-and-red pottery and iron. In the upper levels of these sites the black-and-red pottery gradually yields to the black polished ware characteristic of the Ganges civilization. Farther south in the rest of the peninsula, a similar black-and-red ware is frequently found in association with iron implements, but the upper strata lack the northern black polished ware. Thus, in the southern areas directly bordering the Ganges civilization, the introduction of iron is soon followed by black polished pottery—that ubiquitous symbol of an expanding and unifying northern empire. Farther south this pattern of political and cultural dominance does not occur. Instead, the comparable period (500–200 B.C.) is defined by the emergence of a culture known by a distinctive burial complex involving the erection of aligned stone monoliths, rock-cut chambers, pit-circle graves, and cist graves. Black-and-red pottery and uniform types of iron tools are found in all the graves. The similarity of some of these grave types to those in central Asia, the Caucasus, Arabia, and the Levant have led to wild speculations as to the origins of this culture. Although the variety of grave types is such as to suggest some kind of intrusive population, it is likely that only a few of them could be attributed to this source. Similarly, likenesses between these graves and the contemporary practices of tribal groups in central India and Assam are usually dismissed. This dismissal may be hasty, for there is at least one grave type—the aligned dolmen—that not only is consistent with contemporary Dravidian tribal conventions, but also is attested in the early Tamil literature. In the latter the populace is described as erecting standing "hero stones" in honor of a deceased warrior. In my opinion there is no difficulty in assigning the dolmen graves to Dravidian peoples. The uniform iron implements found among the grave goods are clearly derivable from the Ganges civilization, but their presence probably indicates cultural borrowing rather than population movements. The economy of this megalithic culture seems to have been based on shifting agriculture, although ancient tanks (ponds) adjacent to at least one settlement may indicate that the megalith builders practiced tank irrigation.

On the Indian borderlands two neolithic cultures with definite affinities to non-Indian sources developed. In Assam, assemblages of stone axes and pottery with distinctive similarities to Chinese and Southeast Asian types have been found. Most characteristic of the stone tools are shouldered adzes similar to those widely distributed throughout Southeast Asia. A similarly intrusive neolithic culture found in the Vale of Kashmir dates from about 2300 B.C. The settlement consisted of pit dwellings, and the material culture included ground stone axes, bone points, awls, needles, ring stones, and a rectangular chopper unlike anything previously found in India. More notably, dogs were sometimes buried with their masters, and other animals were ceremonially interred. All of these elements are foreign to India, but almost identical with the features of neolithic cultures in north China. In sum, neither these primitive hunters nor the Stone Age farmers of Assam played an important role in the formation of Indian civilization. They are simply isolated outposts of other neolithic traditions.

THREE

THE ORTHODOX PATTERN

Our next records of civilization in India derive from the Āryan invaders who are generally thought to have entered India between 1700 and 1200 B.C. Descriptive terminology for the stages of Āryan occupance and the development of Indian institutions corresponds to the major subdivisions of Vedic literature. This literature is the primary source of information on Indian civilization during the period from 1000 to 500 B.C. The major literary subdivisions are: the four *Saṁhitās* (*Ṛg Veda, Sāma Veda, Atharva Veda, Yajur Veda*); the *Brāhmaṇas* and the *Āraṇyakas* (forest books) appended to the *Brāhmaṇas*; and the *Upaniṣads*. Each of these was composed during subsequent stages of Āryan spread in the order given, and each reflects facets of the process of Āryan/non-Āryan interaction and synthesis. These four classes of literature are often referred to as *Vedas* even though that designation in its narrower sense refers only to the four *Saṁhitās*. The *Saṁhitās, Āraṇyakas, Brāhmaṇas,* and *Upaniṣads* are classed as *śruti* (revealed). They are eternal, have no human authors, and were "seen" by the *ṛsis* (seers). Other sacred literature is classed as *smṛti* (recollection), traditional accounts which have been handed down, but were not revealed.

The *Ṛg Veda* is the book of knowledge of hymns; the *Sāma Veda* is the book of knowledge of chants; the *Yajur Veda* is the book of knowledge of sacrificial formulae; and the *Atharva Veda* is the book of knowledge of prayers and curses. *Āraṇyakas* are allegorical interpretations of the sacrifice intended as a special form of knowledge for those who entered upon the hermit life. As the divisions within the priestly class became more elaborate, each division or school came to be associated with an oral tradition (a *Brāhmaṇa*) consisting of commentary and speculation on the meanings of the *Saṁhitās*. The *Upaniṣads* carry out the program of speculation and allegorical interpretation begun in the *Āraṇyakas* and *Brāhmaṇas*, but, in so doing, effect the development of a great philosophic tradition which stands as the foundation for all subsequent Indian philosophy.

Completed in its present form by approximately 1000 B.C., the *Ṛg Veda* is the most important source for this early period of Indian history. It is a collection of hymns for the king consisting of ten books and a 117-hymn appendix which is sometimes classed as an eleventh book.

The locale of the *Ṛg Veda* is in eastern Panjāb. Evidence for this is derived from references to identifiable rivers, mountains, and other geographical features mentioned in the *Veda*. The Jamuna (Yamuna) River, for example, is mentioned only three times in the *Ṛg Veda*, and the Ganges only once. The River Narmadā (Narbada) is not mentioned at all, nor is there any mention of the Vindhya Mountains.

In the *Veda* the universe is divided into two parts: the *sat* (existence, truth) and *asat* (nonexistence, untruth). The sat—the region of the universe in which men and gods move—consists of the surface of the earth, a vault above, and the atmosphere in between (the middle region). The earth contains heat, light, and moisture. There is permanent light outside the vault, and the chinks in the vault are the stars through which light comes. The asat—the realm of the demons—is without light, heat, and moisture. In the sat, everything operates according to order and law expressed in the word *ṛta* (made to move, law, order, truth). The realm of the demons has no ṛta, it is *anṛta* (chaos). The realm of ṛta is the realm of sat (truth) and the realm of anṛta is the realm of asat (nontruth). (See Figure 3.)

The sat is ruled by the 33 gods, who are in turn ruled by Indra. The gods are divided into three classes: celestial, terrestrial, and atmospheric. The chief celestial divinities are Varuṇa, Sūrya, Savitṛ, Viṣṇu, Uṣas, Aditi, Mitra, Āryaman, the Aśvins. Among atmospheric deities, the most important are Indra, Rudra, Vāyu, the Maruts. Agni, Soma, Bṛhaspati, and Yama are the major terrestrial gods. Many of the gods represent personifications of natural forces. Thus Vāyu is the wind, Uṣas is the dawn, Sūrya is the sun, Agni is fire. Other gods are personifications of ritual. Soma, for example, is a personification of a powerful sacrificial beverage. Still others, like Tvaṣṭṛ (the artificer), are agentive gods. Because they need offerings, the gods can be cajoled into aiding men by the proper performance of sacrifices. Gods and men are interdependent.

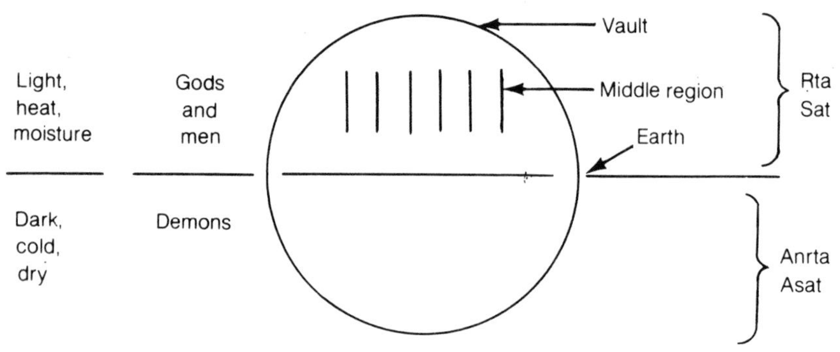

Figure 3. The Āryan cosmos.

The asat is ruled by Vṛtra and his cohorts, the Rakṣases. The Rakṣases aid evil men, or snatch unsuspecting men from the face of the earth. They are most dangerous at night and during the journey of the dead along the path to heaven. Lurking on this path, they drag the unrighteous from it. For the righteous dead, two dogs stand on the path to ward off the Rakṣases.

There are two general cosmological myths in the *Ṛg Veda*: the Deva and Asura myths. In the Deva myth, common to all Indo-European peoples, sky-father (Dyaus) impregnates earth-mother (pṛthivi) with rain and she has offspring who become the gods. Uṣas (the dawn) and the Aświns (horses of the wind) are among the results of this cosmic copulation. The Deva myth is not a particularly important myth in the Vedas while the Asura myth is, in general, the dominant myth. The word Asura in this myth means creature possessed of power, but in later portions of the Veda comes to mean demon. The Asuras originally lived in a house built for them by the god Tvaṣṭṛ (artificer, builder). The house consisted of heaven and earth which at this time were undivided. The sat and the asat were similarly undivided. There are two classes of Asuras: Āditya (antibondage) and Dānava (bondage). The Ādityas stand for expansion, development, and light; the Dānavas for darkness and bondage. Their leader is Vṛtra (the encloser). Neither the Dānavas nor the Ādityas has a parentage; they are personifications of abstractions. Because the Ādityas want to release the "cosmic waters" and the Dānavas want to keep them contained, a war ensues. In this war the three Ādityas—Varuṇa, Mitra, and Āryaman (the number varies)—are being worsted by the Dānavas and need a champion. They arrange for the birth of Indra, who is kept out of sight when first born, but after drinking soma he enlarges to such a great extent that earth and sky fly apart in terror. Indra fills the space in between. He agrees to be champion of the Ādityas only if they make him king of the gods. To this they assent. Tvaṣṭṛ forms a weapon (the vajra "thunderbolt") for him, and with it he slays Vṛtra, cuts him open, and the cosmic waters flow forth—freeing the sat from the asat and making it possible to organize the cosmos and give it order, light, heat, and moisture. Ṛta is established and Varuṇa made the guardian of it. Evil, however, is not completely abolished. The gods still need support in the form of sacrifices, for every day the battle with Vṛtra is renewed. Daylight symbolizes the victory of the Ādityas, and night the encroaching reign of the demons. For this reason, night is an evil time when the demons roam freely until the battle is renewed at the break of day with the morning sacrifice.

In essence, this myth follows the developmental sequence of: (1) in the beginning there was undifferentiated chaos; (2) there is a release of potentiality (energy symbolized by Indra and the life-giving cosmic waters); and (3) the universe is created and order prevails. The central problem of Vedic literature is to keep the universe in operation according to ṛta through the cooperation of god and man against the designs of the Dānavas and Rakṣases. The essential method for accomplishing this end is proper performance of the sacrifices.

Ethical concepts in the *Vedas* are derived from the concept of ṛta. In this natural order of the universe, each man and each god has his proper place with an associated set of duties. Eventually these duties came to be designated in the *Veda* on the basis of occupation, and each man's duty became that of the group to which he belonged. This functional explanation is represented in the division of society into the four varṇas (Brāhmaṇ, Kṣatriya, Vaiśya, Śūdra). The Brāhmaṇs are a priestly class responsible for the sacrifices; Kṣatriyas comprise a warrior class from which the king is selected; Vaiśyas are farmers; and Śūdras are laborers. In addition to unique duties assigned to each varṇa, other duties incumbent upon all men were performance of the sacrifices, and combatting the forces of evil. When both gods and men performed their proper duties correctly, the universe was in harmony, operating in conformance with the laws of ṛta. Conversely, when men and gods failed in the performance of their duties, the universe fell into chaos (anṛta) and evil triumphed.

In the earlier portions of the *Ṛg Veda*, supernaturals of whatever kind are Asuras—that is, creatures possessed of occult power. The Asuras are divided into two classes: Ādityas (gods) and Dānavas (demons). The Ādityas are subdivided into celestial, atmospheric, and terrestrial deities. Dānavas are subdivided into Rakṣases (enemies of men) and Piśācas (enemies of the departed fathers). The whole class of Dānavas are enemies of the gods. The general classification of supernaturals is illustrated in Figure 4.

Asuras (supernaturals)				
Āditya (gods)			Dānava (demons)	
Celestial	Atmospheric	Terrestrial	Rakṣases	Piśācas
Varuṇa, etc.	Indra, etc.	Agni, etc.	Vṛtra, etc.	(various)

Figure 4. The Vedic classification of supernaturals.

In the later *Vedas* as well as in the later portions of the *Ṛg Veda* itself, this classification is superficially transformed. The demons are referred to collectively as Asuras, the gods as Devas. The Ādityas become a mere subclass of celestial deities and are given a dubious parentage. This change is illustrated in Figure 5. Despite these shifts in the denotata of specific terms, there is no substantial structural change in the taxonomy of supernaturals from the earlier to the later *Vedas*. To be sure, there appears to be no head term for the class of supernaturals, but the basic opposition between gods and demons remains unaffected. In this respect it is important to note that much of post-

Devas (gods)			Asuras (demons)	
Celestial	Atmospheric	Terrestrial	Rakṣases	Piśācas
Varuṇa, Ādityas	etc.	etc.	etc.	etc.

Figure 5. Transformation of supernatural categories.

Vedic thought is in some way connected with the missing term denoting supernaturals. The question becomes crucial when the taxonomy of supernaturals is transformed into a process of cosmic evolution. The thing denoted by the missing term then comes to be interpreted as the underlying cause or source of origin even of the gods themselves. In the Hindu synthesis of later centuries the classification of deities is transformed. In place of classification on the basis of taxonomic contrast as represented in Figures 4 and 5, the gods are classified into hierarchic ranks corresponding to the major divisions of society (see pp. 85–86). The classification of supernaturals is thus transformed from a taxonomy to an hierarchic tree in later Hinduism.

The major deities in the *Vedas* are Indra, Varuṇa, Rudra, and Agni. Indra's origin is obscure. He is called "the sun of strength" or "the lord of strength." An atmospheric deity, he is the youngest of the gods and must have Soma three times daily. He is the archetype of the Āryan warrior chief. Other atmospheric deities are associated with him as personifications of his power—for example, Vāyu (the wind), Maruts (storm gods), and Rudra (the roarer, probably thunder). Rudra is an object of fear. Dwelling in the distant mountains he is a divine archer whose arrows bring disease. In his beneficent aspect he is the guardian of healing. Like Indra, he is amoral and capricious. A stern and remote god who abhors evil deeds, Varuṇa is custodian of ṛta and king of the celestial deities. He has spies (the stars) who point out those who violate ṛta. On these offenders, Varuṇa inflicts dropsy, symbolizing their inability to escape from the Rakṣases. Evil men he condemns to the "House of Clay," a gloomy, subterranean hell. Agni is the god of sacrificial fire—in fact, like Prometheus, he is the god of all fire. Agni carries the offerings to the gods in the form of vapor or smoke if he approves of the offering and if the ritual is correctly performed. These offerings were usually ghī (clarified butter), grain, or animals.

Lesser deities include Yama, lord of death, the first man to die, who became guardian of the world of the Fathers where the righteous dead, in a state of eternal bliss, feast on the offerings of the living. Ṛbhus were gnomes who worked in metal. Gandharvas were divine musicians, and apsarases were beautiful nymphs, mistresses of gods and men. Mention should also be made of a mysterious entity called brāhmaṇ.* Sometimes brāhmaṇ is the magical power inherent in sacred utterances, but more often it is a contagious, formless power. One who possessed this power was known as a Brāhmaṇa, a priest or magician, whose words conveyed supernatural power.

At the center of the Vedic cult was the domestic sacrifice (yajña) symbolized by the god Agni. The constant companion of every householder, Agni inhabited the household fire kindled at marriage. Vedic sacrifice was thus preeminently a cult of the family hearth, and all the altars of Vedic sacrifice are but metaphoric extensions of the family hearth. Even in later times the elaborate royal sacrifices performed for the king are simply macrocosmic ceremonies performed for the family of Āryans. The king is to his subjects as

**The word "brāhmaṇ" in its various forms has come to mean several things. For example, Brāhmaṇ denotes both the varṇa and the caste; brāhmaṇ denotes the deity;* Brāhmaṇa *means the text (when italicized), or it meant a priest in earlier times; Brahmā denotes a deity.*

a father is to his family. He is the head of the sacrifice who undertakes to protect his family and ensure fertility.

An altar could be constructed anywhere, for the sacrifice entailed no temples, images, or sacred localities. From the flames of the household fire two sacrificial fires were kindled on separate altars. The first or northern altar was dedicated to the deities, and the second or southern was dedicated to the demons. In the fires of these altars Agni temporarily took up residence as a divine messenger who bore away the sacrificer's gift to the god invoked in the sacred formulae. Taking the sacrifice in his mouth, Agni rose up in the smoke like a bird carrying food to its fledglings. The gods, their strength renewed by the sacrificial food, agreed to defeat the enemies of the householder.

Essential to the sacrifice was the Brāhmaṇ priest who summoned the gods by his prayers and incantations. The pouring forth of magically potent words in the incantation was mystically identified with the pouring of oblations on the sacred fire. Compelled by their divine hunger and the power of the incantations, the gods arrive in their shining heavenly vehicles and take up seats on a litter of holy grass around the altar where they partake of the offerings as honored guests.

The whole point of the domestic sacrifice was to promote universal order and to secure the wealth and well-being of the householder. Through these sacrifices the virtuous householder obtained both the good things of this life and a place in the heavenly abode of the Fathers. The domestic sacrifice thus formed the crucial link between the ideal order of the social microcosm and the heavenly macrocosm, but Vedic religion as expressed in these domestic sacrifices is a sterile, mechanical thing lacking joy, warmth, or wonder. It is a religion in which the individual is subservient to the social order and is forever cut off from closeness with the gods. In the Vedic scheme of things the gods were not particularly virtuous and therefore worthy of emulation, they were merely powerful and therefore worthy of supplication and propitiation. Even their power was chancy, more often than not rendered ineffective through the countervailing power of the demons or the quarreling and bungling of the gods themselves. But, in addition to their power, the gods possessed one trait that separated them from mere humankind—they were immortal (amṛtyu). More than anything, Vedic man desired this godly quality. In comparison to immortality the impermanent rewards of the domestic sacrifice pale into insignificance. Thus, alongside the domestic sacrifice, there is an entirely different sacrificial series whose chief aim is to conquer death with amṛta, the drink of immortality.

Dedicated to the god Soma, the central act of these immortality sacrifices was the meticulous preparation and consumption of an hallucinogenic drink called *soma*. The context of a Soma sacrifice differs significantly from the domestic sacrifices for it entails a rite of consecration and purification. Bathed, anointed, and dressed in fresh garments, the sacrificer sits on a black antelope skin in a special hut near the sacrificial fire. Here he fasts in solitude through the night, generating the mysterious power of heat (tapas). Properly consecrated, the sacrificer quaffs the soma and acquires the power of the gods. Bright visions, the power of flight, enormous strength, and a beatific sense of well-being are the immediate bounty of the soma drinker.

Clearly the Soma sacrifices constitute an ecstatic cult devoted to a mystical exaltation that makes man akin to the divine. At its root it is a cult designed to transform man into a god, to establish an identity between man and god. In its individualism it contrasts with the household rituals devoted to Agni, which are purely rituals of the social order or the kin group, reaffirming the householder's obligations. Unlike the Soma sacrifices they are not designed to release the sacrificer from his earthly obligations or the limitations of his mundane existence. The domestic rites exalt morality and the social order, but the Soma rites are amoral and individualistic. Here it is significant to note the close association between Indra as the amoral warrior or supreme individual, and Soma. In contrast, Varuṇa as the chief symbol of the social order is closely associated with Agni and the domestic rituals.

Vedic religion embodies an essential dualism, opposing the individual and the social order (see Figure 6), and it is the tension and conflict between these two orientations that motivates all later Indian theology. As we shall see, first one then the other predominates until finally in the grand synthesis of Hinduism they are brought into a dynamic equilibrium, each balanced against the other. In the *Brāhmaṇas* exaltation of the sacrifice and elaboration of ritual raised the religion of the social order to preeminence. Later the *Upaniṣads* and heterodox cults repressed this religion of the social order and preached a doctrine of individual salvation through asceticism. In the eventual Hindu synthesis the rituals of the life cycle and the sacrifices of the domestic cult were dynamically joined to the individualistic cults of devotionalism (Bhakti) and asceticism, thus completing what was only inconsistently visualized in the *Vedas*. In recent years this delicate balance between the religion of the social order and the religion of the individual has begun to show signs of strain. A new round of competition between these fundamental categories of Indian thought has been set in motion and we sense in this repetitious struggle something of the dynamic but changeless character of Indian culture, of the shifting substance of dualism within the persistent form of duality.

In the *Vedas* the inherent contradiction between the domestic rites and the Soma rites is not only unreconciled, it is but dimly perceived. To us it seems clear that the Soma rites should have been conceptually linked with anṛta, with the asat, with the undifferentiated state of the cosmos—in a word, with the demons. So it must have seemed to post-Vedic man, for post-Vedic speculation focuses on the central act of the Asura myth—the moment when

Sacrifice (yajña)	
Domestic rites (Agni)	Soma rites (Soma)
Social order	Individual
Varuṇa	Indra
This world/the world of the Fathers	Immortality

Figure 6. Vedic dualism.

Indra, drunk with soma, split the sat from the asat, released the cosmic waters and set the cosmos in motion. The great aim of post-Vedic thought is to recapture the state approximating the undifferentiated plenum that Indra destroyed. In post-Vedic times Indra loses to Vṛtra.

THE RITUAL PARADIGM OF THE *BRĀHMAṆAS*

Between 1500 and 1000 B.C., the first stage of Āryan occupance occurred in eastern Panjāb, south of Umballa, an area known as Brahmāvarta (holy land). In the second stage the Āryans are located in the Ganges-Jamuna doab (area between two rivers) in eastern Uttar Pradesh. In the third stage they moved farther eastward to Bihār. There is an allusion to this movement in the *Śataphatha Brāhmaṇa* (ca. 800 B.C.) where Agni is referred to as burning over the land. This could symbolize either a "slash and burn" type of agriculture or the spread of Āryan sacrifices. Although this is probably a priestly version of the Āryan advance, it indicates that the Āryans were in Bihār by 800 B.C. Slighting references to the eastern part of Bihār in the *Śatapatha Brāhamaṇa* imply that the area east of the Gandak River was not Āryanized before that time. This was the area in which both Buddhism and Jainism came into existence during the fifth and sixth centuries B.C. In addition to this eastern advance, the Āryans were moving down the Indus River to the south in Kathiawār, Gujarāt, and Mahārāshtra. They also moved southward along the western side of the Thār desert. By Manu's time (first century A.D.), the Āryans occupied an area stretching from the Persian Gulf eastward to the Bay of Bengal, and from the Himālayas south to the Vindhya Mountains. This is the area defined as Āryāvarta (land of the Āryas) by Manu. By the latter half of the third century A.D., the Āryans were in Ceylon.

During *Ṛg Veda* times, society was divided into Āryan and non-Āryan elements, with the former subdivided into Brāhmaṇ, Kṣatriya, (Rājanya), Vaiśya, and Śūdra. The Śūdras are regarded in Vedic literature as descendants of non-Āryans who had been conquered by the Āryans and received into the Āryan fold on humble terrms. In the *Vedas* these groups do not appear to have been hereditary, but by the time of the *Brāhmaṇas* they were being further subdivided, and there is some evidence that occupations were becoming hereditary. Marriage restrictions were becoming more strict, but marriages still occurred across group lines, particularly between Brāhmaṇs and Kṣatriyas.

The *Aitareya Brāhmaṇa* defines the relationship of these classes in terms of the king's position. The king's status in the early *Ṛg Veda* had been that of a leader of a tribe in war, but by the time of the *Brāhmaṇas* it had become hereditary and was surrounded with elaborate ceremony. The king is described as having four "precious jewels"—his wife, prime minister, general, and chaplain. The king was also judge of criminal and civil law. Criminal procedure was largely trial by ordeal. Wergeld was practiced with the blood payment ranked in accordance with the status of the person killed. Civil law primarily concerned the division of property among sons. The *Ṛg Veda* mentions two types of assembly: the sabhā and samiti. These assemblies must have consisted of the nobles—probably the Kṣatriyas and Brāhmaṇs—whose major function was selection and censure of the king. That they are rarely mentioned in the *Brāhmaṇas* is probably an indication of their loss of status resulting from the king's acquisition of absolute power.

During the later Vedic period, the king's authority was circumscribed less by the assemblies than by the power of the Brāhmaṇs. Every chieftain had a chaplain (*purohita*) whose ritual assistance was necessary in every undertaking. Extension and elaboration of the sacrificial system far beyond the layman's comprehension contributed directly to the growing power of the Brāhmaṇs. The efficacy of sacrifice, regarded as a mystical force which would irresistibly compel the gods to grant the wishes of men, depended on accurate performance of the ritual. Consequently, the priest became all-powerful, for only he had complete knowledge of every intricate ritual and ceremonial detail. Such great and elaborate state sacrifices as the Rājasūya (coronation) and the Aśvamedha (the horse sacrifice symbolizing imperial authority) developed in the period of the *Brāhmaṇas* are clear indications both of the important position of the Brāhmaṇs and of the king's enhanced position. Also reflecting this trend was the increased specialization within the priestly class. In Vedic times Brāhmaṇs were subdivided into three groups, each of which had special duties to perform at the sacrifice. There were the *hotṛ* (sacrificer), *udgatṛ* (singer, chanter), and *adhvaryu* (ritualist). Associated with each group was a *Veda*—the hotṛ with the *Ṛg Veda*, the udgatṛ with the *Sāma Veda*, the adhvaryu with the *Yajur Veda*. The oral tradition of each group was constituted in its *Brāhmaṇa* which, along with the *Veda*, had to be learned by heart. Gradually even during the Vedic period these priestly schools became great learned associations; as differences crept into the teachings, new schools with new *Brāhmaṇas* were formed. These schools grew by various means. In one, the sacrificial formulae in the *Yajur Veda* were separated from the verses and a new *Yajur Veda* was formed, to be known as the *White Yajur Veda*. The old *Yajur Veda* became known as the *Black Yajur Veda*. In another method, somewhat later, the *Adhvaryu Veda* was compiled and developed a separate set of *Brāhmaṇas*.

In the Vedic period the beginnings of the ascetic tradition were evident in the practice of austerities (*tapas*; literally, "heat"). Various forms of self-torture were inflicted in order to secure miraculous powers or prowess in war, but more important was the view that through tapas one could gain immortality. Thus the gods gained immortality not only through the sacrifice, but also through asceticism. The *Veda* also mentions the long-haired, yellow-robed muni who abandons his body and transcends the profane world. Other supranormal experiences are accorded such mythical figures as Ekavrātya and Vena, who are probably divinized archetypes of ascetics and magicians. A mysterious group called Vrātyas practices asceticism, is familiar with the system of breath control, and in certain of their ceremonies utilizes a form of ritual sexual intercourse. Some of the seeds of the later Yogic and Tantric traditions are thus already attested in the *Vedas*.

Later, at the end of the *Brāhmaṇa* period, the beginnings of an order of ascetics makes its appearance. Living in the forest in huts of wood and leaves are groups of hermits (Vānaprasthas, "forest dwellers"). Their hermitage was called an *aśrama*. They wore coats of bark or skin, their hair was matted, and they practiced austerities. Though tapas was still used to obtain miraculous powers, it was becoming more important as a means of achieving nearness to the divine. A special form of knowledge contained in the *Āraṇyakas* (forest books) was given to those who entered upon this way of life. The *Āraṇyakas* are allegorical interpretations of the sacrifice designed as the basis for meditation.

Philosophical thought begins in the *Ṛg Veda* as indicated by the range of solutions offered for the problem of creation in the Vedic hymns, but by the end of the Vedic period there must have been a dissatisfied group of intellectuals who did not accept the Asura myth—the predominant solution of the *Vedas*. These discontented sages could not accept that the universe had come into existence by the agency of the gods, nor could they believe that the universe operated under the control of an anthropomorphic demiurge. In rejecting the Asura myth these sages sought the undivided state preceding Indra's separation of the sat from the asat. Their mutation of the Vṛtra theme from the Asura myth was expressed in the idea of impersonal force, either as a process of evolution or as an inherent quality, and they found this impersonal force in two different Vedic concepts—brāhmaṇ and sacrifice.

The sacrifice is exalted into a mystic force in R. V. 10.90, the Puruṣa hymn. In this hymn the universe comes into existence through the sacrifice of a primeval being called Puruṣa (man). The four varṇas are created from Puruṣa—the Brāhmaṇ from his head, the Kṣatriya from his arms and shoulders, the Vaiśya from his torso, and the Śūdra from his legs and feet. Puruṣa contained within himself all the constitutive elements of the universe, and out of these elements the gods made an ordered whole through the medium of the sacrifice. The sacrifice thus becomes the mechanism of creation and, through their control of the power of sacrifice, the gods are able to effect the creative act. Creation is not an expression of their own inherent power, it merely expresses their possession of the power of sacrificial ritual.

In contrast to the notion of ritual as the supreme expression of the impersonal force in the universe, R. V. 10.121 develops the idea of supertheism, a god above gods, an unmoved mover. This idea was represented in the god Prajāpati, lord of creatures. The hymn lists all the features of Indra and rejects them, asserting that Prajāpati encompasses all created things. Unlike Indra, Prajāpati is an abstraction. Completely lacking personification, he is the blind force behind all creation.

In the *Atharva Veda* (19.53) an impersonal mechanistic doctrine of creation is advanced. In this formulation everything in the universe is considered to be time, but the Vedic idea of impersonal power inherent in the universe is usually conceptualized as brāhmaṇ. The earliest reference to this concept is the phrase *tad ekam* (that one, sole existent). Tad ekam is the single, impersonal power in contrast to Indra who is merely the *deva ekah* (the one god). As the sole existent, tad ekam contains the elements of creation, and the gods are among these elements in contrast to the Puruṣa explanation which held that the gods were apart from the elements. Tad ekam operates mystically, by its own potency. The *Ṛg Veda* (10.129) asserts that even before the sat and the asat, tad ekam breathed by its own potentiality, not by breath. Tad ekam was born through the power of its own heat (tapas). Desire came upon tad ekam and was the seed of thought. In the beginning then, there is mere unrealized, unactivated potentiality which becomes manifest through its own self-generative powers (tapas). This activity begets desire, and desire causes cognition. The hymn asserts that although the gods do not know of this process the sages do. Through introspection the sages discover the source of being in nonbeing.

At the beginning of the *Brāhmaṇa* period then, two distinct paths of development are evident. The dominant trend manifests itself in the elaboration of ritual, particularly in the service of the king, who stands as a symbol of order and fulfillment of worldly needs. The "less traveled path" of detachment from this world constitutes a rejection of the efficacy of ritual and of its goals. In the *Vedas* the contradiction between these points of view is scarcely realized. In different contexts both are endorsed with equal fervor, but in the *Brāhmaṇas* the idea of ritual is ascendant.

In emphasizing the importance of ritual, the *Brāhmaṇas* effected a major transformation in Vedic thought. Ritual sacrifice (yajña) in the *Ṛg Veda* was a means to an end. It stressed a relation between the sacrificial performance and a result external to the sacrifice. Men sacrificed in order to obtain the good things of life, to ask for forgiveness of sin, to propitiate the demons, or to attain immortality. In this view the sacrifice is a gift which establishes a link between god and man—the sacred and the profane—by means of a victim. Its basic form is simply an invitation to the god to come and partake of the food and drink provided by the sacrificer (yajamāna). The sacrificer does not perform the ritual himself, but has it performed for him by various classes of ritual specialists. When the victim has been consecrated and offered to the gods in the sacred fire, the sacrificer consumes the remains of the offering, thereby establishing not only a mystical communion between himself and the deity, but also acquiring the holy power of the consecrated victim. In the earlier portions of the *Ṛg Veda* there is only a faint suggestion that ritual could compel or coerce the gods to do man's bidding. Instead, the general theme is one of cooperation between men and gods. In their war with the demons the gods depend on sacrifices offered by men. Conversely, men depend on the gods for protection from the demons, for the productivity of cows, crops, and women, and for success in war.

In the later portions of the *Ṛg Veda* a new concept of ritual as a magical spell begins to emerge, and it is this concept which becomes the central theme of the *Brāhmaṇas.* This transformation of sacrifice from gift to spell is first manifested in the notion that the ritual can coerce the gods to do what man desires. The gods are powerless before the magical potency of ritual. The second step in the transformation derives from the first. Because they are powerless in the face of ritual, the gods decline in importance, and in their place the great object of priestly concentration becomes the ritual itself. He who understands and controls its power becomes mightier than the gods. Ritual thus becomes an end in itself rather than an instrument. From here the final step is to see the whole universe as a ritual order. The ritual then is an expression of itself. As in the *Ṛg Veda*, the ritual has cause in it, but it does not depend on some other object. Its causal efficacy is merely an expression of its own potentiality, an idea clearly expressed in the threefold meaning of the word *ṛta*: the order of the universe, the order of the sacrifice, and the order of moral law.

In essence then, the *Ṛg Veda* predicates a "man-sacrifice-gods" paradigm, the *Brāhmaṇas* a "man-ritual-universe" paradigm. In the former the sacrificer acquires the aid of the gods (or immortality, becoming one with the gods). In the latter, the ritualist acquires the power of the universe and becomes greater than the gods. Many Western scholars have condemned the *Brāhmaṇas* as puerile priestly elaborations, but this hasty dismissal neglects the fact that these early priests were working within a conceptual order in itself as sensible and logical as the presuppositions of any priestly cult dedicated to the Faustian proposition that "knowledge is power." That the order of the universe could be identical with ritual and moral order is after all no more ridiculous than the more familiar notions of natural law, the laws of nature, or of scientific determinism. And that man, through right ritual knowledge, could manipulate the universe is no more preposterous or pretentious than the idea that man can immorally manipulate a mechanistically conceived universe through right scientific knowledge.

THE MONISTIC REDUCTION OF THE *UPANIṢADS*

As the concluding portions of the *Vedas*, the *Upaniṣads* recognize the authority of the *Vedas*, but like the *Brāhmaṇas* go on to seek higher truths. Unlike the *Brāhmaṇas* the *Upaniṣads* do not accept the idea of sacrifice as the motivating principle of the universe. Instead they look to the concept of brāhmaṇ, emphasizing a mystical identity between the individual and the impersonal power of the universe. The individual does not acquire the power of the universe through ritual manipulation, but becomes identical with it. There is no longer a relation between the individual and cosmic power, and consequently there is no need for ritual.

Upaniṣadic speculation is thus associated with the elaboration of the ascetic tradition at the expense of the ritual tradition. A new type of ascetic, called parivrājaka (wanderer), bhikṣu (beggar), or sannyāsin (renouncer), appears to reinterpret both the ancient ritual and the ascetic tradition of tapas. Symbolic and allegorical interpretations replace the earlier mechanical explanations of ritual. The ritual act itself is no longer the link between man and the supernatural. Instead, knowledge of the meanings symbolically represented in the ritual becomes the goal. This knowledge, radically interpreted as self-realization, can be attained by those who are adept at meditation. In the *Upaniṣads* the ancient techniques of tapas are thus harnessed to an introspective self-realization which penetrates beyond the flux of things to the underlying ultimate reality. This ultimate reality consists in the equation of brāhmaṇ (the pure absolute) with ātman (the individual self). Brāhmaṇ, envisaged as the transcendent self of the universe beyond manifestation (nirguṇa, "qualityless") and as the transcendent self manifest (saguṇa, "with qualities") resolves the apparent duality between individual selves and the world self.

Brāhmaṇ is the constitutive reality, the cause of the world, the dwelling place of selves. Brāhmaṇ is the ātman of the universe, the self of the individual is ātman, and the universal ātman is identical to the individual ātman. This identity is expressed in the "great affirmation": *tat tvam asi* ("that thou art"). "My self is the infinite self"; *aham brāhmaṇasmi* ("I am brāhmaṇ"). Self-knowledge is knowledge of brāhmaṇ, and he who knows brāhmaṇ is free from the cycle of births and deaths.

In the *Bṛhadāraṇyaka Upaniṣad* (4.3.7 and 2.1.16) attainment of union between brāhmaṇ and ātman is likened to the progression from wakefulness to deep sleep. Here, the sage Yajñavalkya in his conversation with Janaka, king of Videha, postulates three worlds: this world, other worlds, and an area in between. Wakefulness corresponds to this world, dreaming sleep corresponds to the middle world, and deep sleep to the other world. Deep sleep is the state of the ātman in its pure form where there are none of the distinctions of name and form (nāma rūpa). The ability to taste is not lost, but there is nothing to taste; the ability to see is not lost, but there is nothing to see; there is only subject, no object. Identification with Brahmāloka (the place of brāhmaṇ) is complete and the individual ātman and brāhmaṇ are one. Dreaming sleep is metaphysically linked to dying while retaining desires. Dreams are representative of desire which not only keeps the individual ātman and brāhmaṇ separate, but incurs rebirth. The states of the ātman as represented in Yajñavalkya's analysis are all contained in the mystical expression OM (aum). OM is the sound-form of the ātman (*Maitri Upaniṣad* 6.5), and each constituent sound of this word stands for a state of the ātman. Thus: A, this world; U, the intermediate world; M, the other world. The end of the word, when sound ceases, represents an indescribable state in which one has complete self-knowledge (*Praśna Upaniṣad* 5.2).

Just as the *Upaniṣads* radically reinterpret the nature of the universe, so too with notions of the afterlife. In the *Ṛg Veda* the deserving dead go to a vaguely paradisiacal heaven (*svarga*), the abode of the gods and of the Fathers. There they remain, enjoying with the gods the sacrifices offered by the living. In the *Upaniṣads* this simplistic eschatological notion of personal immortality in the paradise of the gods is supplanted by the doctrines of karma and reincarnation. The *Bṛhadāraṇyaka Upaniṣad* (6.2.16) first conceives of the doctrine of reincarnation in purely mechanistic terms. The souls of those who have lived good lives pass into the smoke of the cremation fires, and after some obscure peregrinations, go to the moon, and reside briefly with the Fathers. From there they go to empty space, pass into air, and descend to earth in the rain. There they become food, are transformed into semen, and finally are transmitted into the wombs of women from which they are born again. The unrighteous are reborn as worms, insects, or "whatever there is that bites." From this rather crude conception there developed a sublime notion that linked all forms of life into a single system. Not just the souls of men but the souls of all living things—gods, animals, and plants—the whole of life passed through innumerable changes from life to life in an endless, eternal round of birth, death, and rebirth. This endless cycle is known as saṁsāra.

Karma (literally, action) refers to the inevitable consequences of action, the resolving of one's good or bad actions through many forms of existence. Bad actions incur rebirth in the bodies of lower beings. Good actions incur rebirth in the bodies of higher beings. One's thoughts and deeds in one earthly life have their fruition in a subsequent embodiment. A man's body, character, status, happiness, and sorrow in this life are consequences of past deeds and knowledge. The *Chāndogya Upaniṣad* (5.3) attributes these new ideas to the Kṣatriyas. The Ṛg Vedic idea of paradise is retained only in the notion that death is followed by a brief interval of excarnate existence during which time the deceased enjoys the results of his good deeds. But this brief respite soon ends, for those who have placed their faith in the "unsafe boats" of sacrificial forms and good deeds are eventually reborn. Here the message is clear: those who attend, no matter how diligently, to ritual and good deeds are deluded, for they must return; but those who know brāhmaṇ, who are submerged in brāhmaṇ, who seek the ātman by austerity, chastity, faith, and knowledge, do not return.

Thus the old ideal of cosmic interdependence of man and god expressed in the *Saṁhitās* was gradually transformed, giving way first to the principle of ritual interdependence in the *Brāhmaṇas*, and finally, in the *Āraṇyakas* and *Upaniṣads*, to the monistic doctrine of the identity of brāhmaṇ and ātman. The magnitude of this transformation is scarcely credible. Where the earlier doctrines emphasized the positive values of this life, symbolizing them in rituals whose purpose was to assist men in achieving the good things of this world, the Upaniṣadic ideal is renunciation of these values of the worldly life. If renunciation is the ultimate goal, then the whole intricate structure of ritual and sacerdotal practice so painstakingly elaborated by generations of ritual specialists and now securely in the hands of an hereditary priestly caste is endangered. Yet, in their efforts to seek the cause of the universe, the Upaniṣadic speculators did not repudiate the *Vedas*. Within the encompassing sweep of monism, Vedic gods and rituals could be accommodated as manifestations of brāhmaṇ. Incomplete in the *Upaniṣads*, this accommodation remained implicit until the efflorescence of later Hindu doctrine worked out a systematic reintegration of asceticism and ritual. But this stupendous achievement came only after the sacerdotal tradition was directly threatened by the uncompromising ascetic values of Buddhism and Jainism.

FOUR

THE HETERODOX CHALLENGE

Beginning in the *Upaniṣads* there developed between the seventh and fifth centuries B.C. a tradition of thought that rejected the authority of the *Vedas*, denied the superiority of the Brāhmaṇ caste, denigrated ritual observances, and, in brief, challenged the whole structure of orthodoxy. Because they rejected the metaphysical and social categories of the orthodox tradition, Jainism, Buddhism, and the materialist philosophy of the *Cārvākas* are branded as *heterodox*. This period was marked not only by intellectual ferment, but by far-reaching changes in the structure of Indian society. The old tribal structure of Vedic society had given way to regional kingdoms, and in the less-organized portions of eastern India, the tribal "republics" or confederacies were under constant attack by expansionist centralized kingdoms. Here, in what is now Bihār and eastern Uttar Pradesh, the Āryan class system was less developed and the system of Vedic religion had not yet eradicated worship of local deities (yakṣas and nāgas) at sacred mounds and groves. Here, too, had arisen an influential class of wealthy merchants dwelling in large cities. Doubtless this parvenu merchant class resented the traditional pretensions of the Brāhmaṇ caste, and the transition from tribal to state organization must have created a sense of insecurity and discontent with the sterile sacrificial structure of the *Brāhmaṇas*. Whatever the causes, a wave of pessimism, reflected in the universal acceptance of the doctrines of transmigration and karma, overspread the land. When these doctrines first appear in the *Upaniṣads* there is little suggestion that this life is so full of misery and suffering that the whole aim of life is to escape. Instead, the *Upaniṣads* teach these and the associated doctrine of union with brāhmaṇ as a rare and new form of knowledge whose mystic implications can be mastered only by a select group of specially instructed adepts. Where Buddhism and Jainism emphasize the negative character of life as an argument for the necessity of escape, the *Upaniṣads* emphasize the positive nature of the union between brāhmaṇ and ātman as a higher form of intuitive knowledge.

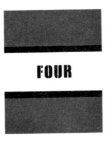

The sources of these heterodox systems can be traced from the *Upaniṣads* through a line of shadowy unorthodox teachers and ascetic sects. Buddhist scriptures mention six "heretics" who taught a variety of doctrines at variance with orthodox thought. The fifth of these teachers was Mahāvīra (great hero), the founder of Jainism. According to Jainist tradition Mahāvīra is the twenty-fourth and last tīrthankara (ford maker) of the present cosmic period. He was preceded by the twenty-third tīrthankara, Parśva, whose teachings and ascetic organization formed the basis of Jainism. A contemporary of the Buddha, Mahāvīra's father was reputedly the chief of the warrior clan of Jñātrikas, and his mother was the sister of a chief of the tribe of Licchavis. Both the Jñātrikas and Licchavis were tribal "republics" in northern Bihār. According to legend, Mahāvīra left home at the age of 30, wandered for 12 years and attained enlightenment at the age of 42. During the next 30 years he taught and founded an order of naked monks. He died in 468 B.C. at the age of 72.

Arising among Kṣatriyas, Jainism eventually flourished under the patronage of one of the emperors of the expanding Mauryan Kingdom. In Jain tradition, the unwritten sacred texts of Mahāvīra were forgotten during the disorganization caused by a great famine. A council of monks was convened to reconstruct the canon, but their efforts only led to schism. Jainism was divided into two sections: the Digambaras (space-clad) and Śvetāmbaras (white-clad). The Digambaras, who insisted on total nudity, did not accept the full authenticity of the reconstructed canon, while the white-robed Śvetāmbaras did. This Jain canon consists of 45 texts composed in the Ardha-Māgadhī dialect of Prākṛt. Probably the oldest and most important are the 11 limbs (aṅga), 12 secondary limbs (upaṅga), and ten miscellaneous texts (Prakīrṇaka).

Jainism is an atheistic, ascetic system build around a doctrine of strict materialism which teaches that the universe consists of six permanent substances: (1) souls (jīva), (2) nonsouls (ajīva), (3) a medium through which movement is possible (dharma), (4) a medium that makes rest possible (adharma), (5) time (kāla), and (6) matter (pudgala). In Jainism the soul (jīva) is finite and has dimension, but it is not an atom. Like the taste of salt in water, it pervades the body it inhabits. Everything in the universe has a soul: men, gods, plants, animals, the elements. These souls are always fettered, enmeshed in matter, their current condition determined by karma. In its pure state the jīva is omniscient and mirrors the universe, but every thought and deed clouds the soul's natural brightness with the subtle matter of karma which flows into the soul through the organs of sense. The goal of Jainism is to free the soul from its immersion in karmic matter. Once cleansed of karmic matter, the jīva is not destroyed, but exists clear, luminescent, with perfect intuition.

The way of deliverance is through the "three jewels" of right faith, right knowledge, and right conduct. Right faith consists in belief in "real existence"—that is, in the tattvas (categories) (p. 59); knowledge of real nature is right knowledge. Practice of the five virtues (nonviolence, truth-speaking, nonstealing, chastity, and nonattachment to worldly things) constitutes right conduct. Knowledge is of five kinds: (1) mati (ordinary cognition, memory, induction); (2) śruti (knowledge derived through signs, symbols, words, and aspects); (3) avadhi (direct knowledge of things at a distance); (4) manaḥparyaya (direct knowledge of the thoughts of others); and (5) kevala (perfect knowledge). The first three are subject to error, the last two are not. The concept of aspects or standpoints (naya) refers to ways of knowing. Knowledge is either of the thing itself (pramāṇa) or of the thing in its relation (naya). As represented in the theory of syādvāda (conditional predication), the naya notion leads to the conclusion that reality, whatever it is, expresses itself in multiple forms. Depending on one's standpoint, reality looks different, is "many-sided." Thus all predications have a point of view, and reality cannot be exhausted in a single predication. This leads to a relativistic doctrine which holds that all knowledge is only probable or partial.

Jainist doctrine teaches nine categories (tattvas) of fundamental truth: (1) soul (jīva); (2) nonsoul (ajīva); (3) merit (punya); (4) nonmerit (pāpa); (5) channels for the entry of karma; (6) obstructions to the entry of karma; (7) bondage of the soul to karma; (8) means of destruction of karmic bondage; and (9) mokṣa (release). Souls are either bound or unbound, and exist in creatures of one sense or two, three, four, or five senses. The last group includes men, gods, the higher animals, and beings in hell. This group is distinguished from the fourth by the possession of intelligence. The fourth group consists of creatures with touch, taste, smell, and sight and includes larger insects. Lacking sight and hearing are such three-sensed beings as small insects. With only the sense of taste and touch, worms and shellfish are two-sense creatures. The final class is subdivided into five subclasses: vegetable bodies, earth bodies, water bodies, fire bodies, and wind bodies. Vegetable bodies may be simple, containing only one soul, or complex, containing countless souls. Each of the five major categories of soul is also subdivided into a sevenfold system which includes, among others, those souls in hell, lower female souls, and higher female souls. Ajīva is divided into two main classes—those without form (arūpa) and those with form (rūpa). Included in the former are motion (dharma), rest (adharma), space (ākasa), and time (kāla); and in the latter is matter (pudgala) which is composed of minute atoms. Since the substances motion, rest, and time are derived from ajīva, it is clear that Jainism is basically dualistic in its cosmology. In a subsequent chapter it will be seen that the oldest orthodox philosophical system, known as Sāṁkhya, has a similar cosmology. The remaining categories of fundamental truth are similarly classified. Thus there are 18 kinds of pāpa which produce evil karma. These include injury to living beings, untruth, eight kinds of pride, greed, and 25 kinds of false faith. There are 82 consequences of sin (pāpa). There are 42 means by which karma may enter, of which 25 are classed as major and 17 as minor. There are 57 obstructions to the entry of karma, four kinds of karmic bondage, and 12 means of karmic destruction comprising six exterior and six interior austerities. The category mokṣa has no karma—it is neither good nor evil. There are 15 kinds of perfected beings.

Actions must be carefully regulated to prevent the influx of karma. Those actions that do no harm and are undertaken from good motives incur very little karma, but even unintentional acts may have serious consequences, and deliberate injury to a living being acquires consequences commensurate with the categorical status of the being injured. Thus the Jain monk will not eat potatoes or other root crops since these complex vegetable bodies contain many souls. He strains his drinking water, wears a face mask to prevent inhaling wind lives, and will not run or stamp his feet for fear of injuring the earth.

For a Jain, the whole world is alive; the universe is a living organism animated by jīvas which circulate throughout it. It is an organism which will never die. Its constitutive jīvas ascend and descend through various states of being, undergoing endless transformations without beginning and without end. The number of souls in the universe is infinite. Most of these have no hope of salvation, and no matter how many obtain release, the number of those that remain is still infinite. Most souls are condemned to eternal transmigration, and this doctrine implies a cosmic conception of time. The universe progresses through great cycles of growth and decay, and each cosmic cycle is divided into two halves, ascending and descending. These two halves are divided into six periods. In the first "very happy" period, men had great size, longevity, virtue, and no cares. The second "happy" stage shows slight diminution of these features, and in the third "happy-wretched" stage sorrow and evil appear, making government, religion, and saviors (tīrthankaras) necessary. Decline continues in the fourth "wretched-happy" period. The fifth "wretched" period, which began three years after Mahāvīra's death and has approximately 21,000 years remaining, will witness the gradual disappearance of Jainism. The sixth "very wretched" period will last for 21,000 years. Men will be pygmies living in caves without morality. Murder, theft, adultery, and incest will be normal. Finally, wild storms will destroy all but a few bewildered survivors. The world will then begin to improve, progressing through these same stages in reverse order.

Unlike Buddhism, which has disappeared from India, Jainism is still a living religion in India. The Digambara sect is largely restricted to the modern state of Mysore, and the much more numerous Śvetāmbaras are found in Gujarāt and Rājasthān. These Jain communities are divided into monastics and laymen. Monks and nuns are expected to observe a rigorous discipline and to keep the five vows. They must not kill, hold property, have sexual intercourse, lie, or steal. The regimen of the monk was, and still is, extreme. At his initiation his hair was pulled out by the roots, he had to fast for long periods, and he was often forced to meditate for hours. The laity may dispense with some of the vows, but should spend the new- and full-moon days fasting at a Jain monastery. Most, however, observe these fasts only at the end of the year when they confess their sins and ask forgiveness for offenses. Full salvation is not possible to laymen. Only by fasting, self-mortification, and meditation can one get rid of karma, and only by the most rigorous discipline can fresh karmic matter be prevented from entering the soul. No layman should take up agriculture, since it involves destruction of life. Jainism thus encouraged commercial careers, and from an early period Jains have predominantly been merchants.

Although Jainism has no supreme deity, it has traditionally made use of iconographic representations of the tīrthankaras as objects of meditation. Jains have also been influenced by their neighboring Hindus. They worship many Hindu gods and perform Hindu domestic rites involving the use of Brāhmaṇ priests. In recent times (eighteenth century) a further schism occurred in the Śvetāmbara sect over these issues. A reforming monk, Vīrāji, argued that true Jainism could not permit iconolatry, foreign ritual, or temple worship. This new sect (sthānakavāsī) has expunged all ritualism and holds its religious services in simple, unadorned buildings (sthānakas).

BUDDHISM

Like Mahāvīra, the Buddha was the son of the chief of a Bihār tribe (the Śākyas). Leaving home at the age of 29 he became an ascetic, gained enlightenment under a sacred pīpal tree at Gāya, and eventually emerged as the leader of a band of yellow-robed bhikkus (monks). According to Buddhist tradition, he died at the age of 80 in the year 544 B.C., after eating a meal of pork in the house of a blacksmith.

In the 40 years of his ministry, the Buddha and his disciples wandered from place to place for eight months of the year, preaching the new doctrine. During the remaining four months, corresponding to the rainy season, they retreated to forest parks where they lived in crude huts meditating and listening to the Buddha's teaching. At this time and during the 200 years following the Buddha's death, the Saṅgha (society, Buddhist order) was but one of a number of rival heterodox sects, probably less influential than the Jains. But soon after the Buddha's death, the first of a series of great councils was convened for the purpose of codifying the Buddha's teaching. As in Jainism, schisms had developed over points of doctrine and monastic discipline. At the third great council, held under the patronage of King Aśoka, many heretics were expelled from the society and the Theravāda (teaching of the elders) was established as the only orthodox school. By this time the Buddhists had abandoned the practice of peripatetic teaching and had settled in permanent monastic communities (vihāras) on the outskirts of towns and villages in the caityas (sacred spots) of the indigenous spirit cult. In these caityas ancient tumuli erected over the ashes of deceased tribal chiefs were transformed into Buddhist stūpas containing the ashes of the Buddha or of revered monks. The sacred trees of the caitya, originally dedicated to spirits of the earth or other fertility deities, were assimilated to the Bodhi (pīpal) tree, that pregnant symbol of the Buddha's enlightenment. Starting from these syncretistic impulses, there gradually emerged an institutionalized religious system replete with an orthodox theological doctrine and monasteries fat with the alms of the faithful. Supported by wealthy merchants and enjoying the patronage of kings, the monks served an enormous lay population. Thus the simple teachings of the Buddha, which encouraged each man to diligently seek his own personal salvation outside the institutional trappings of cult, symbol, ritual, and deity, were gradually transformed, elaborated, and perverted. Occurring over many centuries, this transformation is reflected in the development of doctrine, the rise of competing sects, and the spread of Buddhism not only in India but throughout Asia.

According to Chinese tradition a fourth great council was convened under the patronage of King Kaniṣka (first–second century A.D.). Here were formulated the doctrines which eventually resulted in the division of Buddhism into the "Great" and "Lesser Vehicles" (*Mahāyāna* and *Hīnayāna*). Deriving in part from ideas introduced in the northwest by recent invaders (Greeks, Śakas, and Kuṣāṇas), a new doctrine (*Mahāyāna*) was formulated. This new doctrine, proclaiming its ability to carry many souls to heaven in a great vehicle, soon became popular in India and was carried by Indian monks to China from whence it spread to Japan and Korea. By the seventh century the Lesser Vehicle was almost extinct in India, but it survived in its purest form in Ceylon and was exported from there to Southeast Asia. In eastern India, still the home of heterodoxy in the eighth century, the primitive, pre-Āryan cults, but briefly submerged by the imperialistic eclecticism of Buddhism, still perdured in the form of popular magical doctrines and sexual mysticism. These potent, subterranean ideas were once again incorporated in the form of a Third Vehicle, "the vehicle of the thunderbolt" (*Vajrayāna*). In this new form, Buddhism was established in Tibet in the eleventh century.

The assimilative power which enabled Buddhism to become a popular cult eventually contributed to its decline. Having incorporated so much, it lost its identity for the laity. Buddhism became simply another in a great variety of religious cults, none of which had exclusive rights to the road to salvation. In the ultimate irony, that great atheist, the Buddha himself, was gradually incorporated into the system of Hindu deities, becoming merely the ninth of Viṣṇu's ten incarnations. It is probably true that at no time was Buddhism the exclusive religion of the Indian masses. Even during its greatest efflorescence, Buddhism did not completely supplant earlier faiths, and though the Indian may have supported the monks, he turned to the Brāhmaṇs for family rituals and dared not neglect the dark powers of the village "mother," the earth "mother," or the goddesses of forest, field, fertility, and disease. Such is and has been his practice from time immemorial.

Beginning in the ninth century Buddhism came under more direct attack from a renascent Hinduism which had developed its own order of monks and a devotional cult which it carried directly to the masses in language they could understand. Just as the Buddha had taught in local vernaculars, so did the saints of devotional Hinduism; and just as the Buddhists capitalized on the sterility of Brāhmaṇic ritual conducted in a language the people could no longer understand, so too did the Hindu saints take advantage of the stagnation of Buddhist teaching. Isolated from the people in their fabulous monasteries, the Buddhist monks failed to serve their parishioners. Even before this the Buddhists had begun to lose the patronage of kings, for in the fourth century A.D. the emperors of the Gupta empire gave their chief support to the Vaiṣṇavite sect of Hinduism. Despite occasional Buddhist conversions and the support of the Pāla dynasty down to the twelfth century, the pattern of royal patronage was broken and Buddhism was already a dying tradition in India before its ultimate destruction by Muslim invaders. Even the monastery, one of the signal achievements of Buddhism, proved to be a liability. Cut off now from a laity which they had long ceased to serve effectively, and deserted by their royal protectors, Buddhist monks were dependent on the monasteries for their survival. But the monasteries were easy prey to barbarian Muslims who slew the monks, sacked the great monasteries, and burned their "infidel" libraries. Only in the mountain sanctuaries of Nepal and Tibet did Buddhism survive.

Hīnayāna (Lesser Vehicle)

The essential doctrines of the Lesser Vehicle were probably codified by the third century B.C., but according to tradition were not committed to writing until the first century B.C. Written in Pāli (a dialect of Sanskrit), this canon consists of three sections called "baskets" (*Piṭaka*): *Vinaya* (conduct), *Sutta* (sermons), and *Abhidamma* (metaphysics). The *Vinaya Piṭaka* contains the rules of conduct governing the Buddhist monastic order; the *Sutta Piṭaka* contains discourses or sermons attributed to the Buddha; and the *Abhidhamma* consists of works of Buddhist psychology and metaphysics.

The *Tripiṭaka* ("three baskets") propound a diagnosis of the ills of the world and a system of cure. Basic to this doctrine are the "four noble truths": (1) life is inherently full of suffering; (2) suffering is due to craving; (3) suffering can be stopped by eradicating craving; (4) this can be achieved by following the noble eightfold path, the "middle way" between self-indulgence and extreme asceticism. The eightfold path consists of right views, right resolve, right speech, right conduct, right livelihood, right effort, right recollection, and right meditation. The four noble truths and the eightfold path are common doctrine in all Buddhist sects.

These doctrines derive from the "chain of dependent origination" (paṭicca-samuppāda) or the "chain of causation." The root cause of sorrow is ignorance; ignorance causes imagination, which causes self-consciousness, which causes embodied existence, which causes the six senses, which causes perception, which causes emotion, which causes craving, which causes attachment, which causes becoming, which causes rebirth. Ignorance, the ultimate cause of suffering, is primarily ignorance of the true nature of the universe which is that the universe is full of sorrow (dukkha), it is transient (anicca), and it is soulless (anatta).

All things in the universe are composite and can be classed into five components: form and matter (rūpa), sensations (vedanā), perceptions (saññā), psychic dispositions (saṃkhārā), and conscious thoughts (viññana). Matter consists of the objects of the senses and produces sensations. Perception is the cognition of sensation. Psychic dispositions are emotions. Conscious thoughts arise from the interaction of these psychic processes. Since all things in the universe are composite, they are transient. All of life is a becoming, nothing is permanent, and all forms change according to the law of karma. Even the empirical self is a compound of body, feelings, perceptions, states of mind, and awareness which are forever changing from one momentary configuration to another. Because the universe is in constant flux, there is no immortal soul, no permanent, abiding individuality. There is nothing to transmigrate; one life follows another in an endless chain of causation. The gods are also transient; thus he who seeks salvation has no need of gods. The only way to end the process of rebirth is to achieve Nirvāṇa (bliss) through moral conduct and meditation. Neither being nor nonbeing, Nirvāṇa transcends these poles of existence. He who finds Nirvāṇa passes to this state forever.

Since good conduct constituted the initial step on the path to salvation, the Buddha taught a system of altruistic morality which included doing good to others, generosity, a limited form of vegetarianism, and ahiṃsa. The Buddha accepted the four divisions of Indian society, but significantly placed the Kṣatriya at the head of the hierarchy.

Today, the Lesser Vehicle survives only in the Theravāda sect in Ceylon, Burma, Thailand, Cambodia, and Laos. Other sects adhering more or less to the Hīnayāna tradition existed in the past, but have disappeared.

Mahāyāna (Greater Vehicle)

In the course of time the doctrines of the Lesser Vehicle were modified and elaborated into a new system claiming to represent the final doctrines of the Buddha as revealed to only a select few of his most advanced followers. This new system, which probably assumed its completed form between the first and second centuries A.D., was theistic, had an idealistic metaphysics, and preached a doctrine of saviors (bodhisattvas).

In the *Hīnayāna* doctrine the Buddha is not deified, but is depicted as a great sage who attained enlightenment through his own efforts and taught others how to attain enlightenment. On his death he passed completely beyond the universe and no longer affected it. Yet it is evident that a tendency to regard him as a supernatural began quite soon after his death. Early Buddhist sculpture depicts crowds of adherents worshiping the symbols of the Buddha, and by the first century A.D. there are iconic representations of the Buddha himself. Thus, by a gradual process of absorption, the Buddha came to be worshiped as yet another of the multifarious manifestations of god in human form.

The early doctrine taught a limited notion of bodhisattvas (beings of wisdom). In a long series of previous incarnations, the Buddha performed deeds of compassion, becoming gradually more perfect in virtue and wisdom before his final birth. It was generally believed that the Buddha was only the last of a series of earlier Buddhas. By a simple transformation there evolved a doctrine of future Buddhas who would come to teach the doctrine anew. Since this future Buddha (Maitreya) had not yet been born, he must now already be in existence, gradually perfecting himself for his final birth. And, if there was this one Buddha to come, there must be countless others in various stages of perfection, all looking after the welfare of men. Full of compassion, these bodhisattvas came to be thought of as beings who, even though they are soon to attain Nirvāṇa, refuse to take this final step until all the living things of the universe have reached Nirvāṇa. This savior concept, probably deriving from Zoroastrianism, replaces the earlier idea of the Arhant (worthy), who, having learned the way to salvation, selfishly attains Nirvāṇa without thought for the suffering souls still enmeshed in ignorance. Since these numerous bodhisattvas are capable of carrying many souls to bliss, the new doctrine came to be known as *Mahāyāna* (the Greater Vehicle).

But, if the highest function of those on the road to enlightenment is compassion, why did the Buddha not remain among men to aid them in their attainment of perfection? The answer to this question was given in the doctrine of the three bodies (trikāya). The Buddha had three bodies—the body of essence (dharmakāya), the body of bliss (sambhogakāya), and the created body (nirmāṇakāya). Only the last was seen on earth as an emanation from the body of bliss, which was in turn an emanation from the body of essence. The body of bliss, deified as Amitābha (immeasurable radiance) rules sukhāvatī (happy land), where the blessed are reborn in the buds of lotuses. Pervading the whole universe, the body of essence is the eternal, ultimate Buddha, identified with Nirvāṇa. Thus the body of essence in no way differs from the earlier Upaniṣadic notion of the absolute *brāhmaṇ*. Beginning in heterodoxy, Buddhism eventually returns to mystical monism.

The metaphysical theories of *Mahāyāna* philosophy betray a similar retreat from realistic skepticism to idealism. The principal philosophical schools were Mādhyamika (middle position) and Vijñānavāda (doctrine of consciousness). Mādhyamikas espoused a form of qualified realism in which the perceptual world, although an illusory projection of the mind, has a pragmatic reality for the perceiver. The phenomenal world is unreal, but the perceiver believes it is real and acts upon it as if it were real. Even the great cosmic flux of interdependent events comprising the chain of dependent causation is illusory. As a consequence, Nirvāṇa is also unreal, for what makes the limit of Nirvāṇa is also the limit of illusion; there is no difference between Nirvāṇa and illusion. All that exists is the "Great Void," "Emptiness" (Śūnyatā), that cessation of all thought which is, in fact, the body of essence. This doctrine of ontological nihilism did not lead to skepticism for, if this world and Nirvāṇa are equally unreal and there is no difference between them, all beings already participate in bliss if they but know the doctrine of emptiness. Ultimate bliss is attainable in the immediate world and is open to all. The Vijñānavāda or Yogācāra (way of union) school rejected even the qualified realism of the Mādhyamikas and held that the world exists only in the mind of the perceiver. The only true reality was "suchness" (tathātā), a pure existent without characteristics, similar to the Mādhyamika "void" or the *brāhmaṇ* of the *Upaniṣads.* The way to salvation was through Yoga. By directed meditation the monk empties his consciousness of its illusions, purifying it until it becomes identical to the void of pure being (tathātā) itself.

Vajrayāna (Thunderbolt Vehicle)

Like the "Black Mass" of medieval Christianity, *Vajrayāna* Buddhism is founded on a doctrine of "reversal." Accepting the Mādhyamika doctrine of "emptiness," *Vajrayāna* Buddhism, instead of denigrating the phenomenal world, which is after all identical with universal emptiness itself, insists that the phenomenal world can be used as a means of attaining salvation. For, to the pure, all things are pure. Just as a thorn is used to remove a thorn in the flesh, so a man poisoned by passion rids himself of passion by more passion. Ritual sexual intercourse, meat-eating, drunkenness, animal and human sacrifice, eating of excrement, all impure acts violating normal rules of behavior are but a means to the end of salvation for the adept.

The chief divinities of *Vajrayāna* are "savioresses" (tāras), the female counterpart (wives) of Buddhas and bodhisattvas, symbolizing their force or potency (śakti). Since the male aspect of the deity was transcendent and aloof, he could best be approached through his active aspect—the goddess. This union of active power in the form of the female aspect with the quiescent "prepotency" of the male aspect was symbolized in sexual union.

Knowledge of the proper formula (mantra) or correct magical symbol (yantra) enabled one to coerce these deities to confer magical power on the worshiper. Textbooks containing instructions for compelling the supernaturals are known as *Tantras*, and the sect is sometimes referred to as Tantrism. The magical lore of the *Tantras* was imparted to a select group of initiates by a guru in clandestine meetings.

Although the *Vajrayāna* doctrines seem extreme in many of their forms, they are but one possible transformation of a series of interrelated themes already present in earlier thought. The mystical power of sexual intercourse is already attested in the Vedic practices associated with the Vrātyas. Similarly, the creative notion of divine coitus has Vedic sources. The dualistic notion of inactive male and active female aspects is a potent and frequently recurring motif not only with respect to the gods but is symbolically incarnated in the Sāṁkhya system of philosophy as the opposition between puruṣa (soul, person; literally, male person) and prakṛti (matter, feminine gender). Use of ritual formulae to compel the gods is a constant theme in the *Vedas* and *Brāhmaṇas*, and secret associations in which magical lore is transmitted to specially qualified adepts by a guru or sage are at least as old as the *Upaniṣads.* Finally, the idea that he who possesses secret mystical knowledge has power over the gods, is outside time, and is no longer bound to follow conventional morality is not only a persistent theme, but it is also the great idea animating all of Indian speculative thought. What is peculiar about *Vajrayāna* doctrine is the way these common themes are concatenated, combined and transformed into a unique system which does not conform to the normal Indian pattern of outright rejection of the phenomenal world as a necessary preliminary step on the road to salvation. Instead, it accepts, embraces, exploits the inherent contradictions of the phenomenal world as a means to ultimate rejection of that phenomenal world. In *Vajrayāṇa* doctrine, the phenomenal world is not a barrier to salvation but a means.

The Buddhist Saṅgha (Order)

Recruitment to the Buddhist order was unrestrictive. Low caste, high caste, men, women, young, and old, all were admitted provided they donned the yellow robe, shaved their heads, and proclaimed the vows. The basic profession of faith was the "Three Jewels" and the "Ten Precepts." The "Three Jewels" were: "I go for refuge to the Buddha, I go for refuge to the Doctrine, I go for refuge to the Saṅgha." In the "Ten Precepts," the initiate vowed to refrain from: doing harm; stealing; sexual intercourse; lying; alcohol; eating after midday; participating in dancing, singing, music, or drama; bodily adornment; using a comfortable bed; and receiving money. Supposedly, a monk should own only three robes, a loincloth, an alms bowl, a razor, a needle, and a cloth to strain his drinking water in order to prevent inadvertently killing any microscopic water life. In the beginning, a monk was supposed to obtain his food by begging, but this practice was later abandoned.

A monk's vows were not necessarily permanent, and one who wished to leave the order could do so at any time. Although the monasteries had no powerful central authority and each monk was expected to participate in the life of the monastery without coercion, a committee of elders and an abbot provided direction and decided issues involving admission and expulsion. As part of his duties a monk was expected to do physical labor and to teach novices, but most of his time was spent in study and religious exercises.

CĀRVĀKA

The ultimate heterodox transformation in Indian thought combined the philosophical skepticism of early Buddhism and the materialism of Jainism. This potent mixture produced a thoroughly atheistic school of materialist thought known variously as *Cārvāka* or *Lokāyata*. With inchoate origins even in the *Vedas*, materialist doctrines appear to have attained systematic expression sometime around 600 B.C. These doctrines assert that only the real world exists, there is no future life; religion, god, and immortality are illusory, immaterial categories. The original, ultimate principles of matter are earth, fire, air, and water, which, when transformed, produce body and intelligence. The soul is merely the body transformed by intelligence. When the body dies, the soul is destroyed. Pleasure and pain are essential features of life. The goal of life is enjoyment produced by sensual pleasure, and there is no hell other than the purely earthly sources of pain produced by mundane causes. The *Vedas*, written by fools, are self-contradictory, incoherent, and intended only for those who have no better sense. Chastity is the invention of weaklings and charity was devised by the indigent.

Consistent with their materialism, the Cārvākas maintained that perception was the only source of knowledge. What could not be perceived did not exist. Since we can only perceive particulars and not universals, inference, which depends on a universal connection, is invalid. Not only is the syllogism thus dismantled, but the relation of cause and effect is rejected. Because we cannot legitimately infer what is unperceivable, souls, heaven, hell, gods, all immaterial categories must be abandoned. Since there is no cause and effect and no afterlife, the laws of karma are illusions. There is no supernatural retribution for evil deeds and one would be a fool, deceived by the lies of priests, if he forsook the embrace of a beautiful woman for penances, begging, and mortification, with the false hope of attaining a nonexistent salvation.

Cārvāka doctrines can be reconstructed only from refutation appearing in Buddhist and Hindu treatises, and this absence of any texts testifies to the extreme abhorrence these ideas aroused. Yet, despite suppression and scorn, a subtle thread of materialist thought survived, albeit emasculated and subverted by incorporation into the grand synthesis of Hindu social theory. No matter how distorted, materialist notions are still perceptible in Hindu theories of the state, the duties of the householder, and the technical handbooks of love-making.

FIVE

THE HINDU SYNTHESIS

Āryan orthodoxy was obliterated by heterodoxy, and even though the heterodox cults themselves eventually declined, the pattern of Āryan dominance was forever shattered. Remnants of Āryan culture were to survive the destruction but only in "Dravidianized" form. In every cultural sphere the ancient Dravidian forms reasserted themselves, transmogrifying Āryan doctrines and conventions, reducing Āryan gods to Dravidian gods, replacing the Āryan cult of the family altar with the Dravidian temple, subordinating ritualism to devotionalism, transforming class divisions into caste distinctions, and welding loosely knit tribal confederacies into centralized empires. The Hindu synthesis was less the dialectical reduction of orthodoxy and heterodoxy than the resurgence of the ancient, aboriginal Indus civilization. In this process the rude, barbaric Āryan tribes were gradually civilized and eventually merged with the autochthonous Dravidians. Although elements of their domestic cult and ritualism were jealously preserved by Brāhmaṇ priests, the body of their culture survived only in fragmentary tales and allegories embedded in vast, syncretistic compendia. On the whole, the Āryan contribution to Indian culture is insignificant. The essential pattern of Indian culture was already established in the third millennium B.C., and although the Āryans destroyed the Indus cities, the form of Indian civilization perdured and eventually reasserted itself.

THE SIX SYSTEMS OF PHILOSOPHY (*SADDARŚANA*)

In their frontal attack on orthodoxy, the great thinkers of the heterodox systems developed a form of critical philosophy based on logical analysis. This critical analysis forced the orthodox thinkers to systematize their philosophical views and to formulate logical defenses. Developing over a long period of time, separate philosophical systems gradually emerged. In the beginning these systems provided different and often contradictory solutions to philosophical issues, but there eventually developed a conception which held that these independent systems were but subordinate and complementary parts of a more comprehensive scheme. Each system thus came to be known as a darsána (a way of seeing), and each represented in its own way a practical means of achieving a common goal—salvation.

Despite their seeming differences in method and result, the major systems agree in many essential features. All accept the authority of the *Vedas*, and all maintain that the only legitimate goal of philosophy is salvation. Consequently, reason or logical analysis is always subordinated to intuition, for only intuition enables one to transcend mere self-consciousness. Critical philosophy is an incomplete and inadequate means for the attainment of salvation. By enthroning intuition, orthodox philosophers were able to salvage the great speculative ideas of the *Upaniṣads*. Thus the edge of critical philosophy was blunted by the primacy of intuitive knowledge. All the systems refute the skepticism of heterodox systems and postulate an objective external reality underlying the flux of mundane existence. They also accept the ancient theories of interminable cycles of cosmic creation and dissolution. Neither do they reject the fundamental tenet that the universe is totally ordered in the grand scheme of cause and effect expressed in the doctrine of karma, nor do they challenge the basic order of society represented in the caste system. Conservative to the core, incapable of breaking with speculative tradition, the systematic philosophers were yet able to effectively parry the logical thrusts of the heterodox by relativizing them to the supreme goal of salvation and by subordinating logic to intuition.

The doctrines of the darśanas are written in the form of short aphorisms known as *Sūtras* (literally, threads). Since they are highly compact and terse, the *Sūtras* presuppose much prior knowledge and represent the culmination of a long evolutionary process in which redundancy and repetition were gradually eliminated. Appended to the *Sūtras* are commentaries, glosses, and explanatory notations often reflecting modifications and reinterpretations of the original doctrine.

Of the various systems that must have developed in the course of history, six became predominant. Traditionally divided into three groups of two, which were thought to be complementary, they are: Nyāya and Vaiśeṣika, Sāṁkhya and Yoga, Mīmāṁsā and Vedānta.

Nyāya and Vaiśeṣika

Nyāya (analysis; literally, right, just) is a system of logic or logical proof founded by the teacher Gautama (first century A.D.?). The Nyāya logistic system is accepted as valid by all the other systems. Since clear thinking and logical argument are a means of combatting the ignorance that stands in the way of salvation, logic is given a religious basis. Nyāya classifies the means of knowledge under four types: intuition, inference, comparison, verbal testimony (accepted authority). Of these intuition is the most important. The inferential structure of the Nyāya syllogism has five components: (1) the proposition; (2) the reason; (3) the example; (4) the application; (5) the conclusion. Thus: (1) This hill is on fire (2) because it smokes; (3) whatever has smoke (for example, a kitchen) has fire; (4) so does this hill; (5) therefore, this hill is on fire. Comparison refers to an analogical process by means of which things can be said to be similar or different. Verbal testimony concerns evaluation of sources of information. The *Vedas*, for example, are reliable because the Vedic authors were inspired by divine, infallible intuition.

Attributed to the legendary sage Kaṇāda (atom eater), Vaiśēṣika (from viśeṣa, "particularity") doctrines constitute a physical and metaphysical basis for Nyāya. Their doctrines posit six categories or objects of experience: substance, quality, action, generality, individuality, and inherence (inseparable connection). Knowing the true nature of these categories leads to bliss. The ultimate, indivisible atomic substances are earth, water, fire, and air. Reality consists of these four gross substances plus five inferential substances (ether, time, space, self, and mind). Substances possess qualities (color, taste, smell, number, conjunction, and others) and may express actions (motion). Earth, for example, possesses color, taste, smell, and touch, but ether possesses none of these, being marked instead by the characteristic actions of ingress and egress represented physically by sound. These three (substance, quality, action) can be intuited or directly perceived, but generality, individuality, and inherence can only be known by logical inference; they are not directly perceived.

Conjunction of self with body produces birth; conjunction of self with organs of sense in contact with substances produces cognition (mind). The self is known by revelation and cognition of the referents of "I." Each self has a characteristic individuality marked by its particular status or condition, which in turn is produced by the consequences of past deeds. When one has true knowledge of the categories of reality, the self becomes "seedless," takes up no new bodies (that is, is not reborn), and attains mokṣa (salvation).

Sāṁkhya and Yoga

Probably existing in rudimentary form by the fourth or fifth centuries B.C., the Sāṁkhya (enumeration) is the oldest of the six systems. Its purpose is provision of knowledge which will terminate misery and release the soul from bondage. Since misery is an attribute of the body, the soul's misery derives from its association with the body. The soul's bondage is an illusion caused by ignorance of the true nature of things. Knowing the true nature of things releases the soul from its bondage. Evolving from an uncaused cause, the phenomenal world is an eternal process of unfolding or evolution. The order and regulation of this causal system is knowable by means of perception, inference, and valid testimony.

The Sāṁkhya postulates two ultimate realities, spirit (Puruṣa) and nature or substance (Prakṛti). Underlying this duality is the opposition between subject and object, the knower and the known. Puruṣa, without form, cause or substance, is the all-pervasive intelligence that regulates cosmic evolution. Prakṛti is a cosmic force, the uncaused cause of all objective existence. The power of Prakṛti becomes manifest in three strands (guṇas) or constituents of the objective world. Sattva guṇa is the real, existent; it is the cause of equilibrium, manifested in light. Rajas guṇa, an active component, can move the other guṇas. It is manifest in the force of wind. Tamas guṇa is darkness, obstructive of the tendencies of the other two guṇas, and has the characteristics gravity, mass, weight, and inertia. Prior to the manifestation of the objective world, these guṇas are in perfect equilibrium. Because Puruṣa is formless it cannot act, and Prakṛti being inanimate is similarly unable to act. Puruṣa and Prakṛti are dependent and all manifestation results from their interaction. Because of past action (karma), Prakṛti is "quickened" by Puruṣa, producing the first stage of evolution. Caused by karmic stress upsetting the equilibrium of the guṇas, Mahātattva (cosmic intelligence) evolves. It is a capacity to expand, an urge to develop. Soon afterward, the Ahaṁkāra ("I maker") appears. It is a principle of individuation which brings about differentiation, variety, and self-realization. From the sattva guṇa inherent in the Ahaṁkāra, there arises Manas (mind cognition). From the rajas guṇa evolve the Indriyas consisting of five senses of perception (power to feel, see, hear, taste, smell), and five instruments of action (power to express, procreate, excrete, grasp, move). From the tamas aspect of the Ahaṁkāra the five subtle elements (Tanmātras) are produced. The Tanmātras (essence of sound, touch, form, flavor, odor) are necessary in order for the powers of feeling, tasting, etc., to have objects. Without something to hear, the power of hearing would be useless. Finally, from these subtle elements, the five gross elements of existence (Mahābhūtas; viz., ether, air, fire, water, and earth) arise. Through these vehicles the subtle elements manifest themselves. Thus ether has sound; air has sound and touch; fire has sound, touch, and form; water has sound, touch, form, and flavor; and earth has sound, touch, form, flavor, and odor. All other manifestations of the objective world are built up from the five gross elements.

The person or individual (jīva) is part of the natural world, but within his gross body there is a subtle body, for each individual is a composite of Puruṣa and Prakṛti. Bondage arises when the individual cannot distinguish between Puruṣa and Prakṛti. Bondage is the result of the activity of Prakṛti and release comes from the inactivity of Prakṛti. Like Jainism, the Sāṁkhya sees souls as enmeshed in matter. Salvation results when the obstacle of matter is removed. Salvation can be achieved by virtue and Yoga. Sāṁkhya is the theoretical analysis of how bondage comes about, and Yoga provides the means by which one can become free of bondage.

Although the ultimate Hindu synthesis eventually succeeded in transforming the Sāṁkhya into but one more aspect of the manifold orthodoxy, many features of the Sāṁkhya have led some scholars to conclude that it was originally a heterodox system. Like Buddhism and Jainism, the Sāṁkhya is essentially atheistic and materialistic. It postulates no deity, and it firmly asserts that the material world exists in its own right and is not merely an illusion. With Buddhism it holds that the ultimate nature of existence is pain and suffering, and with Jainism it conceives of the individual self as enmeshed in matter. Unlike Jainism, however, the Sāṁkhya does not view karmic infusions in a mechanistic quasi-chemical fashion, but rather as a mechanical psychological process. Again, like Buddhism, the Sāṁkhya posits a universe in a constant process of evolution or becoming. With Jainism it agrees that individual selves are indestructible. Even after being freed from matter they exist in a pure, luminescent, unconscious state. In contrast to the orthodox solution of Vedānta, individual selves are not merged with anything and there is no consciousness of bliss.

These quite remarkable parallels sufficiently establish a case for the originally heterodox origin of the Sāṁkhya, but even more important in this respect is the character of the dualistic primordial categories of Puruṣa and Prakṛti. In the Sāṁkhya these are the ultimate categories of cosmic evolution. Potentiality (Puruṣa) and the ability to act (Prakṛti) are identifiable as masculine and feminine respectively. The feminine aspect is active and the cause of illusion. The masculine aspect is mere inactive potentiality, the expression of purified selves. The aim of Sāṁkhya is to eliminate the bondage caused by the activity of Prakṛti and to attain the state of pure luminescence characteristic of Puruṣa. Here one sees a total inversion of the Vedic Asura myth (see pp. 44–45), in which the gods stood for growth, development, and evolution; the demons represented inactivity and the withholding of potentiality symbolized by the cosmic waters. The aim of the gods in the Asura myth was to prevent the encompassing and holding back of the power of growth, development, and evolution. Comparing the two myths, it is evident that they are but inverted expressions of a single mythological theme. The Ādityas (gods) of the Asura myth are to growth and development as Prakṛti is to cosmic evolution in the Sāṁkhya. Similarly, the Dānavas (demons) of the Asura myth are to encompassing the power of evolution as Puruṣa is to inactivity in the Sāṁkhya. The correspondences are the same, but, significantly, the Sāṁkhya inverts their relation to good and evil (see Figure 7).

The Sāṁkhya thus is a reworking and transformation of an ancient and primitive myth, homologizing cosmic and psychic evolution. Both the universe and the individual self are the unfolding from a state of quiescent potentiality. The development of self and the development of the universe are identical processes, both creating the parameters of pain and suffering. At this point the Sāṁkhya breaks with the ancient myth and makes its most important contribution. First, it identifies the essential character of existence as pain and suffering. All those things that are conducive to life are mere agents of pain and suffering. Hence the inversion of the relation between the constituents of life and death and good and evil. Second, in establishing the individual psyche and the universe as homologous evolvents, it provides that the mind can recapture or retrace the steps of the whole evolutionary process simply by its powers of introspection. Since the cosmic evolution of matter is eternal, how could the mind comprehend the direction and constituent forces of the endless reshuffling of nature's material? How can a finite means know an infinite process? Here the Sāṁkhya proposes a familiar solution. The relation

	Asura myth	:	Sāṁkhya	
Good (ṛta)	Release of cosmic waters	=	Start of process of cosmic evolution	Evil (dharma)
	Ādityas	=	Prakṛti	
Evil (anṛta)	Dānavas	=	Puruṣa	Good (mokṣa)
	Retention of cosmic waters	=	Inactive potentiality	

Figure 7. Analogical correspondences between the Asura myth and Sāṁkhya.

of mind to cosmic evolution is that of microcosm to macrocosm. Exactly mirrored in the processes of mental evolution are all the processes and categories of macrocosmic evolution. The individual mind is never identified with the macrocosm either as identity (as in advaita Vedānta) or as part to whole (as in dvaita Vedānta). The Sāṁkhya places the identity relation in the processes of microcosmic and macrocosmic evolution. The same processes account for both mental and cosmic evolution. Macrocosmic evolution is knowable because it results from the same processes that account for microcosmic evolution. Knowing the process by which the individual psyche becomes enmeshed in matter establishes the grounds and means of escape. Here the classification of the archaic myth is broken. Because the Sāṁkhya paradigm eliminates the gods and the demons, there is no need for sacrifice. Only man and the order of the universe remain, and because these two result from an identical process, there is no place for ritual. Both the Vedic paradigm of man-sacrifice-gods and the Brāhmaṇic paradigm of man-ritual-universe are violated. There is neither a relation between man and the gods expressed in sacrifice, nor a relation between man and the power of the universe expressed in ritual. Ultimately, there is no relation at all. Man as subject in relation to some object is man encompassed, bound, enmeshed. Only by breaking the relation to an object can man be free. But man thus freed does not enter into a new relation. He merely exists in a state of magnificent, terrifying, eternal loneliness.

It is small wonder that this radical solution should have proved unpalatable to the orthodox traditions. Nor is it surprising that all subsequent philosophizing constituted a concerted effort to replace the missing relation between self and other. What is surprising is that this fundamental reduction prevailed. Thus, when we look for the underlying cognitive categories of Indian culture, we will find that it is this radical transformation of archaic concepts represented in the Sāṁkhya system that comprises the fundamental structure of Indian thought. Conceptions of the social order and of time, ideas of purity and pollution, the gods, and the forms of worship all derive from this seminal transformation. Contrary to popular belief, it is not the monism of Vedānta that expresses the fundamental Hindu attitude.

Traditionally attributed to Patañjali (second century B.C.), the Yoga system is essentially a derogation of the categories of the Sāṁkhya from the universal to the particular—that is, from cosmic to individual spheres. Patañjali makes a basic modification of Sāṁkhya metaphysics by introducing a deity (Īśvara). Īśvara was not a creator, but like the Buddha of the Lesser Vehicle or the Tīrthaṅkaras of Jainism, he was merely an example, a free or exalted soul.

The aim of Yoga is to free the self from citta (mind stuff) which deludes the self into mistaking the noneternal for the eternal. This is accomplished by nonattachment, restraint of the outgoing tendencies of the mind, and union of the individual soul with the universal soul. The practical discipline of the Yoga system is set forth in eight separate stages: (1) self-control; (2) observances; (3) posture; (4) breath control; (5) withdrawal; (6) steadying the mind; (7) meditation, (8) release (Samādhi). The first two consist of following the moral rules of nonviolence, truthfulness, not stealing, chastity, and avoidance of greed. Posture refers to the "seat" or sitting position in which one meditates. Breath control aids in mastering the unconscious functions of the body. In withdrawal, the adept attempts to withdraw his mind from external objects. Steadying the mind indicates the attempt to hold an object of meditation for an instant in which no other object is grasped by the mind. Meditation is simply a prolongation of the preceding step. In the final step, the individual is no longer conscious of the separation of subject and object; he is merged with the divinity.

This classical system of Yoga is known as Rājayoga and forms the basis for all other yoga systems. Others are mantrayoga (the yoga of spells), involving the use of magical words and phrases; haṭhayoga (the yoga of force), which utilizes physical exercises; and layayoga (the yoga of dissolution). The latter is based on an esoteric system of physiology in which a central vein or duct (suṣumṇa) roughly corresponding to the spinal column is conceptualized as having six (sometimes seven) centers (cakras) of psychic force dispersed along it. Inside the skull is the topmost center (sahasrāra), and localized in the genitals is the bottom center (kuṇḍalinī). The kuṇḍalinī (often homologized as a serpent) is naturally quiescent until aroused by yogic practices. By effort and meditation the kuṇḍalinī gradually rises up in the suṣumṇa, piercing the centers of psychic power until it finally reaches the sahasrāra and the yogin achieves salvation. In some tantric systems, the rise of kuṇḍalinī was hastened by sexual practices designed to prevent the outflow of the three "precious jewels" (breath, thought, and semen). Sexual union symbolizes the union of Puruṣa and Prakṛti as the male and female principles of the universe. As the kuṇḍalinī rises from center to center, the yogin inevitably acquires miraculous powers (siddhis). According to tradition, he can, for example, remember previous lives, know another's thoughts, become invisible, fly through the air, or walk on water. In most cases, practice of these powers was discouraged because they did not facilitate attainment of release.

Mīmāṁsā and Vedānta

Mīmāṁsā (inquiry) or pūrva (earlier) Mīmāṁsā is devoted to an analysis of the actions enjoined in the *Vedas*. In its earliest form, it differed from all the other schools in defining salvation as life in heaven rather than a state of ultimate release, but later writers gradually brought Mīmāṁsā doctrine into line with the more prevalent attitude. Mīmāṁsā, attributed to Jaimini (second century B.C.), attempts to prove that the Vedas are authoritative and that actions (conduct) are the essence of human life. Right conduct not only leads to salvation, but provides the basis for future lives. In essence, the Mīmāṁsā is a set of rules for interpretation of Vedic texts. In the process of analyzing actions, Mīmāṁsā thinkers made useful contributions to logic and epistemology. For example, they took the proper position that it was not the truth of a proposition which had to be ascertained, but its falsity. It is customary among Western interpreters to dismiss Mīmāṁsā as a mere survival of Brāhmaṇism, but in view of the Mīmāṁsā doctrine that dharma (right action, law) is independent of sense perception and is instead knowable by means of understanding verbal injunctions, we have, in fact, a very contemporary conception of linguistic usage which is independent of the inadequacies of Nyāya sense-datum theories or of the traditional exaltation of intuition.

Uttara ("last") Mīmāṁsā or Vedānta ("end of the *Vedas*") deals with the religious and philosophical speculations of the Upaniṣads. The Vedāntasūtra is traditionally attributed to Badarāyāṇa who probably lived in the early part of the Christian era, but of more importance to modern Hinduism are the later commentaries by Śaṅkara (eighth century), Rāmānuja (eleventh century) and Madhava (twelfth century).

Śaṅkara is often credited with the remarkable feat of having reduced the contradictory passages of the various *Upaniṣads* to a consistent system. In his system the self is established in a fashion reminiscent of Descartes. Objects of knowledge may be open to doubt, but that something doubts is undoubtable. But this self is undifferentiated, universal. Although the world of objects is dependent, it is nonetheless real; and although real, it is not the ultimate reality. Behind the world of empirical reality is that which originated it, is itself unalterable, and provides the support for the empirical world. This ultimate nonempirical reality is brāhmaṇ—creator, maintainer, and destroyer of the material universe. Both immanent and transcendent, it is the cause of all phenomena. The individual self (ātman) is simply an individuated aspect of brāhmaṇ. Ignorance of the identity between brāhmaṇ and ātman leads to illusion (māyā), but by the practice of virtue and devotion one reaches self-realization (mokṣa). Śaṅkara thus teaches a system of absolute monism (*advaita*, nondualism). Brāhmaṇ and ātman are one.

Rāmānuja's system is referred to as qualified nondualism (viśiṣṭādvaita) because he holds that the individual selves and the material world differ essentially from brāhmaṇ. The self cannot be encompassed by or dissolved in brāhmaṇ, for brāhmaṇ has two forms: selves and the phenomenal world. Selves merely stand in a part-whole relation to brāhmaṇ. Salvation then cannot consist in a merging of the individual ātman with brāhmaṇ. Selves are subordinate to brāhmaṇ and can only worship or reverence brāhmaṇ. Salvation, then, is simply a state of permanent adoration.

Madhava's dualistic system (dvaita) teaches that God, selves, and the world are separate, but that the latter two depend on God. Brāhmaṇ, identified as the deity Viṣṇu, has complete power over selves and the world. Salvation derives from Viṣṇu's grace, which is granted only to those who live moral lives. The damned are condemned to eternal separation from God, while others are doomed to eternal transmigration.

In both Rāmānuja's and Madhava's thinking it is apparent that a new element has crept into the old Upaniṣadic doctrines. The abstract, impersonal brāhmaṇ of the *Upaniṣads* and of Śaṅkara, knowable by intuition, has been replaced by a more-or-less personal deity who may be worshiped, but is essentially other than the devoted worshiper. He is also a deity who rewards and punishes. Both Rāmānuja and Madhava are reacting to the indigenous development of a new religious cult—the cult of bhakti or devotion—and in Madhava's case it is certain that elements of Christianity have been incorporated. Whereas it is clear that the other philosophical systems and even the earlier forms of Vedānta were reactions to the threat of heterodoxy, later Vedāntist thought responds to a different set of challenges. Yet, in each instance, the form of the argument is constrained by the universal questions and underlying predispositions already apparent in the earlier traditions.

THE SOCIAL ORDER

Just as the literature of heterodoxy resounds to the clash of Āryan and non-Āryan religious and metaphysical beliefs, the "secular" literature of early Hinduism resonates to the strains of accommodation between Āryan and non-Āryan societies. The earliest forms of this accommodation are incoherently reflected in the great epics—the *Mahābhārata* and the *Rāmāyaṇa*. Only in such later works as the *Arthaśāstra*, the *Code of Manu*, and the *Pūraṇas* do the full details of the Hindu synthesis become apparent.

Although they derive from martial legends of an earlier period, the *Mahābhārata* and *Rāmāyaṇa* probably were first compiled in rudimentary form during the sixth century B.C. Traditionally attributed to the sage Vyāsa, the *Mahābhārata*, containing approximately 90,000 stanzas, is probably the world's longest poem. Its prodigious length eloquently attests to an eclecticism which, despite priestly exegesis, was never more than haphazard. Beginning as a rather simple tale about a civil war between the Kurus and Pāṇḍavas, the *Mahābhārata* eventually became a vast, jumbled repository of miscellaneous tales, legends, myths, and treatises on law, religion, politics, and theology.

The *Rāmāyaṇa*, traditionally attributed to the sage Vālmīki, tells the story of the capture of Rāma's wife Sīta by the demon Rāvaṇa, the ensuing war, and Sīta's eventual recovery. Like the *Mahābhārata*, this rather simple story was a transformation of earlier and diverse elements. The *Rāmāyaṇa* blends two separate strands of legendary material—Āryan and non-Āryan. The Āryan legends center around the life of Rāma as a prince of Ayodhyā. By contrast, the non-Āryan legends focus on the demons, their hero Rāvaṇa, and their conflicts with the apes. These non-Āryan legends do not mention Rāma nor do they tell the story of Sīta's abduction. Rāvaṇa is the hero in the non-Āryan legends. The Āryan Rāma story was originally little more than an effusion of bardic praise for a famous prince, but, in blending the bardic paean with non-Āryan elements, the *Rāmāyaṇa* eventually emerged as a treatise on dharma. It creates ideal human characters, emphasizes the ideal relations between brothers, father and son, husband and wife, and it delineates the character of the ideal woman and man. Sīta's faithfulness in the face of suffering became the model of every little girl in Hindu society; and Rāma's honesty, bravery, and integrity were interpreted as the norm of Hindu manliness. Rāma, represented as the righteous king who sought to restore and maintain dharma, clearly characterizes the Hindu concept of kingship.

Earlier *Sūtra* literature devoted to explanations of the scriptures and ceremonies gradually gave rise to a form of literature known as *Śāstra* (science, instruction). Central to this Śastric literature is the *Mānava Dharma Śāstra* or lawbook of Manu (ca. second–third centuries A.D.) which deals with human conduct. The *Code of Manu* is essentially a theoretical treatise on social order from the point of view of the Brāhmaṇ caste. Complementing it is the *Arthaśāstra* (science of polity) which treats of the organization and conduct of government from a more secular or Kṣatriya point of view.

Another important class of literature, the *Pūraṇas* (ancient tales), are summaries and compendia of legends, religious notions, quasi-historical events, and genealogies. Although the *Pūraṇas* are late, they contain much material from very early periods.

Dharma

The central theme of the epics and *Śāstras* is dharma. Derived from the root *dhṛ* (to sustain), dharma has many meanings, but basically it refers to religiously ordained duty, morality, right conduct, or the rules of conduct. In a narrower sense it can mean custom, law, or ordinance. Often called "the Foundation of the Universe," the concept of dharma replaced the earlier Vedic notion of cosmic interdependence expressed by the word ṛta. Originally dharma was classified into active and passive aspects known respectively as pravṛtti and nivṛtti. Pravṛtti referred to actions performed in the realm of worldly life. Its opposite, nivṛtti, referred to a period of retirement from the pursuit of worldly goals. Thus the moral content of dharma was relativized to life stages. As a man moved from active participation in the affairs of the world to a life of retirement and contemplation, his moral obligations changed. This classification was later amplified in the concept of varṇāśrama dharma. Pravṛtti was subdivided into two separate life stages (āśrama): student (brahmacārin) and householder (gṛhastha). Nivṛtti was subdivided into: forest dweller (vānaprastha) and ascetic (sannyāsin). The duties and obligations of each life stage differed. Not only was dharma relativized for life stages, it was also relativized for class (varṇa; literally, color). All the epics and *Śāstras* accept the fourfold division of society into priest (Brāhmaṇ), warrior (Kṣatriya), merchant and cultivator (Vaīśya), and servent (Śūdra). Associated with each class (varṇa) was a separate, distinct set of duties and obligations. One's moral obligations were the moral obligations of one's own class. Dharma is not the same for all, and although varṇāśrama dharma is sometimes opposed to sanatana dharma (universal moral obligation) or even to svadharma (personal obligation), it is clearly varṇāśrama dharma that is of paramount importance.

Hindu theoreticians also conceived of man's life as directed to four great goals or ends of life (puruṣartha). The quest of righteousness and virtue is dharma, but activities directed toward material gain are classed as artha. When the object of an activity is love or pleasure, it is classed as kāma. Finally, the renunciation of all activities for the purpose of obtaining release from the wheel of life is mokṣa. The quest for dharma is appropriate to the first three life stages, but to be motivated by artha and kāma is appropriate only to the second. Mokṣa is sought only in the fourth life stage.

Dharma was also relative to time, and the content of dharma changed in accordance with changing circumstances. Time is cyclical, consisting of four great ages (yugas) of different duration. Each of these ages is characterized by a progressive spiritual deterioration. The force of dharma decreases from one age to the next until it is renewed with full force at the beginning of each new cycle. Thus there is no universal, uniform dharma applicable to all ages.

Quite obviously, the subdivision of dharma into pravṛtti and nivṛtti as well as the other life stages represents an accommodation between the ritualism of the *Brāhmaṇas* with their emphasis on appropriate action in this world and the quietistic, "life-negating" search for spiritual release represented in the *Upaniṣads*. Similarly, the class relativity of dharma is a means of reconciling divergent ideas of diverse peoples. Through such accommodation, conflicting doctrines and ways of life were able to persist for centuries in peaceful coexistence.

Pollution

Although dharma is the overt theme of the ancient Hindu *Śāstras*, pollution is the real topic, and every point of dharma is articulated within a conceptual context that presupposes the notion of pollution. All of the texts implicitly or explicitly recognize two major kinds of pollution: permanent and impermanent. Permanent pollution attaches to a person by virtue of his birth in a high or low caste and cannot be removed by purification. Impermanent pollution arises from the normal functions of everyday life and can be removed by purification.

The major sources of pollution involve contact with death and bodily emissions. Every secretion or excretion of the human body pollutes. Blood, feces, urine, semen, saliva, nail parings, and hair cut from the body are ritually impure, and any contact with them renders a person impure. Ingestion of food is impure, and everything surrounding the eating and preparation of food and drink is highly vulnerable to pollution. Thus the kitchen occupies the most remote and private area of the house, and food is consumed in utter privacy with one's close kin or ritual equals. Food itself is subject to classification on the basis of its relative purity depending on who handles it in preparation, how it is prepared, how and by whom it is served. Some foods have special purity, either inherently (milk) or by the process of preparation (fried foods). Further, fried food can be more or less pure depending on the kind of oil used, clarified butter (ghī) being best. Fried food, known as pakkā food, is less vulnerable to pollution than food prepared in water or baked (kachchā food). Similarly, raw (or unprepared) food still in a husk or shell is less susceptible to pollution than food that has been husked or shelled. A Brāhmaṇ, for example, can accept an unpeeled banana or unhusked coconut from an untouchable, but will not accept the exposed flesh of these fruits. Similarly, food served in clay utensils is more prone to pollution than food served in brass utensils. In general, the more food departs from its raw or unprepared state the more important become the questions of its manner of preparation, serving, and consumption. Leftover food is defiled unless it has been consumed by a deity or holy man. Alcohol and meat are inherently polluting and no manner of preparation can remove their impurity.

Obviously, then, the classification of food, its manner of preparation, serving, and so on involve a system of dichotomous oppositions with a logic similar to the varṇa system (pp. 81–86). Like the varṇa oppositions, the classification of food entails a hierarchic ranking, and the ranking provides a ready index of relative purity and vulnerability to pollution. This hierarchic rank is illustrated in Figure 8. The letter A denotes acceptable, U denotes unacceptable. The diagram is read as follows: Is this food vegetarian (+) or nonvegetarian (–)? If vegetarian (+), is it unprepared or not? If unprepared, then it is acceptable. Such a diagram corresponds to a semantic tree in cognitive anthropology. For details, see Tyler (1969, 10–11). The features "plus, unprepared" and "minus, unprepared" correspond of course to Lévi-Strauss's categories "raw" and "cooked." (See, for example, Lévi-Strauss, 1964.) Figure 8

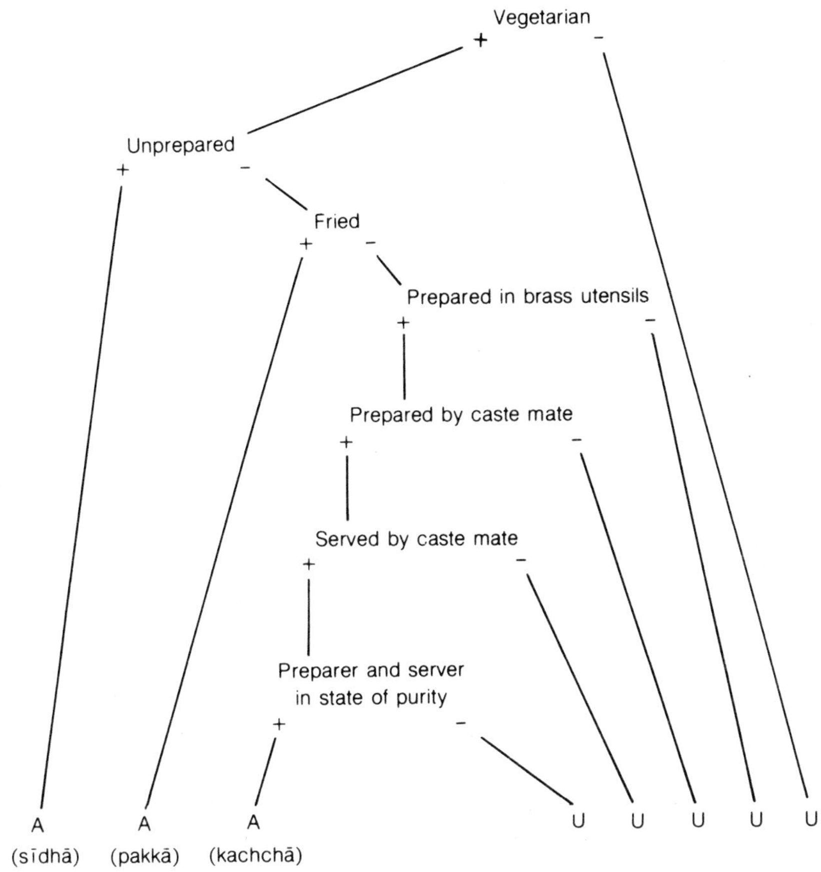

Figure 8. Hierarchy of relative purity in food categories. The letter A denotes acceptable; U denotes unacceptable. The diagram is read as follows: Is this food vegetarian (+) or nonvegetarian (–)?

is a rather simplified outline of a very complex phenomenon, but it does reveal the basic features involved in a decision about accepting food and illustrates that perviousness to pollution is the basis of the classification.

Pollution is contagious. Always transferable by physical contact, it can sometimes radiate from a source and pollute even without actual contact. Birth and death, for example, radiate pollution along the lines of kinship. Close agnatic kin are polluted by deaths and births occurring even outside their immediate families and must undergo seclusion and purification ritual. Sexual relations render the participants impure, and abstinence from sex is prescribed before important rituals. Sexual relations between persons of unequal rank are highly polluting for the higher-ranked partner, particularly if female. Defilement can be so severe that there can be no recovery, and the woman must be evicted from her caste before her pollution contaminates everyone else. Permanent pollution, too, is contagious within a whole caste group. Barbers are polluted because they come in contact with the polluted hair trimmings of their clients, and even though one may never have cut hair or given another person a shave, the fact of being born a barber transmits the impurity of all barbers to oneself.

The hierarchy of relative pollution includes most things in the universe. Species of animals and plants, earth, fire, air, water, and even the gods fall within the range of pollution rankings. Times of danger—an eclipse, a new- or full-moon day—require special precautions against pollution. All things have an inherent degree of pollution, some things being inherently more polluted than others. Purity, too, is inherent and some things are inherently more pure than others. Running water is pure, and the morning bath in water flowing over one's head forms a major part of all purificatory rites. Cleansing must be done to the accompaniment of ritual gestures and words. Other purifying agents include fire, the sun, earth, Sanskrit characters, and especially water from the Ganges. The products of the cow have great purifying power, the most potent purifying potion being a mixture of the five products of the cow (pañcagavya): milk, curds, ghī (clarified butter), dung, and urine.

Purity is essential in the performance of ritual; a man should not even study the *Veda* in a state of ritual impurity. Such purity is a highly transitory state threatened on all sides by possible sources of pollution. Consequently, important rituals are preceded by complicated purificatory rites often lasting up to the very moment of a ritual performance, and inherently pure things are employed to set up a surrounding context of purity. Amulets containing Sanskrit mantras, for example, and ritual places smeared with cow dung and sprinkled with water erect a barrier to the insidious powers of pollution.

These Indian notions of pollution have been compared to the inherent magical power of mana and the avoidance patterns characteristic of taboo (Hutton, 1946, 184–191), and though there is a general correspondence, it is not necessary to look beyond India for the motivating notions underlying the ideology of purity and pollution. The same indigenous conceptual scheme that underlies the ideology of purity and pollution led the Jain thinkers to posit karmic matter as one of the prime elements of the universe, and prompted Sāṁkhya philosophers to identify Prakṛti (matter) as the motivating principle of the universe. In both of these systems, bits of indestructible matter enmesh the living soul, clouding its luminescent purity, and a state of absolute purity is attained only when the soul has been cleansed of the impurities of karmic infusion. Ritual purity and soul purity are analogous, as are matter and pollution. The originally heterodox cults of Jainism and Sāṁkhya philosophy are early sophisticated expressions of the rustic aboriginal Dravidian notions of purity and pollution. Already linked with karma, this archaic and pervasive ideology was eventually grafted onto the varṇa system, transforming it from a system of tribal class divisions into the modern caste system. With this final effort, the Hindu synthesis was complete. Ironically, it was a system scarcely different from the pre-Āryan Indus civilization. A thousand years after their destructive invasion, the rude Āryan pastoralists are all but obliterated in the rise of a new urban civilization that owes most of its genius to the indomitable Dravidians. But for the tenacious Brāhmaṇs and their jealous preservation of Āryan lore, the Āryans, like so many other barbarian invaders, would have been totally submerged by Dravidian culture.

The Varṇas

Already by the end of the Ṛg Vedic period the fourfold division of society was regarded as divinely ordained, and Hindu theoreticians attempted to give a functional explanation for the four classes. A Brāhmaṇ should study, teach, and perform sacrifices; a Kṣatriya must protect the people; a Vaiśya should raise cattle, till the earth, and engage in trade; and a Śūdra should serve all the other classes. Although this explanation was, of course, an idealization never fully attained, it did serve as a model of social organization. These four varṇas were divided into two groups. The first three were classed as twice-born (dvija), indicating their natural birth and later spiritual rebirth when they were initiated and invested with the sacred thread. The Śūdras, having no initiation, were often not even regarded as Āryan.

As a divinity in human form the Brāhmaṇ claimed precedence. Even the power of the king was circumscribed by the ritual authority of the Brāhmaṇ. Many Brāhmaṇs did conform to the ideal priestly pattern, but many others engaged in professions not normally thought to be appropriate to Brāhmaṇs. Administrative positions in government have always been one of their favorite secular professions. Others were agriculturalists, either living on income derived from their tax-free lands or directly cultivating the soil themselves. These secular Brāhmaṇs were generally less esteemed than those who lived by sacrifice and teaching.

The claims and pretensions of the Brāhmaṇ have always been contested by the Kṣatriyas, and many legends, tales, and proverbs hinge on the contradictions entailed by this competition. Because a Kṣatriya's duty is to fight in war and govern in peace, invaders and martial peoples of all kinds have been incorporated into the Hindu social order by ascribing Kṣatriya status to them. Just as Brāhmaṇs had special dispensation (āpad-dharma) allowing them to engage in unauthorized activities in time of need, so too many Kṣatriyas were farmers, merchants, and craftsmen.

Vaiśyas, with their expert knowledge of every form of trade and commerce, were the preeminent business class. Earlier literature had enjoined them to keep cattle and raise crops, but the Vaiśya soon deserted these occupations for more lucrative enterprises. In the sacred literature, Vaiśyas are far below Brāhmaṇs and Kṣatriyas in prestige. In some instances, even their twice-born status is denied. Possibly this discrepancy between their economic and ritual status accounts for their support of the unorthodox religions of Buddhism and Jainism.

Śūdras had few rights and many disabilities. Servants to all, they could be beaten, compelled to work, and expelled from the village at will. They were denied full ritual participation and were not allowed to read or hear the Vedas. The punishment for a Brāhmaṇ killing a Śūdra was the same as for killing a cat or dog. A Śūdra should eat his master's leftover food, wear his discarded clothing, and should not accumulate wealth. Yet, wretched as his state may have been, it was superior to that of the untouchable. Low and defiling, the Śūdra still had a recognized position in the social order. Even though they were sometimes referred to as pañcama (fifth class), the untouchables were outside the system. They could not dwell within the boundaries of the village and had to perform all sorts of unclean tasks—cremation of corpses, scavenging, removal of dead animals. Often even their appearance was regarded as polluting and they had to warn the clean castes of their approach.

Although India was never economically dependent on the institution of slavery, slaves (dāsa) were certainly a part of the Indian social system. Those vanquished in battle were held to be subject to enslavement, a free man in distress could sell himself and his family into slavery, and the children of slaves became the property of their parents' masters. Even so, Indian slavery was less barbaric than that of many other civilizations. Slaves might be bought and sold, but masters had obligations to their slaves. They could not abandon them in old age nor beat them more severely than they might beat a wife or younger brother. Masters were encouraged to free their slaves as a pious act, and some law books permitted slaves to own and inherit property.

In summary, Indian society was divided first into Āryan and non-Āryan components. Āryans were divided into those who were twice-born (dvija) and those who were not twice-born. The twice-born were divided into those who had dominion over men and those who had dominion over animals. Those who had dominion over men were divided into those with a priestly or sacerdotal function and those without a sacerdotal function. Non-Āryans were divided

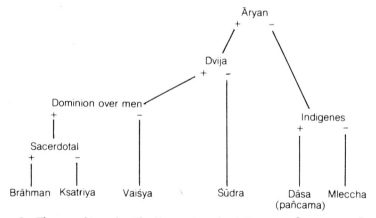

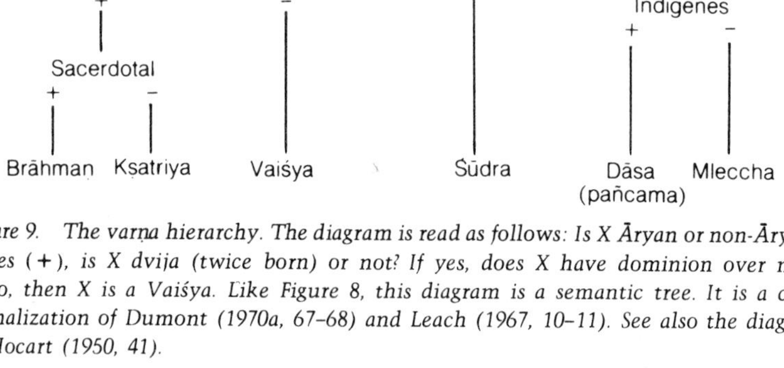

Figure 9. The varṇa hierarchy. The diagram is read as follows: Is X Āryan or non-Āryan? If yes (+), is X dvija (twice born) or not? If yes, does X have dominion over men? If no, then X is a Vaiśya. Like Figure 8, this diagram is a semantic tree. It is a clear formalization of Dumont (1970a, 67–68) and Leach (1967, 10–11). See also the diagram in Hocart (1950, 41).

into indigenes (dāsa) and foreigners (mlecchas). Figure 9 represents this system of social classification. It will be noted that the number of plus signs in Figure 9 for any one of the four varṇas gives an automatic index of relative status. The Brāhmaṇ has four plus signs, the Kṣatriya three, the Vaiśya two, and the Śūdra one. Thus, the higher the number of pluses, the higher the status. This distribution of classificatory attributes produces a scalogram of status rank. Letting S = sacerdotal, D = dominion over men, T = twice-born, A = Āryan, we can construct the scalogram in Figure 10. This diagram indicates that the relative status ranks of the four classes derive from the sum of attributes appropriate to each class. The higher the number of positive attributes, the higher the rank.

Historically, the competition between Brāhmaṇs and Kṣatriyas has been expressed as a disagreement over the attributes "sacerdotal" and "dominion over men." By embracing Buddhism and Jainism, the Kṣatriyas invalidated the sacerdotal attribute and thereby challenged the Brāhmaṇ's claim to higher rank. Similarly, the rejection of Brāhmaṇic ritual involved an assertion that the Brāhmaṇ's claim to dominion over men through the power of ritual was illegitimate. The pivotal attribute or attributes that separated one class from another have always been the focus of claims to higher status.

This elaboration of the varṇa system only partially reflects the course of accommodation between Āryan and non-Āryan societies. It is clear that the fourfold division of society is an ancient Āryan class system, for similar divisions of society existed in other Indo-European communities. More important as indices of accommodation are the division of society into Āryan and non-Āryan components, the extensive literature on "confusion of class," and the evolution of hierarchically ranked subunits within each of the varṇas.

Earlier sacred literature insists on a fundamental distinction between Āryan and non-Āryan. The chief criterion of Āryanness was adherence to Āryan sacraments. Those who did not follow Āryan ritual practices were dāsas or dasyus (demons) or mlecchas (foreigners, barbarians). In later days, those who were without Āryan sacraments were either untouchables or, if sufficiently warlike, Kṣatriyas who had temporarily forgotten the sacred rites. While the distinction between Āryan and non-Āryan could thus be maintained by a flexible criterion of sacramental adherence, the distinctions among the four classes were constantly threatened by wrong marriages. Theoretically, the four classes were endogamous—marriage being permitted only between members of the same class—and kings were constantly exhorted to prevent class confusion through miscegenation. Hypergamous marriages between a man of higher

	S	D	T	A
Brāhman	+	+	+	+
Kṣatriya		+	+	+
Vaiśya			+	+
Śūdra				+

Figure 10. Scalogram of varṇa status rank.

class and a woman of lower class were sometimes permitted, but hypogamous marriages between a woman of higher class and a man of lower class were not. Hindu theoreticians argued that both these forms of marriage produced offspring who were technically members of neither parent's class. The theoreticians attributed the development of various "mixed" classes to such unorthodox unions. This confusion of classes through irregular marriages was regarded both as a threat to the social order and as an explanation for the proliferation of social groups that did not fit easily into the four theoretical divisions of society.

Since it is unlikely that the thousands of distinct social groups in the caste system could have thus originated from the four varṇas, this explanation is faulty. Even though faulty, it is important because it chronicles the development of the complex system of social groups known as castes, and it demonstrates the pervasiveness of an ideal order based on the assumption that the underlying relativity of human nature should be materially expressed in hierarchical social groups. The Hindu theorists were confronted with a world containing a multiplicity of social groups of diverse origin and variant customs—a world seemingly incompatible with the ancient fourfold scheme. Significantly, they did not abandon this ideal model in the face of nonconforming facts. Instead, they conformed the facts with the ideal model. It mattered little that existent social groups were more numerous than the ideal four classes; what was important was that the proliferation of social groups could be attributed to lapses in the observance of the rules of dharma. Even more importantly, these lapses themselves validated the ideal scheme. The four varṇas were the immutable forms of which the confused plethora of social groups were but distorted and inconstant representations. Finally, when the idea of karma was deliberately grafted onto the varṇa system, the implications of this profound rationalization were fully realized. Karma, denoting the consequences of past actions, provides an explanation for a man's current status. Rewards for doing one's duty and punishments for failure to do it are expressed in rebirth and determine the conditions of rebirth. One's current life condition results from past deeds; consequently, one's present varṇa status results from past deeds. Birth in a high varṇa is a reward, birth in a low varṇa a punishment. Persons born in high varṇas are morally, intellectually, and spiritually superior to those born in low varṇas. A low varṇa person could not have the capacity to understand ritual; and because he was a lower order of being, he could not be expected to behave in accordance with the higher moral principles. Standards of acceptable behavior were naturally different for each varṇa. What might be a terrible sin for a Brāhmaṇ was merely normal behavior for a person of a lower varṇa. Human nature was not universal; moral obligation was not the same for all men. One's essential nature and moral obligation were given by caste membership.

Relativity of human nature is accurately and explicitly denoted by the word jāti—the indigenous word for caste. Jāti denotes species or kind, and members of different jātis are members of different species. Each species has its own duties, obligations, and standards of behavior, and when each behaves in accordance with its own rules of conduct, it contributes directly to the maintenance of dharma or cosmic order. To behave in conformance with the rules of one's own jāti thus became the highest expression of morality.

By means of this notion of human relativity, the Hindu theoreticians successfully wrought an accommodation of conflicting doctrines and contradictory codes of behavior. The bewildering variety of un-Āryan behavior, customs, and codes did not invalidate the varṇa system, but merely expressed the natural order of things. A fundamental by-product of this theoretical formulation was a magnificent tolerance for strange and peculiar customs. From an egalitarian point of view, the inherent tolerance of a system of thought founded on a doctrine of relativity in human endowment represents a profound paradox. From a Hindu point of view, an egalitarian doctrine founded on the notion that all men are created equal and which yet results in systematic intolerance is a paradox within a paradox.

The varṇa system was also given a functional interpretation by valorizing it in terms of the sacrifice. Just as the earliest reference to the varṇas (R.V. 10.90) attributed their origin to the sacrifice of a primeval man (puruṣa), the varṇas themselves were homologized as functionally interdependent roles in the sacrifice. Thus the Brāhmaṇ performed the sacrifice, but he performed it for the king. The components of the sacrifice were provided by the Vaiśyas, and the Śūdras were necessary for performing certain impure acts associated with the sacrifice. Theoretically, each varṇa had a prescribed role in the sacrifice, and the sacrifice signified the ritual interdependence of the varṇas. Corresponding to these ritual roles, each varṇa was assigned a color (varṇa = color), with the basic contrast between light and dark. The Brāhmaṇs, Kṣatriyas, and Vaiśyas were associated with light colors: Brāhmaṇs with white, Kṣatriyas with red, Vaiśyas with yellow. The Śūdras were associated with blue or black. Similarly, each varṇa was assigned a point of the compass: Brāhmaṇs to the north; Kṣatriyas to the east (toward the rising sun, symbolizing the victory of the gods of light over the powers of darkness); Vaiśyas to the south; and Śūdras to the west (toward the setting sun, symbolizing the powers of darkness and death). Finally, each varṇa was assigned a yuga (a period of time; see pp. 92–94).

A further series of cosmic homologies symbolized varṇa interdependence. The early Brāhmaṇ was associated with the divine priest Bṛhaspati, and in his role as intermediary between gods and men, he was identified with Agni, the messenger of the gods. The Kṣatriya, as the varṇa from which the king was selected, corresponded to Indra, lord of the gods, or to Varuṇa, lord of law, guardian of order, and punisher of evildoers. Vaiśyas were homologized to classes of lesser deities such as the Maruts, who were assistants of the high gods. The Śūdras were associated with the demons, the powers of darkness. Thus the twice-born varṇas were assigned to the gods of light, the Śūdras to powers of darkness. The twice-born were differentiated from one another by assigning each to deities of different rank and function. In short, the organization of human society was a replica of divine society, and central to both human and divine societies was the concept of a cosmic order maintained through the sacrificial interdependence of men and gods. This series of homologies is represented in Figure 11.

	Light			Dark
Supernatural class	Devas (gods)			Asuras (demons)
Social class (varṇa)	Twice-born (dvija)			Non-twice-born
	Brāhmaṇ	Kṣatriya	Vaiśya	Śūdra
Sacrificial role	Sacrificient	Sacrificer	Provider of sacrificial goods	Performance of unclean acts associated with the sacrifice
Color	White	Red	Yellow	Blue, black
Direction	North	East	South	West
Time	Kṛta yuga	Dvapara yuga	Treta yuga	Kali yuga

Figure 11. Cosmological homologies of the varṇa categories.

The Four Life Stages Āśramas

Just as society was divided into four classes, a man's life was divided into four stages (āśramas). The four āśramas and the conception of duties and obligations specific to each cannot be traced to Vedic sources; it is possible that this scheme arose in response to Buddhist and Jainist preaching which encouraged young men to abandon family responsibilities and take up the ascetic life. Whatever its origins, the system of four life stages, like age-grading systems in many other cultures, provided a theoretical basis for the smooth transfer of authority from generation to generation.

In the classical expositions of the āśrama system, a man's life and sacramental obligations began before his birth and continued beyond his death. A man was said to be born with three great debts: a debt to the gods, a debt to the sages, and a debt to the ancestors. Lifelong performance of ritual repaid the debt to the gods, study of the *Vedas* liquidated the debt to the sages, and special rites dedicated to the deceased paid the debt to the ancestors.

Of the forty or so sacraments (saṃskāra) commemorating life stages, three were performed before birth. The garbhādhāna promoted conception, the puṃsavana encouraged the birth of male children, and the sīmantonnayana ensured the child's well-being in the womb. At the birth ceremony (jātakarma) the child was fed a mixture of honey and ghī and given a secret name. The child's parents were ritually impure for ten days after his birth and were prohibited from participating in religious ceremonies. At the end of this ten-day period, the child was given a public name. Other ceremonies were performed on the occasions of the piercing of the child's ear, his first look at the sun, his first feeding, and when his head was shaved leaving only a topknot.

Of all these ceremonies, probably the most important was the upanayana or initiation. Among Brāhmaṇs initiation was performed at eight years of age, among Kṣatriyas at eleven, and among Vaiśyas at twelve. Before his initiation, a boy was not Āryan; he could not really participate in religious observances and could not commit sins. The upanayana ceremony signaled a son's second birth and accession to Āryan status. In this ceremony the boy was dressed in ascetic costume, the sacred Gāyatrī was whispered in his ear, and the sacred thread was draped over his right shoulder and under his left arm. Once invested with the sacred thread, he could remove it only at the risk of ritual impurity. The cord itself consisted of three threads, each of nine strands. For Brāhmaṇs the thread was made of wool, for Kṣatriyas of cotton, and for Vaiśyas it could only consist of hemp. The Gāyatrī is a verse from the *Ṛg Veda* addressed to the sun god Savitṛ. Repeated on all religious occasions, it is the most holy passage of Hindu scripture.

First Stage: Student (Brahmacārin)

When a child was invested with the sacred thread he became a full member of the Āryan community and entered the first life stage (brahmacārin, "student"). As a brahmacārin he was expected to lead a celibate life studying the Vedas in the home of his teacher (guru). He was exhorted to treat his guru as a divinity, to revere and obey him, and in some instances to beg food for him. Under the guidance of the guru, the student learned to perform the sandhyā (morning, noon, and evening devotions) and committed the Veda to memory. He was taught to restrain his senses and was expected to master the six vedāṅgas (limbs of the Veda), consisting of: kalpa, the performance of sacrifice; śikṣā, phonetics; chandas, composition; nirukta, etymology; vyākaraṇa, grammar; and jyotiṣa, astronomy. In some schools he received supplementary instruction in philosophy, sacred law, and mathematics.

Second Stage: Householder (Gṛhastha)

After twelve years of study, a young man returned to his home and, after a ritual bath and special homecoming ceremony, prepared to enter the next life stage (gṛhastha, "householder"). In order to provide his father with descendants who could perform the ancestor ceremonies, he was expected to marry soon after his return. Marriage was arranged by the parents, who selected a spouse after special consultation, the casting of horoscopes, examination of genealogies, and a lengthy discussion of dowry payments. Although the ideal was for a man to marry a girl one-third his own age, this seems not to have been the practice. In a later period girls were expected to be married before puberty, but this custom was not sanctioned by sacred law.

The marriage ceremony as outlined in the law books called for the groom and his party to proceed to the bride's home where they were greeted by the bride's father with a ceremonial drink of honey and curds. The wedding ceremony was enacted in a special pavillion constructed in the courtyard. Seated separately on either side of a curtain in the pavillion, the bride and groom listened to the chanting of sacred verses and waited expectantly for the Brāhmaṇ to draw the curtain. When the curtain was drawn, the bride and groom saw one another, often for the first time. The bride's father then presented her to the groom, who swore to behave with piety and provide her with wealth and pleasure. After the traditional offering of ghī and rice were made to the sacred fire, the couple's garments were knotted together and the groom led the bride around the sacred fire. Next, the bride stepped on a millstone. Then the couple, still joined together, took seven steps, the bride treading on a small mound of rice with each step. The couple was then sprinkled with holy water. Although there were variations on this pattern, most writers were agreed that a proper marriage ceremony had to include homa (offerings to the sacred fire), paṇigrāhana (taking the bride's hand), and saptapadi (seven steps).

After completion of the main ceremony, the married couple entered the bride's house and offered sacrifice to the domestic fire. In the evening they gazed at the Pole Star, a symbol of faithfulness. They were expected to remain continent until the fourth night, when the marriage was finally consummated.

According to the sacred authorities, marriage itself was a sacrament directed toward fulfillment of dharma (religious obligation), praja (offspring), and rati (sexual pleasure). The marriage of a Śūdra was said to be for sexual pleasure only. The essentially religious character of marriage was signified by a series of sacramental obligations. It was the duty of the householder and his wife to offer five great sacrifices (pañca mahāyajña) to brāhmaṇ, ancestors, gods, demons, and men during the morning, noon, and evening devotions. Brāhmaṇ was satisfied with the recitation of Vedic verses, principal among which was the Gāyatrī (hymn to the rising sun). Ancestors (pitṛs) were given offerings of food and water in addition to the annual ancestor rites (śrāddha). Gods were given oblations burnt in the sacred fire. Other offerings were scattered in various directions to satisfy miscellaneous spirits and demons. Respect to guests was a duty, and men were honored by hospitality. Finally, in a corner of the house, the householder left food offerings to dogs, outcastes, crows, and insects. According to Manu, the man who does not neglect these sacrifices is untainted by sins committed in the five places of slaughter (i.e., hearth, grinding stone, broom, pestle, and mortar). Thus life taken intentionally or unintentionally in the round of daily activities incurred no sin for the man who performed the five great sacrifices.

A newly married couple did not set up a new household, for the ideal of family life was for brothers, uncles, cousins, and nephews to reside in a common household. The ideal family thus was a patrilineal joint family. All males descended from a common ancestor shared jointly in the family property and lived together in an extended household. Usually, the eldest male in direct line of descent from the founding ancestor was the head of the house. This group was held together by common ownership of property, common residence, joint responsibility for revenue, and ritual observances. Of the latter, the most important expression of family unity was the ancestor rites. These śrāddha ceremonies called upon descendants to honor three generations of deceased ancestors in the male line with offerings of rice balls (piṇḍa). Those who were entitled to participate in the ceremony were sapiṇḍa, descendants of a common male ancestor. The concept of sapiṇḍa later came to mean those who were born of one body and was extended to include one's mother's ancestors. Sapiṇḍa eventually came to designate a rule of exogamy—a man could not marry a sapiṇḍa. This group included anyone with a common ancestor up to the eighth generation in the father's patriline and the sixth generation in the mother's patriline.

In theory a family should continue as a joint estate until the death or retirement of the male head, but in fact the partition of an estate occurred at varying times. According to one modern school of family law (the mitākṣarā), descendants had rights in family property even before the death or retirement of the male head; but in another school (the dāyabhāga), rights in family property devolved to descendants only after the death of the paterfamilias. The mitākṣarā also provided that a man's property could be subdivided with his consent, agreement among descendants, or in cases of senility and incompetence. Sons shared equally in the partition of an estate, and though the law books differ on this point, women generally were excluded from equal inheritance. When a man died without male heirs, his property was inherited by his male agnates and in some law books by his wife and daughters.

In much of south India the patrilineal joint family was not the norm. Instead, many castes had matrilineal joint families with descent and inheritance traced exclusively through females. Sons had no (or strictly circumscribed) rights to family property, and family authority was vested in the mother's brother rather than the father. Southern rules of exogamy also differed substantially from the Āryan model expounded in the books of sacred law. Where the Āryan model prohibits marriage between close relatives, marriage with a cross-cousin (mother's brother's daughter or father's sister's daughter) or niece (older sister's daughter) was (and is) regarded as the most desirable form of marriage in the south. The Āryan law books often attempted to reconcile these variant patterns with the Āryan model by invoking the notion that, since each caste might have its own rules and customs, such deviant forms were permissible. Yet, despite their access to the idea of moral relativity, most law books expressed an underlying sentiment of repulsion for these southern customs that took distinctly un-Āryan and reprehensible forms.

Third Stage: Forest Dweller (Vānaprastha)

The *Code of Manu* clearly states that the householder is the most important life stage. Because men in all the other life stages depend on the support of the householder, he is essential and is accorded a high status. Once, however, he has lived the second part of his life according to the laws and duties incumbent on a householder, a man should depart into the forest either alone or in the company of his wife. Having made over his property to his sons, he should dwell in the forest without attachment to worldly goods. Possessing only the sacred fire and those artifacts necessary for the domestic sacrifices, he should obtain his food by begging and sleep on the bare ground without care for shelter. Dwelling in the forest, he should study the *Vedas* and *Upanisads* and perform the rites practiced by the sages. The vānaprastha (forest dweller) occupies a life stage intermediate between the first two and the final life stages. He is still bound by dharma, but the other worldly motivations (artha, kāma) do not apply to him.

When a man enters the final life stage (sannyāsin), he completely abandons the things of this world and is beyond dharma. Having taken the sacred fire into himself, he should become a celibate, wandering alone, indifferent to everything, meditating and concentrating his mind on brāhmaṇ. Desiring neither life nor death, he should practice the postures prescribed by the Yoga. Be detaching his senses from the objects of sensual enjoyment and by practicing austerities, he eventually possesses true insight, is no longer fettered by his deeds (karma), and attains union with brāhmaṇ and freedom from rebirth.

By this scheme a man's life was essentially divided into two major segments, one devoted to the things of this world and dominated by the motivations of artha, kāma, and dharma, the other devoted to attaining release from the things of this world (mokṣa). This segmentation is denoted by the words pravṛtti and nivṛtti. Pravṛtti included three separate stages (trivarga)—brahmacārin, gṛhastha, and vānaprastha—which are oriented to the pursuits of the world and are ruled by dharma. Nivṛtti (or apavarga, "completion, end") eventually came to refer only to the last life stage, in which dharma is no longer a central concern. The domain of dharma refers only to the first three life stages, while mokṣa dominates the last life stage. Figure 12 illustrates these relationships.

Dharma			Mokṣa
Pravṛtti			Nivṛtti
Brahmacārin	Gṛhastha	Vānaprastha	Sannyāsin

Figure 12. The domains of dharma and mokṣa.

The position of the vānaprastha in Figure 12 is rather ambiguous. Even though the vānaprastha is not actively engaged in the pursuits of this world, he is still ruled by dharma. His attachment to dharma is signified by the fact that he must still perform domestic rites (in particular, the five sacrifices), and by the fact that he does not take a vow of celibacy. By contrast, the sannyāsin takes a vow of celibacy, renounces his wife, and does not perform any of the domestic sacrifices. His renunciation of the world and liberation from the dictates of dharma are symbolized in a ceremony in which his topknot is cut off and his sacred thread severed. Since cutting off the topknot is customary in funeral ceremonies, its removal when a man becomes a sannyāsin symbolizes his worldly death and proclaims him free from the obligations and customs of the world. He no longer participates in the affairs of the world and is not required to follow the norms of everyday society. The difference between the vānaprastha and the sannyāsin is again manifested in funeral ceremonies. A vānaprastha receives the same ceremonial treatment as any ordinary human—his body is cremated on the funeral pyre. A sannyāsin, however, is buried rather than cremated. Further, no defilement or pollution is associated with a sannyāsin's funeral, whereas the principal mourners at a vānaprastha's funeral are polluted by contact with death and must undergo purificatory rites to remove the pollution. Finally, none of the śrāddha (ances-

<table>
<tr><td colspan="3">Dharma</td></tr>
<tr><td colspan="2">Pravṛtti</td><td>Nivṛtti</td></tr>
<tr><td>Brahmacārin</td><td>Gṛhastha</td><td>Vānaprastha</td></tr>
</table>

Figure 13: The earlier subdivisions of dharma.

tor) rites are performed for a sannyāsin. All these differences signify that the vānaprastha's status is governed by dharma, while the sannyāsin's status is determined by mokṣa. Despite his retirement from active life, the vānaprastha is still a member of ordinary society and is bound by those rules. The sannyāsin is dead to ordinary society and is bound only by the extraordinary goal of mokṣa.

This opposition between dharma and mokṣa reflects an historical pattern of synthesis between conflicting social goals. Earlier classifications of life styles did not entail a disjunction between this-worldly and other-worldly aims and motivations. Both motivations were simply the active and negative aspects of dharma (earlier, ṛta). In this historically prior classification of life stages, represented in Figure 13, the whole of society is ruled by dharma, which has active and negative aspects. The ascetic (sannyāsin) and his goal (mokṣa) were originally accommodated to this classification as aspects of nivṛtti, but gradually mokṣa came to be recognized as the opposite of dharma. Thus, when the quietistic teachings of the *Upaniṣads* and the ascetic traditions of the Buddhists and Jains were ultimately reconciled with the ritualism of the *Brāhmaṇas*, the vānaprastha was displaced by the sannyāsin. Nivṛtti was radically reinterpreted to denote not just retirement from activity in the world but a rejection of this world. Consequently, mokṣa, signifying the opposite of all that dharma stood for, was incorporated into the system. In the final synthesis, the dialectical opposites of dharma and mokṣa were relativized as complementary rather than contradictory life orientations.

Transformation and Hierarchy

At this point it is instructive to note the relationship between this transformational sequence and the similar transformation wrought by the Śāmkhya philosophical system (see pp. 70–73). It is clear that pravṛtti and nivṛtti are the societal corollaries of the Śāmkhya prakṛti and puruṣa. Thus pravṛtti is to activity in this world as prakṛti is to cosmic force, and nivṛtti is to withdrawal from this world as puruṣa is to inactive potentiality. We see then that just as the abstract philosophical systems represent a transformation of earlier metaphysical conceptions, this same transformation was also carried over into the realm of social theory. Both exemplify the same logical transformation.

Here, too, we must observe that the four ends of life constitute an hierarchic ordering of the four life stages identical to that of the varṇa system (pp. 81–86). Although the basic contrast is between dharma and mokṣa, dharma itself is subdivided into two categories: artha and kāma. In essence, then, one is oriented to life in this world and the obligations of society (dharma) or not (mokṣa). If one is oriented to this world, one desires the material wealth of the world (artha) or not. If one desires the material wealth of the world, one

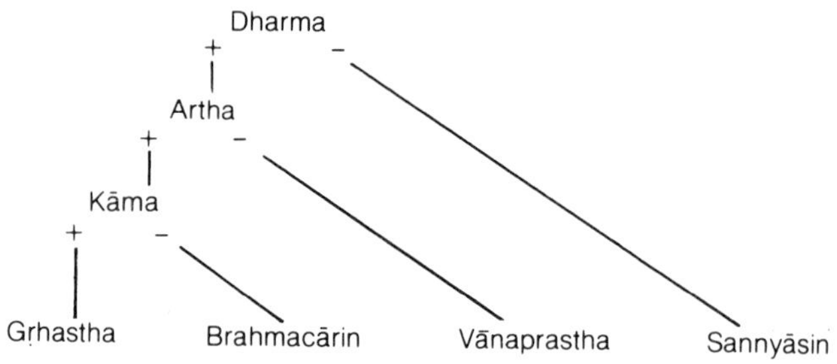

Figure 14. The hierarchy of the four stages of life.

also desires desire (kāma) or not. Figure 14 illustrates these relationships. This hierarchy is particularly interesting because it constitutes what one might call a double hierarchy. That is, the householder (gṛhastha), as Manu declares, is clearly the highest and most important life stage, combining the highest number of positive attributes. But it is the highest if and only if dharma constitutes the original choice—that is, only if one is oriented to the things of this world. If mokṣa (represented in Figure 14 as minus dharma) is the original choice, then the sannyāsin is at the top of the hierarchy and the householder at the bottom. Just as the householder is the most perfect expression of man in society, the sannyāsin is the most perfect expression of man outside society. In this double hierarchy we must clearly perceive the Hindu genius for synthesis through the reconciliation of opposites.

Time

Vedic speculation elevated time to the status of a creator. Without beginning or end, time was a mystical power, the first cause of the universe. The Upaniṣadic seers dethroned time and asserted that brāhmaṇ was beyond time. Time was likened to a wheel whose ceaseless revolutions were measured by the sun. This cyclical notion of time (already adumbrated in the Vedic reference to the year as a "five-spoked wheel") was significantly elaborated in Jainism, and by the time of the *Pūraṇas*, Hindu theorists had incorporated the Jainist doctrines and worked out a more-or-less consistent theory of cyclical time.

In the Pūraṇic system the whole cosmos passes through eternal cycles of cycles. One human year is but a day and night of the gods; 360 human years constitute a divine year; and 12,000 divine years equal one four-age period (caturyuga). A caturyuga consists of one kṛtayuga of 1,728,000 human years (4,800 divine years), a tretayuga of 1,296,000 human years (3,600 divine years), a dvaparayuga of 864,000 human years (2,400 divine years), and a kaliyuga of 432,000 human years (1,200 divine years). Kṛtayuga is a golden age with dharma at its fullest power. In each subsequent age the power of dharma declines, and morality, strength, happiness, and longevity progressively diminish until the cycle begins again with a new golden age. 1,000 caturyugas equal one kalpa or day of Brahmā. The world is created and lasts one day of Brahmā. At the close of Brahmā's day the world is dissolved and absorbed into the god's sleeping body where it remains through one night of Brahmā.

360 days and nights of Brahmā equal a year of Brahmā, and 100 such years is the life span of Brahmā.

The universe thus alternates between states of activity and states of mere potentiality. The active state is a day of Brahmā, and the potential is a night of Brahmā. In this two-stage cycle of time the dualistic categories of Sāṁkhya philosophy have obviously been incorporated, but this is not the end of synthesis, for another cyclical notion of time was reconciled to the system of kalpas. Within the cycle of kalpas is a series of secondary cycles (manvantaras). One manvantara equals 71 caturyugas, and 14 manvantaras equal one kalpa. Between each manvantara there is a short period when life comes to an end before it is re-created by a new Manu. Manu is a regent of Brahmā responsible for creation at the beginning of a manvantara. During the brief period of dissolution at the end of a manvantara, the Manus, the minor gods, and the ancestors ascend to a higher plane for one kṛta period.

This conception of vast, repetitious cycles of time is consistent with the doctrines of karma and rebirth. Death is not the end of one's existence, but merely the end of one existence in a series of existences extending infinitely into the past and future. Only those few who have learned the identity of brāhmaṇ and ātman have escaped this ceaseless round of birth and death. The endless passage of the soul from body to body (saṁsāra) is the lot of the majority of humanity. Because every action has its consequences, a man is condemned to pay for his deeds. He may pay immediately or some misdeed committed many existences previously may suddenly come due. One misstep can send him plunging to the lowest form of existence in a future life. Not even the most exemplary life can put an end to rebirth. Credits for a good life can be accumulated, but they merely lead to rebirth in a higher form of existence. Man is trapped in a web of his own deeds. Hence the great aim of Hinduism is to find a means of escape from the wheel of time.

Underlying the conception of time as an endless cycle is a primordial classification reflected not only in the dualistic alternation between activity and potentiality but more importantly in this notion of existence outside or beyond time. Here the basic themes of opposition in the Asura myth are realized as time and timelessness (that is, time is to ṛta as timelessness is to anṛta; see p. 44). Both the past and the future are in time, but there is another state corresponding to the eternal present that is without past or future, has no history and generates no future. All the rites and duties of the social order are in time; they have a past and engender future consequences (karma). Because all these rites and obligations of the social order engender the consequences of time, one who merely lives an exemplary life according to dharma cannot escape from time. Time and its consequences realized through the social order are identified with māyā (illusion). All that is within time is māyā, and the rites of the social order merely serve to bind the individual closer and closer to the consequences of time. Escape requires that the individual sever his ties with the group, abrogate the rites and obligations of the social order. Individualism is not possible in time, only outside it. Traditionally it was asceticism that provided the means of escape from time, but in the later Hindu synthesis devotionalism (bhakti, pp. 101–103) provides an

Time	Timelessness
Illusion (māyā)	The real (brāhmaṇ, etc.)
Social order (dharma)	Individual (jīvan mukti)
Bondage (karma)	Freedom (mokṣa)
Ritual (yajña)	Asceticism (yoga) and devotionalism (bhakti)
(ṛta)	(anṛta)

Figure 15. The implications of time.

easier method of escape. To be in time then is to be part of an illusion, to be bound to the social order and the obligations of ritual. To be outside time is to participate in brāhmaṇ (the real) as a free individual. The distribution of these concepts within the categories of time and timelessness appears in Figure 15.

It has often been noted that the Hindu conception of time is antithetical to history. As the record of what has happened in the realm of illusion, history is irrelevant and merely inanely repetitious. There is no progress; there are no significant developmental stages or directional changes in the social order. Development implies dissolution, not progress.

Kings and Councilors

Beginning with the Mauryan Empire of the third century B.C., the basic pattern of Indian political organization was set. The unification of northern India under Candragupta Maurya effectively destroyed the competing forms of political organization represented by the conquered oligarchies and tribal confederacies. In their penchant for centralized authority the Mauryans were the legitimate heirs of the Indus civilization, reestablishing a pattern of political life that had been only temporarily interrupted by the Āryan tribals. While it is true that such ancient texts on the science of polity as the *Arthaśāstra* and *Nītiśāstras* give only an idealized version of what a proper kingdom ought to be, it is still a fact that they presented a model of kingship and political authority that every Indian ruler could look to as a source of inspiration. Similarly, though one can argue that other ancient texts espouse a contractual theory of kingship, the predominant motif of both texts and practice was the semidivine status of the king. As protector of law (dharma), the king was homologized with the god Indra. The chief sacrificer, he stood at the head of the sacred rites as the one for whom the rites were performed.

The political organization envisioned by the *Arthaśāstra* was a centralized kingdom with a semidivine king as the ultimate authority. To assist him in his duties, the king had a royal council of advisors consisting of a chief councilor, a chaplain (purohita), a tax collector or treasurer, a councilor on war and peace, a general, and a chief record keeper. Beneath the council a bureaucratic army of clerks, secretaries, and minor officials carried out the royal decrees. Although the *Arthaśāstra* specifies a system of cash payment to ministers and civil servants, the more usual practice was for the king to grant them the tax revenue of a village or district. The king ruled by royal decree, interpreting dharma and established custom. According to the *Arthaśāstra*, the king's chief function was to protect society, and the whole apparatus of government was but a projection of the king's role in carrying out this purpose. The state was thus never an organization transcending society. In protecting society the king's main duty was to ward off external aggression and uphold dharma. He ensured the proper order of castes and the inheritance of property, protected and supported the Brāhmaṇs and temples, and punished adultery, thieving, and extortion. He ruled by daṇda (coercion, punishment). According to Manu, if the king did not inflict punishment, evildoers would triumph and the order of society would crumble. The king who failed to inflict just and impartial punishment would incur the sins of unpunished criminals and suffer in hell. In addition to vigorously upholding dharma, the king was expected to patronize the arts and learning and was urged to refrain from indulging in gambling, wenching, and drinking.

In foreign affairs the *Arthaśāstra* proposes the theory of maṇḍalas (circles). Any kingdom adjoining one's own is an hereditary enemy, any kingdom adjoining the kingdom of an hereditary enemy is an ally, and so on in an ever-widening series of concentric rings. In the conduct of foreign affairs the *Arthaśāstra* encourages every possible Machiavellian device, including psychological warfare. The king was encouraged to extend his empire and become a "universal emperor" (cakravartin), ruling all of Jambudvīpa and extending the boundaries of righteousness. The ancient texts clearly distinguished between righteous conquest and other, less desirable forms of conquest. Righteous conquest was the ideal except in the more secular *Arthaśāstra*, which encouraged the king to extend his empire for whatever purpose. Other sources held that because warfare was the Kṣatriya's dharma, it was justified. In more orthodox sources the rules governing warfare transformed it into a kind of tournament, but not so in the *Arthaśāstra*. Warfare in the *Arthaśāstra* was an all-or-nothing affair; such chivalric deceits as humane conduct toward noncombatants or mercy for the wounded were reserved for psychological ends, not as rules of conduct to be rigidly followed. The *Arthaśāstra* endorsed no code of military honor except as an expedient, and unlike the epics did not encourage the defeated king to burn himself, his family, and retinue alive in their quarters. Theoretically, the king was supposed to be drawn from the Kṣatriya varṇa, but many kings were foreigners, Vaiśyas, and even Śūdras. No matter what his origin every king was a *de facto* Kṣatriya. Succession to kingship descended in the male line by primogeniture, though accession of women both as regents and as actual rulers was not unknown. Exceptions to primogeniture were allowed in the case of disability. Princes were often contentious, constituting a threat not only to one another but to the king as well. The court was often filled with the intrigues of sons lusting for power.

The king's revenue came chiefly from a share of the produce of the land. His proportion seems to have varied between one-sixth and one-quarter of the yield. The cultivator also paid assessments on the use of irrigation water, and sometimes on houses, livestock, and implements of production. Merchants paid road tolls and tariffs at city gates, and craftsmen were expected to contribute a day's work per month. Exempted from this revenue system were the Brāhmaṇs and religious establishments. These frequently were given perpetual revenue-free rights to the produce of the land. This extensive revenue system entailed a bureaucracy of record keepers, surveyors, and collectors. The king's right to a share of the produce of the land was justified as a payment for his protection, but other sources have been interpreted as saying that the king was the "owner" of all the land. It is a mistake to attribute the concept of ownership to this system. In effect, no one owned the land, but all those who were tied to the land by varṇa status had a right to a share in the produce of the land. Each caste in a local village had a right to a share of the landholder's produce by virtue of his participation in a traditional system of mutual exchange of goods and services. The king was merely the preeminent landholder who apportioned a share of the revenue among his servants in the civil administration. The land itself was a deity and could not be possessed by mortals. They had rights only in the fruits of the land, and these rights were conditional on varṇa, caste, and dharma. Similarly, some authorities have mistakenly seen a form of feudalism in the partitioning of rights to revenue among the king's civil servants. This is a complex issue, but here we may note that the devolution of rights to the produce of the land was ultimately not articulated within a paradigm of fealty, vassalage, and overlordship. Instead, these rights were homologized to ritual interdependence. Each person who had a right to a portion of the revenue was in fact a petty king surrounded by ministers, armies, and ritual analogous to the king's court. Each level in the hierarchic devolution of rights to revenue was simply a smaller scale replica of the level above it. At the apex stood the king, the supreme landholder, and at the bottom was the village landholder. The "king's" position and right to revenue at whatever level in this hierarchy was conditional on his participation in a system of exchange. In return for revenue he provided protection and upheld dharma through punishment of criminals and participation in the sacred rituals designed to ensure dharma.

Corresponding to this hierarchic devolution of rights to revenue, the kingdom was divided into provinces, districts, and various other subdivisions. From early times the governorship of these revenue subdivisions tended to become hereditary. Incorporated in this subdivision were the kingdoms of conquered rulers. The usual practice was for the defeated king to swear loyalty to his victor and to agree to pay tribute and provide weapons and men at arms during times of war. In order to guarantee the proper working of this system, the *Arthaśāstra* recommended a system of spies. This secret service system kept close watch on all officials, maintaining records of births, deaths, income and expenditure, and visitors. Prostitutes were employed as spies to keep track of thieves and other evildoers. Any potential plots against the king were supposedly forestalled by this intelligence information. The lowest level in the administrative system was the village, ruled by an hereditary headman in some areas and in others by a council composed of the important men of the village. Like the larger councils of the cities, the headman and the council were responsible for collection of revenue, maintenance of streets and irrigation works, and settlement of disputes. They also had the important function of interceding between the villager and government officials. In many areas the headman was a petty chief responsible for protecting the villagers from cattle thieves and other brigands.

This complex system of hierarchic administrative subdivisions was constantly threatened by dissolution. Powerful vassals watched carefully for any sign of weakness at the center and when the opportunity was ripe they set themselves up as independent rulers and immediately embarked on a campaign of imperialist expansion. The record of empire in India has a pulsating character. Empires form and dissolve into constantly feuding petty kingdoms until a new power emerges and subjugates the others. Frequently those who were once powerful overlords became the vassals of their former vassals. In addition to internal dissension, kingdoms were constantly threatened by external aggression. Thus the Āryans destroyed the Indus civilization, Alexander briefly conquered parts of northern India, the Huns established short-lived empires in the northwest, and invasions of Islamic peoples in the eleventh century eventually resulted in the Moghul empire which extended over the whole of north India and most of the peninsula.

The Moghuls did not put an end to the Hindu system of polity. Instead they adapted it in inconsequential detail and continued it right down to the coming of the British. The empire of Akbar in the sixteenth century was a system of administration consisting of zamīndars who held hereditary rights over land, and jagirdars who held nonhereditary rights to revenue in payment for services to the empire. Other lands known as khālisa were directly controlled by the central government. Zamīndars and jagirdars were supervised by government officials who kept detailed records of revenue collection. Holders of rights to land were expected to contribute men, weapons, and service to military campaigns. The nonhereditary jagirdars constantly threatened to become hereditary, and the Moghul empire was faced with the same problems of fission and dissolution that had plagued the earlier Hindu empires. In all this we see that nothing basic has changed, only the names are different. Even the British were unable to radically alter the system; it persisted in part despite the British and in part because of them.

HINDUISM

The syncretistic pattern characteristic of Hindu views of society is also apparent in the development of the religious system known as Hinduism. Here, too, preexisting non-Āryan religious features were gradually incorporated into the body of Āryan belief. In the process many of the Āryan gods were degraded, and others were accommodated to non-Āryan gods. A reverse process either identified non-Āryan deities directly with Āryan deities or assigned them to an Āryan deity as one of his aspects. Most significantly, non-Āryan female deities came to occupy an important position in the orthodox pantheon. Just as the Āryan pantheon suffered considerable alteration, Brāhmaṇic ritualism was gradually diminished by the force of non-Āryan patterns of asceticism and theistic devotional worship (bhakti).

The New Gods

The character of Śiva and Viṣṇu, two of the most important Hindu deities, clearly reflects the elements of this syncretistic process. The Vedic deity Viṣṇu gradually accumulated a number of popular divinities who came to be regarded as his avatāras (incarnations). Of his traditional ten avatāras, some, like the boar and the man-lion, were theriomorphic divinities. Others, like Rāma, were human heroes elevated to divine status by martial tradition. Most important of his incarnations is the god Kṛṣṇa, himself the product of earlier syncretisms. Different aspects of the Kṛṣṇa legend indicate that he is a composite of a hero-god, a fertility deity associated with pastoralism, and a child-god. Since the name Kṛṣṇa means "black," it seems clear that Kṛṣṇa in his pastoral aspect evolves from the pastoral deity Māyōṉ (the black one) of early Tamil literature. The whole theory of avatāras itself is probably a non-Āryan innovation, for it seems to derive from the Jainist and Buddhist doctrines of a line of Tīrthaṅkaras (ford-makers) and former Buddhas who, like the avatāras, were incarnated in order to save the world from disaster. Thus, not only does Viṣṇu represent a composite of numerous non-Āryan divinities, but also the very theory that rationalizes these divinities as his incarnations derives from non-Āryan sources. Even the divine character of Viṣṇu approximates closely to the characteristics of the Tīrthaṅkaras and Buddhas. Like them, Viṣṇu is a benevolent deity whose incarnations are devoted to the needs and welfare of human beings. In sum, a long line of Āryan apologists gradually incorporated both the content and mechanism of non-Āryan traditions.

Unlike Viṣṇu, Śiva has a dangerous aspect. As death and time he is the divine destroyer who wears a garland of skulls and haunts burning-grounds and battlefields. But he is also the ultimate ascetic sitting on a tiger skin on Mount Kailāsa high in the Himālayas. Through the power of his meditation he maintains the world. As the lord of dance (Śiva Natarāja) he is the patron deity of that art; and of the many dance forms ascribed to him, the most famous is the tāṇḍava—a drunken orgiastic dance that destroys the world at the end of a cosmic cycle. The chief form of Śiva worship is a fertility cult centering around the liṅga, a phallic symbol. Although Śiva derives in part from the Vedic deity Rudra (the roarer), his more important aspects derive from non-Āryan sources. In his terrifying aspect, his association with the mountains, and in his role as the great dancer he seems clearly related to the Tamil deity Murukaṉ whom early Tamil literature depicts as a mountain god whose worshipers engaged in orgiastic dances and who with his terrible mother Koṟṟavai feasted on the corpses of those slain on battlefields. A part of the Śiva cult represents the persistence of an ancient non-Āryan fertility cult, the earliest instance of which is a deity depicted on a seal from the Indus civilization. On this seal is a horned deity seated in yoga posture and surrounded by animals. In general, these themes correspond to the contemporary concept of Śiva Paśupati (lord of beasts). Similarly, the Śiva liṅgas (short cylindrical pillars with rounded tops) correspond in form and function to the fertility pillars of the Indus civilization. It is also likely that the hero-stones (stone pillars erected to commemorate a great hero) found throughout the south and mentioned in early Tamil sources were aspects of a megalithic fertility cult and were incorporated into the composite form of the Śiva cult.

It is sometimes said that Śiva and Viṣṇu together with Brahmā constitute a trinity comparable to that of Christianity, but the Hindu trimūrti (triple form) was not really a monotheistic conception. In the first place, separate functions were assigned each of these deities. Brahmā was the creator, Viṣṇu the preserver, and Śiva the destroyer. Secondly, even though Hinduism incorporates a notion that each individual deity is but a different aspect of one divinity and that worship directed to any deity whatsoever is actually a form of reverence to the underlying unitary godhead, this is an expression of tolerance, not monotheism. In practice, a worshiper selects one of the many possible deities from the Hindu pantheon as the object of his worship. On separate occasions he may worship many different deities, but the object of his worship on any single occasion becomes—for that occasion—the high god. And since he worships only one god (as the high god) at a time, he is not a polytheist. Despite the fact that most Hindus are members of one of the two predominant sects of Vaiṣṇavism (worshipers of Viṣṇu) or Śaivism (worshipers of Śiva), this does not prevent them from occasionally paying homage to other deities. As in the case of divergent social customs, Hindu theoreticians did not attempt to extirpate nonconformist practices. Instead they utilized the underlying theory of relativity of manifestation as a means of reconciling discrepant religious conceptions.

In part, this syncretistic logic has its roots in the Ṛg Veda. In their eagerness to praise the god to whom a particular hymn was dedicated, the Vedic seers did not hesitate to appropriate some aspects of other deities and temporarily assign them to the deity currently being honored. Exalting above all others the deity of one's immediate attention was thus an early Vedic practice. Since a divinity's aspects were not purely inalienable, it is easy to see how deities could rise and fall in importance over a long period of time. Similarly, it is for this reason that there is probably no single exhaustive list of all the gods, goddesses, and godlings who are members of the Hindu pantheon, for the process of syncretism continues even in the contemporary period. New deities are added to the list, old ones are deleted, and new and old alike are constantly assigned and reassigned to other deities. Like all things of this world the deities are subject to change.

Among the more universally honored deities are Indra, Varuṇa, Yama, Kubera, Sūrya, Skanda, Gaṇeśa, and Hanumant. The first four are known as Lokapālas, guardians of the four directions of the universe. Of these four, Indra, Varuṇa, and Yama were important Vedic deities whose status declined in post-Vedic times. Sūrya, the sun god, is actually a composite of several solar deities. Skanda is the war god, and Gaṇeśa is the elephant god, remover of obstacles and patron of literature. Hanumant, the monkey god, is a beneficent deity whose sacred monkey troops frequently infest temples and villages unmolested.

Lesser deities comprise both good and evil spirits. Predominant among the former are the snake spirits (Nāgas), the Yakṣas, the Ṛsis, and the Siddhas. Serpents, and the ant hills in which they frequently live, are almost universally objects of veneration; they are capable of bestowing boons on humans. Yakṣas are fairies who are generally beneficent. As the original composers of the *Vedas*, the seven Ṛsis were exalted to the status of gods who are worshiped through study of the *Vedas*. Siddhas are local saints and religious teachers whose pious lives put them in the class of minor deities. Thus, for example, the sage Āgastya was a local saint who, because he was credited with bringing Āryan religion to the Dravidian south, was elevated to the status of Ṛsi. Evil spirits and dark forces abound in Hinduism, the chief class of demons being the Asuras. In the *Vedas* the Asuras were simply spirits possessed of power, but in Hinduism they came to be spirits whose power was directed toward evil ends. They seldom intervene directly in the lives of men but are regarded as being constantly at war with the gods. Rākṣases are demons capable of assuming many forms for the purpose of capturing and devouring humans. Piśācas inhabit places of death where they live on corpses and harm the unsuspecting. Those who have died violent deaths and have been denied the ancestor rites became dangerous ghosts (bhūta, preta). Their anger and malevolence, frequently expressed in sickness or unusual misfortune, are usually directed toward their living and negligent relatives.

Although she has no specific goddess form, the cow is sacred and her five products (pañcagavya)—milk, curd, butter, urine, and dung—are often combined into a mixture which is a potent purifying agency. Similarly, certain plants are significant religious objects—for instance, the pīpal tree, tulasī (basil), and kuśa and darbha grass. Finally, hills, mountains, and streams are sacred spots.

The Feminine Principle

Associated with fertility and disease, the cult of the mother goddess represents one of the most ancient and persistent expressions of Indian religion. Since mother goddesses are practically nonexistent in the earlier Āryan religious works, it is almost certainly a cult of non-Āryan origin. And, even though the earlier sacred books of the Āryans are silent on the subject, there is no doubt that mother-goddess worship continued among the lower orders and non-Āryans right through the period of Āryan predominance. No matter what heights of theological sophistication may have been reached by the learned, the peasant and the tribal then as now clung tenaciously to their mother-goddess cults. Eventually, through its persistence and pervasiveness, this cult made its influence felt in exalted orthodox theological speculation. Even as early as the Sāṁkhya philosophy we find the notion of power or potency associated with a female principle (prakṛti). Significantly, this female principle is the counterpart of an inactive but immanent masculine principle (puruṣa). In this dualistic formulation, the Sāṁkhya incorporates a notion that was to become prevalent in the Hindu conception of the dual sex characteristics of deities. This notion was expressed in Śaktism and in the idea of divine consorts.

Śakti, the strength or potency of a divinity, is manifest only in his female counterpart or consort. Although they appear to be separate, both the female and the male are aspects of a single godhead. In Tantrism these passive and active aspects were homologized to time and eternity, and their divine sexual union accomplished the primordial creative act. The most important expression of this conception centered around Śiva and his consort, known in her benevolent aspect as Pārvatī, Mahādevī, Satī, or simply as the mother (Mātā, Ammai). In her malevolent aspect (Durgā, Kāli, or Caṇḍī), she is depicted as a terrifying hag with huge tusks, bulging eyes, lolling tongue, and wearing a garland of skulls. As Durgā she is worshiped in the form of a phallic symbol known as a yoni. Thus combined in these higher forms of the mother-goddess cult are the twin aspects of the ancient cult—the mother as a benevolent fertility symbol and as a malevolent bringer of disease and death. In the medieval period this cult was enormously popular, with large, well-endowed temples in place of the rude shrines of the folk cult. These temples were located at holy places where the ashes of Pārvatī's yoni fell after her legendary act of self-immolation. Today the cult has declined among the urban, educated elite; only the Kāmakhya temple in Assam still functions with something of the previous display and ceremonial of the cult's heyday. Though the great temples and mass followings in urban centers have declined, the small, crude village shrines are still as important today among the mass of Hindus as they were at any time in their long history.

Although the fully developed form of Śaktism focuses on Śiva and his consort, its implications are equally evident in the assignment of female consorts to each of the major male divinities. Thus Brahmā has Brahmāṇi or Sarasvatī, Indra has Indrāṇi, Viṣṇu has Lakṣmī. Some of these goddesses, whose names are derived by adding feminine terminations to the names of masculine deities, are obviously unimportant priestly inventions designed in the name of pedantic symmetry, but Lakṣmī and Sarasvatī are important goddesses in their own right. Lakṣmī is the goddess of fortune or good luck. She is also worshiped as Sīta, wife of Rāma, and as Rukmiṇī and Rādhā, favorite consorts of Kṛṣṇa. Sarasvatī, divine inventor of the Sanskrit language and Devanāgarī script, is the patron of art, music, and literature. While the consorts of some of the original Āryan masculine deities are insignificant, in the Dravidian village tradition it is the husbands of the goddesses who are mere appendages of their spouses.

The main source of the mother-goddess cult undoubtedly is non-Āryan, but the rudiments of the feminine principle (Śakti) are traceable to the Vedas. Many of the major Vedic deities have spouses, and there is at least one important dual-sex deity. In the case of the former, however, it is clear that the wives are mere abstractions, mythological necessities, or later inventions. Of the dual-sex deities the pair Dyavapṛthivi, heaven and earth, are central figures in the primordial Indo-European myth, but they are not particularly important in the Vedas. In fact, the male aspect of this divinity erodes in later portions of the Veda, leaving only the prevailing feminine aspect. These developments are to be interpreted, at least in part, as early instances of the influence of the mother-goddess cult and Śaktism. The process of incorporating these non-Āryan conceptions had already begun when the Vedas were composed.

Bhakti

Some form of theistic devotional religion (bhakti) emphasizing worship and personal devotion to a deity rather than sacrifice seems to have existed as early as the first century B.C. and received its most important and lasting literary statement in a late appendage of the *Mahābharata* known as the *Bhagavad Gītā*. Although the main doctrine of the *Bhagavad Gītā* can be interpreted as a rationalization for militarism and as an orthodox defense of the relativity of human capacities enshrined in the varṇa system, there is throughout a theme of adoration and worshipful subjugation to a transcendent deity. In fact, the *Bhagavad Gītā*, like much of the early Bhāgavata (devotional) literature, is simply Sāṁkhya philosophy compounded with a dash of theism. As in the *Purāṇas*, the *Gītā* accepts the spirit-matter dualism and general metaphysics of Sāṁkhya, but adds to it the monism of Vedānta and the notion of a personal omniscient, omnipotent, and transcendent deity who confers grace on the worshiper who surrenders fully to him.

From this synthesis began a series of devotional movements which, through their widespread appeal to the Indian masses, were ultimately to overshadow both ritualism and asceticism. The main literary sources for these movements were the epics and *Purāṇas*. The latter not only described cosmography and cosmology, they dwelt at length on different incarnations of the deity, holy places, and forms of worship. They were, in fact, handbooks of popular Hinduism. The *Bhāgavata Purāṇa*, for example, tells of the Kṛṣṇa incarnation, stressing the ecstatic worship of the gopīs (female cowherds). It maintains that the deity is immanent as well as transcendent, that he manifests himself in different incarnations for the benefit of humanity. Even though he appears in manifold forms and engages in the activity of this world, he is not contaminated by the karma of his actions. He thus becomes the exemplar of human action which should be undertaken without regard for its fruits (i.e., naiśkarmya). By abandoning one's self and acting through him, by complete surrender to him, by praying to him, by singing and composing hymns and poems of adoration for him, by worshiping his image, and by venerating his immanence through respect for all forms of life, one attains salvation. In many cases, the relative merits of these various forms of worhsip were the source of sectarianism—each sect stressing one or another form of worship. The major devotional movements accepted Viṣṇu, Śiva, or one of the principal mother goddesses as the supreme deity.

The theme of ecstatic love for the deity, which came to be the predominant message of all devotional movements, had its first beginnings in the south in the early Tamil hymns of the Āṟvārs (devotees of Viṣṇu) and Nāyaṉārs (devotees of Śiva). From there the practice of composing hymns in regional languages spread to the whole of India, and in the process led to the flowering of literature in each of the regional languages. The peripatetic saints who sang and preached the doctrine of devotionalism came from all classes of society. Some, like Tukarām of Mahārāsthra, were Śūdras; others, like Lallā in Kashmir, were women. Unlike the earlier orthodoxies, bhakti was unrestrictive. The message of devotionalism thus was carried directly to the people in ordinary language by those who were familiar with the lives and needs of the common man.

The Vaiṣṇavaite sects of the south trace their beginnings to the twelve Āṟvārs whose hymns were gathered into a collection known as *Nālāyira Prabhandham*. Often referred to as the *Tamil Veda*, these popular hymns are still used in Vaiṣṇava temples. The viśiṣṭādvaita (qualified monism) school of Vedānta founded by Rāmānuja (see p. 75) drew its inspiration from this collection. Eventually, the Vaiṣṇava followers of Rāmānuja split into two groups, the northern (Vaṭakalai) and southern (Teṇkalai), over the issue of god's grace. The northern school taught salvation on the analogy of the monkey. Just as the monkey's infant must exert effort in clinging to the safety of its mother's body, a human believer must exert effort to attain salvation. The southern school taught salvation on the analogy of the cat. Just as the kitten is irresistibly picked up in its mother's teeth, men are saved without effort on their part. In north India Vaiṣṇava sects are roughly divided into those devoted to Kṛṣṇa and those devoted to Rāma. The latter derive from Rāmānanda, a follower of Rāmānuja who migrated to the north after a quarrel with his preceptor. Rāmānanda was influential in spreading bhakti doctrine in the north, but perhaps the two most famous devotees of Rāma were Tulasīdās and Tyāgarāja. Tulasīdā's Hindi *Rāmacaritamānasa* (a "devotionalized" version of the *Rāmāyana*) became the Bible of the Rāmaite sects. A Telugu, Tyāgarāja was a great composer whose songs and compositions form the cornerstone of Indian music. The Kṛṣṇa sects found literary expression in the *Bhāgavata Purāṇa* and Jayadeva's erotic *Gītā Govinda* (cowherd song) which celebrates the love of the cowherds for Kṛṣṇa. As in the south, the Vaiṣṇavaite and Śaivite sects of the north are divided into adherents of Śaṅkara's monism, Rāmānuja's qualified monism, or Madhava's dualism (see pp. 75–76).

Although Śaivism has its origins in Sanskrit texts known as *Āgamas*, the real source of modern Śaivism is found in the devotional teachings of the Tamil Nāyaṉārs. Fourteen of these texts constitute the *Śaivasiddhānta*. Tamil Śaivism teaches a doctrine of qualified monism. In salvation, the soul is united with, but is not identical to, the deity. By contrast, Kashmir Śaivism is monistic. The duality of soul and deity is merely an illusion, and salvation consists in the realization of the fundamental identity between the soul and the deity. A more radical Śaivite sect is that of the Liṅgāyats or Vīraśaivas in modern Mysore. Basava, the founder of the sect, rejected the *Vedas* and the authority of the Brāhmaṇs. He founded a new priesthood called Jangamas, opposed pilgrimage and sacrifice, taught the equality of women, permitted widow remarriage, and forbade the practice of cremation.

Pūjā

In the *Vedas* the principal religious rites were sacrifices (yajña) performed at the family altar, but in Hinduism worship (pūjā) becomes more important than sacrifice, and temple worship partly displaces the family altar. The temple itself enshrines a deity usually represented in the form of an icon. The deity is fed, bathed, entertained with music, taken through the streets on festival days, and honored with garlands. Attached to the shrine (Vimāna) is a "tank" (pool of water) or stair access to a stream where purificatory ablutions can be made. Some temples also have large pillared porches or halls (maṇḍapam) leading to the shrine entrance. Larger temples have halls (choultries) where pilgrims may spend the night, and extensive accommodations for resident priests. The whole complex is surrounded by an enclosing wall with towers (gōpuram) at the entrance gates. Worship, in contrast to the fantastically sculptured and carved temples, is simple. Several times a day the temple priests bathe the god, dress him in new flowers and jewels, and feed him, to the accompaniment of Vedic hymns. Old flowers and the unconsumed gross part of the deity's food (prasād) is then distributed to the assembled worshipers. After entering the temple enclosure, worshipers circumambulate the temple, enter the shrine, give a brief prayer, and then merely sit and observe the proceedings. Sermons or instruction are not part of the worship, but a devotee may attend discussions in the maṇḍapam or seek separate counsel from one of the temple priests if he wishes.

The heart of the temple is the shrine where the deity has taken up residence, and the essence of worship is the brief moment of adoration offered to the deity by the devotee. Consequently, simple shrines inhabited by snake gods, various other deities, and minor godlings can be found almost anywhere. The devotee worships at these insignificant shrines with as much piety and devotion as he displays in the large, ornate temples.

PART 3

CONTEMPORARY SOCIAL ORGANIZATION

In the poruḷ sections of the ancient Tamil *Tolkāppiyam*, it is written that the first principles of this world are time (kālam) and place (tiṇai). We have already dealt with time, but the problem of place remains. Tiṇai (place) is more than mere location in space; it denotes an ecological region with a particular combination of birds, plants, men, settlement patterns, music, chieftains, economy, and deities. There are five tiṇais: (1) The *hilly regions* (kuṟiñci) are inhabited by Kuṟavar (hill people) who hunt and practice slash-and-burn (swidden) agriculture in the middle of the forest. The Kuṟavar live in small, impermanent villages and have fierce, warlike chiefs and bloody, orgiastic cults devoted to the mountain god (Murukaṉ). (2) The *fertile plain* (marutam) is inhabited by peaceful peasants living in large, permanent villages, practicing settled wet-rice agriculture, and worshiping Indra. (3) The *littoral* (neytal) is occupied by fishermen whose thatched huts dot the coast. Varuṇa is the tutelary deity of the seacoast. (4) *Grasslands* (mullai) are the home of pastoralists following their herds from place to place and worshiping the god Māyōṉ. (5) The fifth tiṇai, the *desert* (pālai), is a purely fictional category.

Although these divisions were invented as a sort of thematic and contextual versifying guide for the ancient Tamil bards and poets, they suggest totemic divisions, that pattern of thought which arbitrarily classifies groups of kinsmen, plants, animals, directions, features of the landscape, gods, demons—in short, everything in the cosmos—into mutually exclusive taxonomic categories and considers those men, plants, animals, and so on who are in the same category as inherently related (cf. Lévi-Strauss, 1966, 35–74).

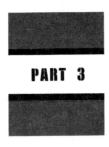

The tiṇai classification is especially interesting, for it reflects a society differentiated by divisions of labor. Rather than consanguineous kin, the men in any given tiṇai category are practitioners of the same occupation. In the Tamil system sameness of occupation has replaced sameness of kinship relation as the classificatory feature, but it is clear that a totemic system of classification underlies the tiṇais. We seem to have here an account of a society at a critical point of transition from tribal to caste society, for the tiṇai occupations are not the only divisions of labor. Carpenters, masons, bards, and numerous others are mentioned in the Tamil poems, but it is clear that these are subordinate to the dominant occupations and are in some way dependent on them. In these dominant occupations, then, we see those who control access to the produce of a region (cf. Lévi-Strauss, 1966, 112–115). Thus the tiṇai occupational categories both represent the basic pattern of ecological adaptation to a given region and name the economically dominant occupational group. Everything else in the region, including men who follow other occupations, is defined in relation to the dominant group. Each of these dominant territorial groups is under the leadership of a chief and is defended by warriors drawn from its ranks.

The ancient Tamil literature thus presupposes an aristocratic social organization consisting of warriors (Cāṉṟōr) and commoners (Iliciṉar). The warriors are either those who have anciently held chief rights to the produce of a region or are recent military adventurers who have wrested control of the region from defeated aristocrats. Because land is the chief resource, we shall see that this ancient pattern is still viable, for those who control land invariably claim warrior status even in modern India. Too, Indian society is still divided into two broad divisions: those who control land and consequently have power, and those who do not control land and consequently depend on those who control land. Finally, there are those among the commoners who are more base and degraded than the ordinary run of men. Known in the ancient Tamil literature as Pulaiyar, they are the forerunners of the untouchables of modern India. The total society of this literature consists of the dominant, the dependent, and the degraded. This hierarchic pattern is represented in Figure 16. The logical parallelism between this system and the varṇa system (see pp. 81–86) should be noted. Significantly, the Tamil hierarchy lacks a separate sacerdotal category. In early Tamil society priests counted for little.

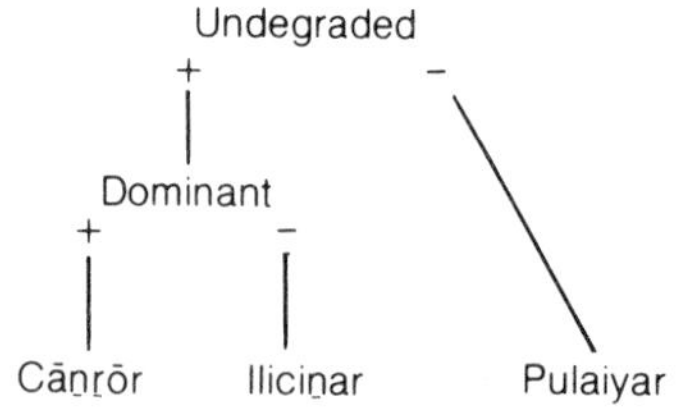

Figure 16. Hierarchic pattern of early Tamil society.

In a somewhat different sense the divisions of the poruḷ sections of the *Tolkāppiyam* reflect a psychological dimension that persists into modern times. The emotional orientation of the tiṇais betrays an essential opposition between the hill peoples (Kuṟavar) and all the others. Tamil love poetry ascribes the themes of erotic love to the hill region, but the other regions are consistent only with love situations involving separation, quarreling, and sulking. In essence, there are but two situations: eros and heroism; and these correspond to the basic divisions of Tamil poetry: akam (subjective) and puṟam (objective), respectively. The masculine subject of a poem is almost always a warrior-hero who finds love in the hills, but saddens the heart of his lady love (now his wife) when he leaves her to find fame and fortune in the field of battle. There are then two central themes: union and separation; and two situations: the tribal life of the hill people and the civilized life of all the other regions. To the ancient Tamil poet as well as to his modern descendant, tribal society and the culture of hill peoples represents something dark, mysterious, fecund, and ultimately sexual. In the Indian mind tribal society has always been associated with the unclean but omnipotent and ultimately free. The independence, individualism, freedom, spontaneity, and orgiasticism of tribal life is felt to be in complete contrast to the subservience, dependence, and inhibitions of caste society. This Rousseauean conception is a palpable element in every significant sacred text. Hindu speculation allows only two kinds of individualism, the tribal and the ascetic, and these are diametrically opposed to the corporate hierarchy of caste society.

Patterns of dependency and hierarchy are fostered in the joint family and reenforced in rules of marriage alliance and the obligations of kinship. In the aristocratic society characteristic of the heroic theme, eros must be subjugated, made subservient to the social order. It must be regulated and channeled into appropriate categories of social class and kinship relation. The heroic theme thus entails order, society, bondage, marriage regulation, aristocracy, and ritual, but the erotic theme stands for chaos, the individual, freedom, sexual license, egalitarianism, and orgiasticism. These dependencies are illustrated in Figure 17.

In its most general sense the heroic theme signifies differentiation, the erotic theme undifferentiation. The erotic theme thus corresponds to the undifferentiated state of the cosmos in the Asura myth (p. 44), to the Puruṣa of Sāṁkhya philosophy (pp. 70–73), and most significantly to mokṣa, the goal of all Indian speculation. The identity between eros and mokṣa makes the sexuality of Tantrism and many of the Bhakti cults understandable and demonstrates that these religious movements

Heroic (puṟam)	Erotic (akam)
Order	Chaos
Society	Individualism
Bondage	Freedom
Marriage	Sexual license
Aristocracy	Egalitarianism
Ritual	Orgiasticism

Figure 17. Dependencies in the heroic and erotic themes.

are more in the mainstream of Indian thought than are the supposedly orthodox cults.

SIX

TRIBES AND PEASANTS

In many ways the mythopoeic vision of anthropologists corresponds to that of the ancient Tamil poets. Tribal society is homogeneous, undifferentiated; the tribe occupies a specific territory, possesses a common ethos, and exists as a totality. Contrasting with tribals are peasant societies, which have internal functional differentiation, lack territorial integrity, are pluralistic, and exist as part of a larger society. In fact, this dichotomy is largely mythical, and in India as elsewhere it is often difficult to discriminate between tribes and peasants. In a very general way groups designated as tribals in India do not have caste distinctions, but may themselves be more or less part of a local caste hierarchy. Too, they usually live in isolated hill or jungle areas and follow a form of shifting cultivation, hunting and gathering, or pastoralism. Quite frequently they speak a different language than that spoken in the surrounding plains, and participate less completely in the higher forms of Hindu religious ceremonial. To this list the Indian would add that tribals are simple, unclean, orgiastic, and possessed of great magical powers.

TRIBES

Tribals may be undifferentiated from the Hindu point of view, but to outsiders it is apparent that their forms of religion, social organization, ecological adaptation, and linguistic affiliations differ widely from group to group. In fact, from this standpoint India's tribals are far too varied for brief summary. Consequently, the simplest means of contrasting them with peasants is their mode of subsistence, their dominant occupation. In a very general way those whom Indians refer to as tribals can be classed as hunters and gatherers, swidden cultivators, or pastoralists, even though many in fact are peasants or at least incipient peasants. Rough though this classification may be, it accurately reflects the Indian attitude. Those who make their living in one way must be categorically differentiated from those who make their living by some other means.

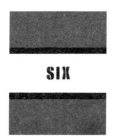

Hunting and gathering is characteristic of many Indian tribal groups residing in remote mountain and jungle areas. Although regional and local variations abound, the basic components of this mode of production involve exploitation of the wild plants and animals by small groups seldom exceeding 50 people. These groups usually consist of several independent and often unrelated families who have temporarily gathered together to exploit some local product of the forest. When the forest produce in one area is exhausted, the group breaks up and each family moves off to another territory, where they may be joined by other families migrating from different territories. The only permanent group is an elementary or sometimes extended family. There is no permanent settlement, and wider kin groups such as clans and lineages are relatively unimportant. Some hunting and gathering groups in the south are matrilineal while others are patrilineal.

Most food is immediately processed and consumed. There is neither occasion nor real necessity for complicated and time-consuming processing and storage. Seasonal migrations from one part of the forest to another permit "harvesting" of different forest products when they become ripe.

In most cases there is a rudimentary division of labor in which men hunt game and women dig for tubers and pluck berries, wild grains, leaves, and fruit. Small-game hunting can be carried out by individuals or a family, but hunting large game requires larger groups. Similarly, larger groups may combine to dam up and fish out a section of a small stream, but most fishing is an individual affair.

Because none of these activities requires sophisticated tools and also because complicated paraphernalia would impede migration, these hunters and gatherers utilize only a limited technology. Digging sticks, axes, knives, bows and arrows, a few baskets, and metal containers constitute the major items of material culture. Nowadays many of these items are purchased from merchants at bazaars or local fairs held at the edge of hill and jungle. Money for these purchases comes from sale of honey, skins, and other forest products.

Swidden Agriculturalists

Frequently hunting and gathering is combined with a form of agricultural production in which domesticated plants and animals provide the major items of consumption. One widespread form of this type of production is swidden or "slash-and-burn" agriculture. Again, there are many variations, but the basic pattern involves cutting over a section of forest, allowing the cut plants to dry, burning them, scattering the ashes over the soil, and planting seeds in the burned-over ground. Crops are grown on this plot usually for no more than three years. The plot is then allowed to revert to jungle and a new plot is cleared and planted. When the territory is large enough, a plot will lie fallow for 15–20 years before it is again cleared. To protect the growing crops from marauding animals, house and village sites are frequently moved when the distance between house and field becomes too great.

Since most swidden agriculture is practiced in hilly country on rather steep slopes and the newly cleared land often contains roots and stumps, animal traction and plows are not used. In fact, the soil is seldom tilled. Seed is usually planted by punching a hole in the ground with a sharp-pointed stick or broadcast and roughly scratched under the surface of topsoil and ash with a hoe.

The cropping complex consists of millet and legumes often sown together with taro, marrow, yams, cucumbers, and climbing beans planted near the borders of the field. In most places, two crops are grown each year, with the second crop planted in between the young plants of the first crop. Weeding is minimal on newly cleared land, but during the second and third years of cultivation crops must be weeded several times. When the grain crops are harvested they are threshed by hand, winnowed, dried, and stored in large woven baskets.

The agricultural year begins in December during the cold weather when the farmers cut trees and shrubs. A slack season follows, lasting until late May when they fire the cut-over jungle. With the arrival of the monsoon in early June the planting season begins. Harvesting commences in late August and continues intermittently as different crops ripen until the last crop is harvested in late November or December.

A special ritual or ceremony normally accompanies each of these phases of production. Thus selection of a swidden site is determined not only by vegetation type, soil type, topography, and distance from the village, but also frequently by divination. Sowing is usually preceded by a sacrifice dedicated to the earth mother, and the harvest of each crop is marked by a ceremony in which the first fruit of the harvest is offered to the deities responsible for its successful growth.

Animal husbandry involving cattle, goats, and pigs is definitely subordinate to this horticultural pattern. These domesticated animals are frequently kept by swidden farmers, but only as a supplementary source of food.

Most swidden farmers, as subsistence agriculturalists, convert nearly all their crops into food products which they consume. They grow very little explicitly as a cash crop, and what little cash return a swidden farmer receives comes from such subsidiary pursuits as casual labor for timber companies or marketing of miscellaneous forest products.

Swidden agriculture is consistent with various types of social organization. Settlement patterns, for example, may be nucleated or dispersed, permanent or shifting. Village size may vary from one or two isolated houses to large settlements containing 20 or 30 houses. Similarly, village kin groups may consist of a few extended families, a widely ramifying group of bilateral kindreds, or large localized corporate lineage segments. Descent and inheritance may be matrilineal or patrilineal. Lineages may be territorially organized with rights of usufruct in a local area deriving from lineage membership, or they may entirely lack any form of territorial integrity. In general, the extended family is the preferred form of family organization among swidden cultivators. Although there are some exceptions, most tribal groups following a swidden subsistence pattern lack extreme status differences among individuals, families, or lineages. On the whole, swidden cultivators are characterized by a kind of rough egalitarianism. And even in those instances where differences in wealth and status are institutionalized, access to a higher status frequently involves costly ceremonies which have the effect of redistributing accumulated wealth.

The division of labor is based primarily on age and sex critèria. Men do the heavy work of cutting and burning the forest as well as most of the planting and sowing. Women are mainly responsible for weeding, and both men and women share in harvesting and winnowing. The very old and the very young have the primary task of protecting the fields from wild animals and birds. Livestock grazing is usually entrusted to adolescent males. Collection of supplementary food products from the forest is largely women's work, and hunting is a male prerogative. Since almost everyone cultivates, little full-time occupational specialization occurs in such areas as blacksmithing, basket-making, pottery-making, or weaving. What the swidden cultivator cannot manufacture for himself, he prefers to buy in the weekly markets or from itinerant peddlers.

It has long been popular to criticize swidden cultivation as wasteful of forest products and deleterious to the soil. Many administrators argued that burning over the forests destroyed valuable trees and promoted flooding and soil erosion on the denuded hillsides. The first argument makes sense only from the point of view of an outsider who has other (to him) "more important" uses for timber. In fact, it was not so much the fear that swidden cultivators were destroying the forest that led British administrators to curtail swidden cultivation, but instead a simple desire to exploit the natural resources of the forest in a different way. Where population densities remain low, there is little danger that swidden cultivation will destroy a forest. Low population density allows cut-over areas to lie fallow long enough for new forest to replace the former one. Because the amount of cultivated land is always small in relation to the amount of forest in a swidden area, there is practically no danger of greatly increasing water runoff and consequently causing widespread erosion and flooding. Only where the area available for swidden cultivation has been drastically reduced either by encroachments of alien populations or misguided government policy has swidden cultivation had adverse ecological effects. The truth of the matter is that swidden cultivation is probably that mode of agricultural production which is best suited to many semi-tropical areas.

Pastoralists

Some tribes, principally in areas adjacent to mountains in the north and the northwest, depend for subsistence on nomadic pastoralism combined with agriculture. These pastoral peoples keep large flocks of sheep and goats and herds of cattle and donkeys. Pastoralism has various patterns. Sometimes keepers of small herds in areas with dependable grassland are able to live in permanent villages located in the middle of a grazing area. In other cases, the requirements of the herd and sparseness of vegetation prohibit permanent village settlements, and herders must live in transitory camps. Between these two extremes is a combination of permanent village settlement and shifting camps, the latter usually characterized by a seasonal migration (transhumance). In late spring and summer herds are moved to pastures at higher elevations where the shepherds live in impermanent camps. During the fall and winter the herds are brought back to the permanent settlements at lower elevations or in the plains.

The extent to which agriculture constitutes a significant contribution to food supply depends largely on the type of pastoralism. Where herders must constantly shift residences, there is little or no opportunity for tending crops; but where pasturage and grazing techniques permit residence in permanent settlements even for part of the year, it is possible to engage in agriculture—providing soil conditions and rainfall are adequate. Grain crops such as winter wheat and barley combined with root crops often not only adapt well to the same environmental conditions as grazing, but also their growing and harvesting cycle complements the seasonal labor requirements and migratory patterns characteristic of the herding complex. Furthermore, grain crops provide food and roughage necessary for wintering over the livestock. In turn, livestock pastured on the stubble of grain fields or kept in pens and sheds during the cold weather contribute valuable manure for fertilizer.

Although pastoralism is sometimes a simple subsistence economy, it is more frequently a form of production organized around a market demand for such products as wool, draught animals, meat, milk, butter, and beasts of burden. Consequently, extreme status differences based on wealth often characterize pastoralist groups. Production for a market also ties the pastoralist more closely to a wider economic and social system. With the exception of the Todas in south India, Indian pastoralists lack religious systems that are in any way distinctive or significantly different from those characteristic of the wider society to which they are tied. Thus in the northwest the pastoralists are Moslems, and in Nepal they follow Tibetan practices.

Social organization varies considerably among pastoralist groups in India. In the northwest, large semicorporate lineages are the norm, but in most other areas there is more of a tendency toward bilateral kin groups. With the exception of the Todas, descent among pastoralists is universally patrilineal, and extended families are everywhere the preferred form of family organization. Given the highly variable patterns of nomadism exemplified by Indian pastoralists, it is not surprising that many of these groups have developed occupational and craft specialization. Where pastoralists are directly tied to a regional economy, some members of pastoralist groups become involved in marketing or in secondary production to the exclusion of other forms of economic activity.

PEASANTS

Hunters and gatherers, swidden cultivators, and pastoralists account for only a small portion of the Indian population. More numerous by far are peasant cultivators. In one form or another permanent field cultivation of crops directly geared to a market economy is the dominant mode of economic production in India.

Peasant Agriculture

Two types of permanent field cultivation are practiced, often simultaneously but more frequently as separate, distinct agricultural patterns entailing highly different capital commitments, crops, labor organization, and ecological adaptation. These two contrasting types are dry-field and wet-field cultivation.

In dry-field cultivation, associated with wheat, barley, and some millets, the peasant has little or no control over water resources and must depend on moisture supplied by the monsoons and scattered rains of other seasons. In general, wheat and barley are grown in more arid areas and millets in areas with somewhat higher rainfall. Because these crops are adaptable to either late or early seasonal sowing and require little tending between planting and harvest, they can fit in with other modes of production either as a subsidiary or alternate activity. Thus in the north dry-field farming is often combined with pastoralism and in the south with wet-field cultivation.

Wet-field cultivation, based on control of water resources, is most often associated with the growing of rice. Irrigation techniques vary widely, the most simple form consisting of rude terraces or small earthen embankments (bunds) thrown up to catch the runoff from monsoon rains. Somewhat more complex are small earthen dams thrown across seasonal streams. The impounded water is then gradually released to flood fields lying beneath the dam. These ponds or "tanks" are sometimes strung out along the entire length of a small stream, the lower ones catching surplus water from those above. Canal irrigation may also be accomplished very simply in alluvial plains by cutting shallow ditches (inundation canals) parallel to the flood plain. When water rises in the adjacent stream, these canals fill and carry water to the fields. Such inundation canals may also be used in association with "direct-lift" mechanisms such as Persian wheels or pumps which raise water directly from the stream to the canal. Perennial canals are more complicated, requiring extensive headworks that regulate and control the supply of water over a large area. In small areas frequently irrigated by wells, water is lifted either by pump or more traditional methods similar to the Persian wheel. Since well irrigation is expensive and serves only a small area, it is primarily used only for intensive cultivation of high-yield garden crops produced for urban markets.

In many areas two and sometimes three crops are grown each year; thus crops are broadly classified according to their planting season. The two major cropping classifications are dry season and wet season, widely known as kharif and rabī respectively. Wet-season crops, sown at the onset of the monsoon (June–July), are harvested in autumn. Dry-season crops are sown after the monsoon and harvested in the spring. In rice-growing regions, late-maturing rice and millets make up the principal wet-season crops with early-maturing rice and millets the major dry-season crops. In the wheat and barley regions of the north, however, millets are a wet-season crop and wheat and barley are dry-season crops. In both regions, subsidiary crops such as ginger, onions, garlic, oil seeds, coriander, pulses, and maize fit into this same pattern.

Several patterns of rice cultivation prevail; the simplest method merely requires that the rice be sown broadcast in the plowed and leveled fields before the monsoon. When the rains come, the plants, approximately a foot high, are nourished by water trapped and held on the fields by embankments or terraces. A more complex method entails growing rice sprouts in specially prepared nursery fields. When the fields are flooded either by the monsoon or by other means, the sprouts are transplanted. Both methods have advantages and disadvantages. Broadcast sowing requires less labor at planting time, but since the crop must be weeded, additional labor is necessary later. Broadcast sowing also produces a lower yield per acre. Transplanting requires large amounts of labor during the critical transplanting season, but because water is held on the fields over a longer period, the crop does not need weeding. Even though transplanting requires less seed and produces higher yields, it will do so only if there is adequate control of water resources. Reliable rainfall or complex irrigation techniques must be present for the transplanting method to be successful. In general, capital and labor requirements and yield per acre are higher for transplanted rice.

When millets are grown as a wet-season crop, their culture corresponds closely to that of broadcast rice. Because they are more tolerant of drought, millets are more dependable than rice and they are also much less labor-intensive, but their yield and cash return per acre is lower than rice. Unlike rice, which requires fertilizer in the form of manure or artificial products, millets are frequently intersown or rotated with leguminous pulses which add nitrogen to the soil. The high capital investment in land under irrigation usually makes crop rotation and fallowing impractical on rice lands. Like the millets, wheat and barley are often grown in rotation with pulses or on fields which have been fallowed.

With the arrival of brief showers in April the agricultural season begins. Peasants plow and level their fields and prepare the nursery plots. In late April and May they sow rice and plow and plant millet fields. By the middle or end of June the monsoon arrives and rice is transplanted. Weeding continues from May through July and August. Harvesting commences in September and continues through October and November as different crops mature. In the wheat and barley regions, plowing commences again with the millet harvest. By mid-October the wheat and barley fields are planted. In March and April these winter crops mature and are harvested.

Plowing, a man's job, is done with a wooden moldboardless plow drawn by a team of oxen or buffaloes. Since the plow scratches a trench but does not turn the earth, fields are plowed several times in a crisscross pattern. When the fields have been plowed they are leveled or harrowed with a simple plank or log through which spikes have been driven. Rice transplanting is women's work. Frequently working in the rain, gangs of women carrying bundles of rice sprouts wade in lines through the mud and water of the rice fields thrusting the shoots firmly into the mud at more-or-less regular intervals. Transplanting is backbreaking work and women suffer from chills, colds, fevers, stiff joints, and dry, itchy skin brought on by the constant wetness. At harvest time, men and women cut the stalks of grain and transport the sheaves from the field to the village in a bullock cart. In the village are specially prepared threshing platforms made of earth and clay with a hard layer of cow dung spread on the surface. Here the sheaves are spread out and ten or twelve cattle tied to a hitching post in the center of the platform are driven round and round over the stalks. When the grain has been separated from the stalks it is winnowed, dried, and stored in woven baskets plastered on the interior with cow dung.

Despite the large number of cattle in India, animal husbandry is comparatively unimportant to the peasant agriculturist. Even so, cattle are valuable. Oxen are used for animal traction, and cows and buffaloes provide milk and manure. Milk, either whole or in the form of butter or ghī (clarified butter), is an important source of cash income. In fact, in areas where peasants cannot produce a surplus crop, these dairy products become the main source of cash income. Cattle-keeping and the importance of cattle varies according to the amount and availability of pasturage. Where intensive rice agriculture constitutes the predominant pattern, there is often insufficient land available for pasturage and few cattle other than those necessary for plowing can be supported. Because of religious sanctions against killing cows, cattle are not raised for meat. For the same reason, hides are an important source of income only for Muslims and untouchable castes. Goats and sheep, raised primarily for sale in local markets, are sometimes kept as a source of food. A few chickens and other fowl, which receive little or no special care, and the ubiquitous scavengers called pariah dogs complete the inventory of the peasants' animals.

Most of the peasants' food supply and income is produced in his own fields, but whenever possible he supplements his food and income by hunting and collecting in the forests and wastelands, by growing garden crops, and by working elsewhere. Wood, honey, wild fruits, herbs, and vegetables are regularly gathered and added to the family larder or sold in the market. Garden crops can be an important source of additional income. Squash, melons, eggplant, areca nuts, chillies, jack fruit, mango, plantain, tamarind, oranges, sago, turmeric, tapioca, ginger, cashew nuts, and betel leaf can all be sold in local markets or contracted out to merchants. During slack seasons, rope-making, weaving, and basket-making are frequently resorted to as a means of providing additional income.

The peasants' access to outside employment is restricted by the demands of his own crop and by the general lack of available alternate forms of employment during the seasons when he does have some free time. Except in unusual circumstances, outside employment is a hit-or-miss affair which adds little to income. Even so, that little often makes the difference between having enough to eat and not. Because most peasant agriculture in India is subsistence production with only insignificant surplus product, contingent expenses deriving from the cost of marriage ceremonies or the death of a bullock drive the peasant into the waiting arms of the local moneylender or into the already glutted pool of casual laborers. Similarly, drought or damage to the harvest temporarily push the peasant out of his fields and into the labor market. Since his land and livestock are usually perennially burdened with debt, his only option is to sell his labor; but since labor demands are highly seasonal in rural areas, this can often mean that he or one of his sons must temporarily migrate to an urban area to find work. Relying on a network of contacts with relatives or other fellow villagers who have previously migrated to urban centers, a peasant endeavors to find work and lodging in a foreign and, to him, frightening environment. If he is successful, he attempts to live frugally and make regular remittances to his family in the village. In many instances this temporary sojourn in the city becomes permanent.

Despite drought, crop failure, and other disasters, peasants sometimes prosper and even accumulate wealth. Savings are first reinvested in land and livestock, but when these needs are met extra cash goes into jewelry, a convenient hole in the wall or floor, or is loaned out at interest. Peasants neither understand nor trust banks; in any event, banking facilities are available only in urban centers.

Sometimes a peasant who has acquired capital from urban employment or a lucky windfall is tempted into a commercial venture. Sweet shops, tobacco shops, tea stalls, and transportation are favored enterprises. An ancient truck, for example, can put a peasant in the trucking business, but on the whole these ventures are only marginally successful and even less secure than farming. The business staggers along from crisis to crisis for a few years and, as operating capital dwindles, gradually collapses.

Under appropriate local conditions, a peasant may be encouraged to shift from predominantly cereal production to other, more profitable cash crops. In villages near large urban centers truck farming can be highly profitable. Similarly, where irrigation and fertilizer are ample, sugar cane produces a comparatively high revenue. But cane production is risky: in the north early frost can ruin the crop, and in the south waterlogging and salinity threaten constantly. The coconut palm is an important cash crop in the south, but because trees do not bear in the first ten years, new coconut groves must be carried through their immature period by other sources of income. Cotton, the chief cash crop of the Deccan, has declined in importance in recent years. Most of the cotton grown in India is short or medium staple and has not competed successfully with imported long-staple cotton. Madras, Orissa, Bihār, and Bengāl have large acreages of jute. In the south tobacco is often grown as a contract crop. A peasant contracts to plant a fixed acreage in tobacco and agrees to sell it exclusively to one of the large tobacco companies. Tobacco is a good cash crop, but it requires reliable irrigation and is susceptible to a number of diseases and wilts.

Peasant villages are not self-sufficient. They depend on larger centers for marketing their crops and for the products of the city. In small towns throughout the countryside weekly markets serviced by traveling merchants are patronized by the peasants. In many cases this is the only market necessary. Here a peasant can market his surplus product, buy such necessities as salt, sugar, oil, cloth, and bangles, or transact business with official agents. Once or twice a year, however, he must go to a permanent market or bazaar in some larger town or city. Lower prices and a greater variety of merchandise encourage the peasant to frequent these larger markets, but these advantages are offset by the personal relationship that a peasant and a local merchant have established over a long period of time. There is often a close personal tie between a peasant and his local merchant and the peasant feels that he can depend on his local merchant to take back a defective item or extend credit in times of need. The local merchant also gives advice on unfamiliar matters. The higher cost of what the peasant buys and lower price of what he sells in the local market is considered to be a small payment for convenience and additional service. Itinerant peddlers pass through the village two or three times a year selling pots and pans or bangles and trinkets, though news and local gossip are their most valued wares. Annual fairs are held at various regional centers, and a peasant may attend two or three in a year. Although some marketing is done at fairs, they are more for diversion and entertainment. A peasant will occasionally set up a concession for selling sweets or tea at a fair, but usually he squanders his earnings on trinkets, liquor, women, or betting on wrestling matches.

Land Tenure and Revenue

Indian peasants hold their lands under a bewildering variety of tenures ranging from outright ownership to multiple subtenancies with diverse rights and obligations. Under the British, landholding was broadly classified as ryotwari or zamīndari. In the former, the individual peasant held title to his land directly under the state. Zamīndari rights over large estates were held as grants with variable rules of inheritance and restricted rights of alienability. In theory the state retained actual ownership of the land, but in fact the zamīndars (the holders of zamīndaris) were absentee landlords. Since Independence much has been done to eliminate zamīndari holdings, but they still exist.

If he does not own his land, a peasant may have a leasehold based on a cash payment to the owner for the right to cultivate or sublet a fixed amount of land for a given period. In addition to the rent which is paid on a yearly basis, the tenant pays an interest charge on the balance of the total amount of rent payable over the term of the lease. At the end of the lease period the tenant must pay a renewal fee in order to continue the lease for another period. A simpler variety of leasehold merely requires the tenant to pay a yearly sum in rent plus a renewal fee at the end of the lease. Under both these forms of lease, the owner has only limited rights of eviction, and under the latter, the tenant frequently has restricted subletting rights. When a peasant rents a parcel of waste or uncultivated land with the intention of bringing it under cultivation, the amount of rent is often prorated to take into account the fact that the tenant will receive little or no return from the land while he is improving it. This type of lease is also frequently used when a tenant plans to plant a coconut grove or orchard which will not bear for five or ten years. With this form of tenure there is also a renewal fee equal to the produce of the grove or orchard for the 18 months preceding the renewal date. Should the tenant fail to improve the land within the terms of the lease, the owner has the right to evict him. The simplest and most widespread form of tenantry is sharecropping. The tenant rents the land on a yearly basis and pays the landlord a percentage (usually half) of the year's crop. Sharecropping has many varieties depending on whether the tenant pays all, part, or none of the land revenue, or provides all, part, or none of the cattle, seeds, implements, and fertilizer.

In many villages there is a class of tenant living on rent-free inalienable land. Hereditary village servants and priests are frequently granted such tenures. The land is cultivated in perpetuity on condition of obligatory village service, but the tenant does not have title to the land nor is he liable for the revenue. As long as the servant or priest keeps up his traditional service obligation, his tenure is fully heritable. Variations on this pattern are found not only from region to region, but often within a single village. The most important variant requires the tenant to pay either the whole or some fixed proportion of the revenue. Land held under these tenures may be sublet to other tenants. Closely related to these occupancy tenures are rent-free (or nominal rent), tax-free, inalienable lands granted by the state to temples for their upkeep. The land is managed by a temple committee which sublets the land to other cultivators or to temple priests and servants.

This whole system can become exceedingly complex, for a single parcel of land may be sublet or subsublet under more than one of these tenures. For example, a man may own ten acres of land which he rents to a tenant for five years for a cash payment plus interest. The tenant sublets half the land to another tenant for a yearly cash payment. He, in turn, sublets the land to another tenant on a sharecropping basis and rents the house to a different tenant for a year's term with monthly rent payments. It is obvious that the possibilities for litigation in such a system are high, and in fact tenure disputes are one of the most frequent causes of litigation.

Because of the fragmented nature of their holdings, peasants who own their land frequently rent out distant parts of their holdings and lease other fields more conveniently located. Thus many tenants are simultaneously owners, tenants, and landlords.

Even when a peasant owns his land, his rights are conditional on paying revenue to the government. As in leaseholding, revenue assessment varies widely from region to region and state to state. In some places revenue is assessed on the standing crop. In others the land is measured and revenue assessed on the basis of expected yield per acre under normal conditions. The latter system employs a sliding scale geared to type of land. Wet land is assessed at a higher rate than dry land. Remissions of revenue are general in times of famine, flood, or crop failure. It is probably safe to say that peasants and revenue officials have thoroughly exploited all the potentialities for graft and corruption in this system.

In the north there are two types of private ownership. One type entails rights in the village common, the other does not. In the past, many villages in the north were joint-ownership villages—that is, all the villagers held land as a joint estate and were jointly responsible for the revenue. As joint occupants they had rights to the uncultivated wasteland (common) within the village boundaries. Villagers unrelated to the founding lineage or corporation might acquire private property in a joint village, but could not acquire rights to the common. For revenue purposes these joint villages are still assessed as a unit estate. In theory the headman or headmen of different sections of the village are responsible for the revenue payment, but in practice each individual owner pays his proportionate share of the revenue to the headman who in turn makes the revenue over to the state. In the south this pattern of joint ownership is not widespread. There revenue is assessed directly on the individual owner.

Land Problems

The average size of a peasant's holding is small, probably less than 10 acres. Since it is generally felt that a man with one team of oxen can cultivate 10 to 20 acres, the size of holding in relation to available oxen and manpower is often uneconomic. Because of subdivision and fragmentation the peasant's holding has tended to become even smaller and more uneconomic. In most areas sons inherit equally and subdivide the family estate into equal shares. This not only has decreased plot size, but also has caused the holdings to be excessively fragmented. Each son has a right to inherit an equal portion of each kind of land in the estate—so many acres of wet land, so many acres of dry land. The practice of cultivating more than one type of land does spread the risk, but it also means that a peasant must constantly shift activities from one small plot to another.

Small plots also inhibit innovation and change. Because fencing such small plots is uneconomic, a peasant must pasture his stubble when others do and harvest when they do; he cannot depart too far from the routine and practices of his neighbors. Some peasants make an effort to consolidate their holdings by renting their own distant plots to others and leasing plots contiguous to theirs, but this solution is not always feasible. The whole system of subdivision and fragmentation is full of potentialities for conflict and produces an almost unbelievable amount of litigation. Heirs squabble over the subdivision, tenants and landlords disagree, neighbors' cattle get into the grain fields, plot lines get moved, water gets diverted, irrigation levees and bunds get broken down, and so on.

Settlement Patterns

Settlement patterns in peasant villages vary almost as much as systems of tenure. In very general terms there are three main types of settlement pattern: nucleated, dispersed, and "strip" or linear. Nucleated villages have their houses located in a central cluster. In a dispersed village there is no central cluster of houses; dwellings are randomly scattered over the landscape at some distance from one another. Frequently, one or two adjacent houses will be surrounded by a fence. "Strip" or linear villages have one or two rows of houses on high ground parallel to a road, bluff, or stream.

Villages are internally subdivided into distinct, caste-specific hamlets. Each caste tends to occupy a contiguous block of houses. In nucleated villages the clean castes occupy the central portion of the villages, and the unclean castes live in hamlets on the outskirts or peripheries. Each hamlet will often have a separate well from which it exclusively draws water. Along the main village lane in larger villages there will be a market place for the weekly bazaar, a few shops, tea stalls, and tobacco booths. Located near the market place are the office of the village council and government offices such as the post office, police station, dispensary, residences for traveling government officials, village development office, and schools. In or near the hamlets of the clean castes there will be a temple dedicated to one of the deities of the Sanskritic tradition. Purely village and local deities of non-Sanskritic origin have their temples and shrines located near the hamlets of the unclean castes.

The houses of the wealthier and higher castes are often substantial structures of masonry with tile roofs, cement floors, and surrounding walls. Fronting on the street is an open verandah used as a reception room or as a sleeping room in hot weather. Behind the verandah and along one side is a group of living rooms around a roofed-over interior terrace and facing onto a courtyard. On the opposite side of the courtyard are the kitchen, storage room, shrine, and sometimes cattle stalls, manure pits, and haystacks. Houses of the poorer castes are built of wattle and daub or mud with thatched roofs and dirt floors coated with cow dung. A small open verandah at the front leads directly into the one-room interior. There are many variations in house styles depending on local tradition and availability of building materials.

Village Hinduism

Village Hinduism consists of a set of beliefs and practices which cannot be directly traced to the orthodox Sanskritic tradition. To be sure, villagers honor many of the Sanskritic deities and adhere to many of the beliefs contained in the ancient religious classics, but more important to their daily lives are beliefs about the supernatural which either do not have the sanction of orthodoxy, or are in various ways only vaguely homologized with the orthodox tradition. Many of these beliefs and practices are purely local customs restricted to a few communities or a geographical region, but many others, like the Sanskritic tradition itself, have an all-India spread.

It is difficult to summarize even the rudimentary substance of a single local tradition, but underlying the specific content of all local traditions are a few generalized principles which manifest themselves in various guises. First, it is important to recognize that there is no complete disjunction between the natural and the supernatural. Not only are supernatural events embodied in naturalistic phenomena, but purely natural events themselves are manifestations of supernatural forces. Secondly, village Hinduism is predominantly, if not exclusively, dedicated to earthly well-being, and concerns itself but little with such abstruse problematics as the ultimate fate of the soul or nature of the godhead. Its manifestly this-worldly orientation is directed toward two primary goals: fertility and health. Fertility of crops, cattle, and women, preeminently symbolized in cults and observances dedicated to the earth mother and the village mother, is a universal feature of village Hinduism. Similarly, freedom from sickness is a motivation expressed in a wide variety of forms in every village. Finally, the logic of village Hinduism is deterministic and causal. Things simply do not happen for no good reason. Crop failures, disease, sterility, family quarrels, drought, and death result from a distant predetermined chain of causation or can be traced to the more immediate machinations of some malevolent supernatural agent. That events could be remotely predetermined and still attributed to an immediate cause is only apparently contradictory, for the immediate cause is but the final link in the chain of causation. Sometimes directly homologized with the Sanskritic notions of karma and rebirth, these workings of past deeds and events are essentially beyond man's control. They may be interfered with, but that interference itself is but part of the unalterable course of events.

The numerous and varied supernatural agents include hosts of gods and goddesses, ghosts, sprites, ancestor spirits, and animal spirits. Most important of the goddesses are the earth mother and the village mother. The earth itself is a deity which may be worshiped in a variety of forms, but usually in one of the aspects of divinity responsible for successful planting and harvest. In some areas where there are clan deities with traditional territories, the earth goddess may also be worshiped in the form of the clan goddess. The village mother is closely related to the earth mother and is generally responsible for protecting the villagers from disease and other calamities. Nearly as important as these goddesses are those responsible for smallpox and cholera. They must be annually propitiated to protect the village from epidemics of these diseases. Other diseases and ill fortune can be caused by any one of a number of supernaturals—an offended ancestor spirit, malevolent ghosts, or a neglected household god. Many of these deities can be induced by worship, sacrifice, or vows to attack an enemy, and when something goes wrong the villager consults a local shaman who diagnoses the cause and recommends appropriate ritual action. Typically the shaman calls upon his own personal deity, becomes possessed by him, and makes a diagnosis through the wisdom of the god. In other instances an exorcist is called upon to induce the supernatural to speak through the patient. In still other cases a diviner consults the configuration of seeds in his winnowing fan and determines the cause of the illness.

Many supernaturals have the ability to possess their worshipers, and a regular feature of many ceremonies involves someone being possessed by the god. One who is possessed trembles, his eyes roll, his speech becomes unintelligible, and he begins to dance wildly. The god may then speak through the person possessed, answering questions, issuing orders, making predictions, and demanding sacrifices.

Village Hinduism differs markedly from the Sanskrit tradition by the nature of the sacrifices offered to deities. In many cases the sacrifice consists of a slaughtered animal. This practice is not universal, but as a general rule the supernaturals of village Hinduism have a fondness for bloody sacrifices. From the point of view of the orthodox tradition, such worship is unclean and impure. For this reason, clean castes frequently do not participate directly in these sacrifices, preferring to let the lower castes perform the rituals, or at least their bloodier aspects, for them. These sacrifices are condoned because the higher castes tacitly recognize that these deities must be dealt with even though they are outside the competence of the Brāhmaṇ.

Places of pilgrimage are held in high esteem by villagers. Wondrous cures and miracles regularly occur at these holy places, and anyone suffering from an intransigent illness will be advised by his shaman to undertake a journey to some distant holy spot. Most of India's sacred geography associated with the Sanskritic tradition is in the north at such places as Hardwar, Allahabad, Gaya, Badrinath, Benares, and Kedarnath, but almost any place with a well-known temple or a famous festival with a high reputation for successful cures will suffice.

Feasts and festivals play an important role in village Hinduism. In addition to agricultural rituals and family and caste ceremonies, there are numerous calendrical festivals. Though many festivals are practically universal and have common features in all parts of the country, the majority of festivals observed in any single village are peculiar to a local region. Among the more commonly observed festivals are Holī, Dīpavālī, Śivarātrī, Naurātrā, Daśarā, Kṛṣṇa Janam Aṣṭamī, and Sankrāntī.

Perhaps the most popular of Indian festivals, Holī commemorates the burning of Kāmadeva, the god of love. Often preceded by month-long preparations, Holī is celebrated in February or March. Holī celebrations involve reversals of ordinary, everyday patterns of respect. Women, for example, may beat men, juniors may behave disrespectfully toward their elders, and persons of authority may be ridiculed and made sport of. People throw mud, cow dung, dust, colored water, and colored powder on one another.

Dīpavālī (Dīvālī) or "festival of lights" is one of the most important Hindu festivals. The celebration extends over a two-day period in September or October. Before the break of dawn on the first day women wave lighted lamps before their husbands, imitating a rite otherwise reserved for worship of gods. Then houses are cleaned and refurbished, and later in the day the household gods are worshiped. In the evening dozens of little earthen lamps are lighted in front of the house. On the second day, cows and bullocks are washed and decorated with multicolored designs, necklaces, garlands, and bells, and fed a special gruel. In the evening the lamps are again lighted. Dīpavālī commemorates the defeat of the demon King Narkasūra at the hands of Kṛṣṇa, but is usually devoted to worship of Lakṣmī, goddess of wealth.

In January or February villagers observe a fast in honor of Śiva. Those who observe Śivarātrī abstain from food and drink until the evening worship ends. Early in the evening, worshipers go to the Śiva shrine or temple, offer food to the god, and return home to eat specially prepared foods. Theoretically, one should keep an all-night vigil, but most go to bed sometime shortly after midnight. During this vigil, villagers listen to a program of dramatic performances and engage in devotional singing.

Naurātrā or "nine nights" held in September or October is dedicated to the goddess Durgā (or to all aspects of the great goddess Devī—that is, Kālī, Pārvatī, Sakti, and the other spouses of Śiva), but more often than not it involves worship of one or another village mother goddess. In many cases this ceremony is carried out only by the women of the village and usually involves construction of clay images of the goddess. The women worship these dolls and sing devotional songs before them during the nine nights of the ceremony.

Daśarā (the tenth) follows immediately after Naurātrā and climaxes that ceremony. Daśarā commemorates Arjuna's victory over the Kauravas and is a day on which people are expected to settle old quarrels and make up their differences.

Kṛṣṇa Janam Aṣṭamī commemorates the birth of Kṛṣṇa. At midnight, the hour when Kṛṣṇa is believed to have been born, the members of a family place specially prepared food offerings before a picture or representation of the god. This ceremony is either preceded or followed by an all-day fast.

Sankrāntī (or Makar or Til Sankrāntī) occurs in December or January on the winter solstice when the sun ceases to travel southward toward the abode of death. Sankrāntī marks the beginning of the day of the gods. Special foods are prepared and eaten, charity is given to Brāhmans and cattle, and it is a good day to patch up quarrels, particularly those between mother and daughter-in-law. Technically, Sankrāntī is the first day of every month, marking the date on which the sun traverses from one constellation to another, and in some areas every Sankrāntī is a festival, but in most places only the Sankrāntī of the winter solstice is important.

Almost every one of these festivals (and others as well) is marked by a special and fairly consistent set of activities reflecting important underlying conceptions. Ritual bathing and purification must precede every ritual observance and great care must be taken to prevent contact with any polluting substance that would make the worshiper unfit to participate in the ceremony. Among the higher castes, part of the preparations for ritual observances must include fasting—either totally or simply by avoiding certain kinds of food—and this provision also carries over to ordinary villagers when they participate in many of the ceremonies dedicated especially to the gods of Sanskritic tradition. Special foods are prepared and offered to the deity. When the deity consumes the essence of the offering, the worshipers share the remains (prasād). In general, leftover food is highly polluted, fit to be consumed only by wives or the lowest untouchables. Eating leftovers is a sign of subordination; by eating food left over by the deity, worshipers symbolize their inferiority and subordination to the deity.

Village Organization

Like the rest of Indian society, the peasant village is segmentary, comprising several different caste groups and local lineages. Single-caste villages are not unknown, but by and large a peasant village contains a multiplicity of castes. In general, one may expect to find a priestly caste or group of castes, a group of influential landholding castes, a group of agricultural castes, a group of artisan castes, and a group of servant or menial castes. The priestly castes correspond to the Brāhman varṇa of sacred tradition; the landholding castes are homologized to the Kṣatriya varṇa; and all the others are Śūdras. Frequently the agricultural castes are subdivided into those who cultivate and those who tend cattle. There are traditionally five artisan castes: goldsmith, brass and copper smith, carpenter, blacksmith, and stoneworker. The servant and menial castes are subdivided into those who are clean and those who are unclean (for details, see Chapter 8 and Appendix II).

Usually the landholding castes effectively dominate village affairs. They control most of the land and most of the nonlanded wealth, and hold or control through subordinates most of the important village offices. All the other castes are allied to them as dependents, performing tasks and receiving their pay in a share of the grain at harvest time. If the other castes are not directly tied to them as clients in the traditional system of economic exchange, they depend on them indirectly through their need for loans and other forms of assistance. Frequently the landholding castes have Western-educated sons who are important in regional and state politics and government administration. The landholding castes thus control local economics and politics through traditional means, and they have also managed to control whole regions and states through the mechanism of Western education and modern politics.

In the traditional scheme of things these separate castes are interdependent. Each caste has a traditional occupation, the performance of which entitles it to a share of the landholder's harvest. This system of grain payment is known as the jajmānī system (see Chapter 8). It expresses the mutual interdependence of villagers and reflects the dominant position of the landholding castes. In modern times the reciprocal and redistributive character of the jajmānī system has been largely replaced by contractual obligation and cash payment.

All village segmentation is not a function of caste. Perhaps even more important are factional cleavages made up of persons from numerous castes. Powerful and influential villagers, usually from the landholding castes, are always eager to recruit new clients and thereby build their influence. Each powerful man competes for clients, binding them to him by multiple ties of economic dependence. The origin of a factional division may be long forgotten, but the purpose of factional division is not. Villagers are allied in factions in order to get their share of life's necessities. In return for his support a peasant has a ready source for loans of money or seed during planting time, and he has a powerful patron who will speak for him in village affairs and look after his interests when government officials and police inspectors threaten. A client is expected to help his patron at harvest or other times of peak labor demand, but without a patron a man has no influential people to call on in time of need and would find it difficult to survive.

Because of the competition between factional leaders, every village ceremonial or joint economic effort becomes the setting for a test of strength between factions, for every village event has its potential implications for factional dominance. When factional leaders cannot restrain their adherents, physical violence results. A temple festival becomes a street fight, or a village council meeting becomes a riot. Some factional alignments are continuations of long-standing rivalries between dominant castes; others are more recent, originating as different responses to changing political and economic institutions. Still other factions seem to be channeled along lineage lines. Segmentation within a dominant local lineage entails realignment of all the castes and lineages previously allied to it—some lining up with one branch of the old lineage, some allying themselves to the other branch, and a few taking the opportunity to make more effective alliances with totally different lineages. In many villages each new issue sees a regrouping of alliances, while in other villages the allied castes remain relatively constant for long periods. It frequently happens that no faction or leader has enough power to organize the village for constructive action. Each faction is only strong enough to block any proposed action. When this happens a village drifts along from crisis to crisis without much hope of coping with problems or instituting new lines of action. In the face of such pervasive factionalism the normal offices of village administration are ineffective. The village headman, even if he is not already a member of one of the factions, would be powerless to force the factional leaders into compromise. Similarly, the village council, in all likelihood already fine-tuned to village factions, would merely reflect the distribution of factional power and would be hopelessly split.

Although the real power in the village resides in the well-to-do landholding castes and the leaders of parties or factions, villages also have official functionaries with limited power. The village headman links his village to the government. He collects the land revenue for the central government and receives a commission along with some tax-free land. He is also the local link with the police. Responsible for maintaining order in his village, he supervises the watchmen and reports any violence to the police inspector. Perhaps his most important job is to look after any visiting government officials, providing them with food, lodging, and servants. Officials who are well cared for do not file damaging reports and are more likely to be lenient in punishing any laxity. The headman's position is usually hereditary and his power derives almost entirely from the force of personal character rather than the office. A weak man in the office is only a cipher, but a man who is good at settling quarrels and handling government officials can often exert more power than the office warrants.

Of the resident village officials, the next in importance is the village accountant, charged with all the intricacies of the village land records. The accountant usually is not native to the village in which he serves, and as a bureaucratic appointee he can be transferred. Despite the comparative tentativeness of appointment, most accountants spend their lives in a single post, often acquiring power and influence far beyond that entitled to their office. Because most villagers are illiterate, they have no idea what the accountant records in his books. In order to keep on his good side villagers pay various additional charges and are careful not to offend the accountant lest he record their land as sold or encumbered with debt or in arrears in revenue payments.

While much of the day-to-day government of the village is in the hands of the headman and accountant, villages also have a formal assembly (panchāyat) to cope with their internal problems. Composed of the elders and influential men of the landholding castes, the panchāyat takes into consideration secular disputes, ritual offenses, and acts of violence between members of different castes. Technically, a caste panchāyat should deal with infractions of caste custom committed by persons of the same caste. Some village panchāyats also assume responsibility for well cleaning, road repair, temple upkeep, and village festivals. The deliberations of the panchāyat are first of all a means of indicating public opinion, and secondly a method of arriving at consensus. When agreement cannot be reached, the meeting is adjourned until another time. Once a decision has been reached the panchāyat undertakes its enforcement with the powers at its disposal. If penalties and fines do not bring about the desired result, a culprit generally is deprived of all village services and finally, if he is still unrepentant, expelled from the village.

Rural Problems and Planned Change

Peasant villages are infinitely variable, yet wearisomely alike. A constant factor is the land. The rhythms of a man's whole life follow the demands of the land—the need to get a crop in, to get it harvested, or to convert it to edible food. When, like passion spent, last year's harvest is only a poignant memory, the peasant must start anew to plant and weed and harvest. The cycle is only briefly interrupted by calamity. Wars, drought, pestilence, flood, famine do not for long interfere with the peasant's work. When the armies have marched away or the pestilence has run its course, the land still waits with the promise of another crop, another harvest.

The peasant's field has always been the solid base of Indian government. Land revenue has been and is the dominant source of income for the rulers of India. It is not surprising then that many of India's most critical problems involve the land. Thus the total amount of arable land expands at a rate less than population growth, land is inequitably distributed, and the peasant's plots of land are fragmented or subdivided into uneconomic holdings. Production of cash crops has climbed, but production of basic food crops has declined. Productivity has been increased but is still low, and much of the harvest is still lost to spoilage or to pests because of inadequate storage and transport. To meet some of these problems the Indian government has initiated land-tenure legislation and land-reclamation programs, has constructed vast irrigation schemes, and has built fertilizer factories, but most spectacular of all these government activities is the community-development program.

Beginning in 1952 the community-development program has attempted to deal with all rural problems. Under the program India was divided into project areas covering some 18,000 of the country's half a million villages. Each project area was to receive intensive treatment over a total of ten years. Each village in a project area was to get two wells or tanks, adequate drainage facilities, one-half of cultivable land under irrigation, a primary school, and a road within half a mile of the village. The villages in a project area were also to have access to a veterinary service and agricultural-extension service. Other facilities and services were to be provided in regional centers for each group of 25 villages. Supplementing the community-development program is the national extension service, a less-intensive form of community development designed to cover a larger area.

The entire administrative system of the community-development program was established as a separate and largely autonomous bureaucracy. Theoretically, development, revenue, police, and other departments were to be separate but not overlapping. Liaison between departments was to have been effected through consultation. In reality, the departments overlap and conflict with one another. Similarly, the "inner democratization" of the bureaucracy never became a fact; the community-development administration remained as authoritarian as the old Indian civil service. Directives issued from the top by those with no knowledge of local conditions characterize the administration. Village-level workers charged with carrying out these unrealistic demands concentrated their efforts on intensive "drives" corresponding with the visit of some high-ranking official, and lapsed into ineffectiveness with his departure. Many of the changes brought about by these methods are naturally superficial and impermanent. In fact, most of the changes so far have been in the material aspects of life, with practically no change in institutional organization and rural attitudes. Naturally, the permanency of material changes ultimately depends on institutional and additudinal changes.

In many ways the development program is naive. It assumes that the constituent groups of a village have common interests that will bind them together, and it implies that these different groups are sufficiently alike to benefit equally from planned change. In fact village groups have dissimilar interests in the program and derive quite inequitable benefits from it. The castes in power have no interest in relinquishing their power or fostering the economic independence of other village castes. Then, too, the government is suspect. Its traditional role has been to extort revenue and maintain the status quo, not promote change. Peasants cannot believe that the community-development administration is really not a new adjunct of the police and revenue administration. The villagers are quite right in suspecting these officials, for traditionally administrative officials have used their power and position to benefit their own caste or group at the expense of the villager, and the peasant has no reason to believe that things have changed. The program has had little success in working with the village leaders. Administrators either mistook the headman as the real source of village authority or circumvented him and went to the important and influential men of the landholding castes. In either case they offended someone and often merely succeeded in adding fuel to factional fights.

Other traditional patterns persist. Śramdān (giving of labor) quickly falls back into the old pattern of begār (forced labor). Village elites welcome Śramdān, for it gives them new roads over which to transport their cash crops and provides them with new advisory positions. The landholding castes assume supervisory roles and leave the labor to the lower castes who have no cash crops to transport and consequently derive no benefit from their labor.

On the whole it is doubtful that the community-development program will be successful in achieving any of its anticipated goals. Villagers will remain divided in interests, production will continue to lag behind population, and so on. But one may be certain that there will be unanticipated changes and that most of them will be undesirable. Community development, change stimulated from the rural sector, belief in the essentially democratic, agrarian village—all are symptoms of a kind of romantic folly. Sooner or later one must learn that peasants are peasants and the virtuous Jeffersonian ideal of free, independent yeoman cultivators has been able to exist if at all only for short periods under highly specialized frontier conditions. The rest of the time the world's cultivators have been subjects of those who controlled the land or the market for the produce of the land or both. Changes in society will not emanate from the fields and villages of India any more than from the rice paddies of China or the yurts of Kazakhstan. The dream of peasant revolution, like the dream of the democratic yeoman, is only a dream.

SEVEN

FAMILY AND KINSHIP

In India one's family and kin are a constant in an otherwise dangerously variable world. The responsibilities and reciprocal obligations of family and kinship relations bind groups of kin together, and most of one's daily life is spent with close kinsmen. Domestic rituals, work, and play are all conducted within the context of kinship relations.

THE JOINT FAMILY

The ideal model of family organization in India is and has been from time immemorial the joint or extended family incorporating a man and wife, their unmarried daughters and sons, and the spouses and children of sons. Each male offspring is entitled to an equal share in the proceeds of the family estate, and married brothers should remain together as co-sharers of a joint estate. As a legal corporation the members of a joint family are jointly responsible for payment of revenue and other government assessments. Female children are expected to leave their natal families and reside in the homes of their husbands. Under ancient law daughters, wives, and widows had no rights in family property but were entitled to maintenance by their male kin. Recent legislation has provided rights in family property for females, but the new laws are generally disregarded by villagers.

Joint ownership of an estate implies that those who have rights in the estate will constitute a common residential unit engaging cooperatively in the production and consumption of goods and participating in common religious observances. Ideally, authority relations within the joint family are determined by sex and age. Men have authority over women and elders have authority over their juniors. The head of a joint family is typically the eldest male. Unless they are incapacitated by illness or senility, fathers retain authority over their sons until death or retirement. If the joint family does not segment at the father's death or retirement, his eldest son assumes the position of family head. Similarly, the wife of the head of the household has absolute authority over all the younger females of the house, and strong-willed women sometimes even assume effective control of the household on the death of their husbands.

Degrees of "Jointness"

This idealized picture of a group of close kinsmen living in the same household, eating, working, and worshiping together is subject to a number of variable empirical expressions. Thus a joint estate may still be legally joint even though some male family members do not live in the same house, share the same cooking fire, dine together, work together, or worship together. In fact, there are various degrees of "jointness." Some joint families may merely meet together for religious functions, refusing to eat, work, or live together. Others may continue to work together and even live under the same roof, but refuse to cook and eat together. Even among those who live under the same roof, the house may be extended and successively partitioned off into semiprivate quarters for each married son. In these subdivided households, each nuclear family cooks, eats, and sleeps together as a partially isolated unit.

These variations in degree of jointness reflect a tendency toward segmentation, and indicate that cooperation between family members becomes increasingly difficult as soon as sons take spouses. The sons' wives feel oppressed by their mother-in-law, often dislike one another, and become jealous over imagined or real favoritisms within the group. Sons chafe at subordination to their father and quarrel with one another over the allocation of family work and income.

Counterbalancing these divisive tendencies are inducements to maintaining close relations. Newly married couples are often psychologically immature and materially dependent on the husband's family. In difficult times the members of a joint family are expected to assist one another, and the larger group provides a strong, united front against the outside world. Both psychologically and materially the combined resources of a joint family are more effective in meeting the world's demands and obligations than the isolated, independent nuclear family. Particularly for small children the joint family provides a warm, secure psychological atmosphere, and the child is not completely at the mercy of one set of parents. Often the very real advantages of joint family life outweigh the annoyances of living together. A man's reputation is partly conditional on his whole family, and a successful joint family demonstrates to the outside world that its members are reliable and respectable people. The various degrees of jointness then simply represent compromises between the strains of close family life and the advantages of jointness.

The degree of jointness or length of time a family remains joint is affected by economic factors. Families having substantial landholdings capable of supporting a large group are more perfectly joint and remain together longer than those that do not, and in general those with considerable wealth are more cohesive than the poor. Similarly, when some members of the family must seek full- or part-time employment outside the natal village, joint-family solidarity is threatened. A woman's contribution to family income may also affect the joint family. Thus a man whose wife brings in substantial income, either from outside employment or by inheritance or other assistance from her natal family, is economically less dependent on his own family and unafraid of asserting his independence. His wife, too, is much less willing to be subjugated by her mother-in-law and will press for an early division of the joint-family estate. As a general rule, economic factors promoting independence either out of necessity or incidentally are detrimental to jointness.

Joint-Family Ritual

The joint family is the locus of many rituals associated with the welfare of the family and the life cycle of family members. The most important act of corporate worship centers around the household god. Every household has a resident deity installed in a niche or sanctified corner of the house. Often only a crude clay figure or cheap oleograph of one of the Hindu gods, he is given daily attention by the wife of the head of the house in the form of food offerings and brief prayers. On special occasions coinciding with important festivals or life-cycle rituals, he is given more elaborate worship in which all family members participate. His general function is to protect the members of the household from harm. Although the intricate series of ceremonies prescribed for important life stages in the ancient texts has been considerably attenuated in all but the more orthodox and high-caste families, rituals associated with life stages are still important. Those most commonly observed are the ceremonies associated with marriage, the birth of a male child, initiation rites for twice-born castes, death ceremonies, and ancestor rites. All of these rituals involve persons other than joint-family members, but their major burden falls on those who belong to the same joint family.

Marriage

Marriage, a risky business surrounded by both human and divine precautions, cannot rationally be left to the caprice and immature judgment of the young. Marriages are a sure indication of family status, for whom a family gives daughters to and receives brides from defines its position in the status hierarchy. In general, one should bend every effort to give daughters to higher-status families and reluctantly receive brides from families of lower status than one's own. Choice of an appropriate mate thus commands all of a family's resources and ingenuity. First of all, a prospective bride and groom must be members of the same caste, but in the north they must not be previously related within varying degrees of distance either on the mother's or father's side. A general rule prohibits marriage within eight degrees on the father's side and six degrees on the mother's side. In the south, by contrast, one ought to marry a close relative, either a mother's brother's child, a father's sister's child (that is, a cross-cousin), or, in the case of a male, an elder sister's daughter.

Once these preliminary conditions have been met, careful negotiations are set afoot, usually through an intermediary who functions as a marriage arranger. The prospective bride's and groom's families carefully investigate one another's background, wealth, connections, and prospects. If these are within reason, horoscopes must be taken and checked for compatibility of signs and indications of future fortune. Next, the proposed amount and appropriateness of gifts must be carefully assessed. Some of these are purely traditional and involve little more than the ceremonial exchange of cloth, but the gifts from the girl's family must be substantial, reflecting not only their ability to pay but indicating clearly the status difference between the two families. The greater the status difference between families the higher must be the price paid in the form of gifts by the girl's family. If negotiations do not break down at this stage, the astrologer is once again called in to set an auspicious day and hour for the marriage ceremonies. In more progressive families there will usually be an opportunity for the prospective bride and groom to meet before negotiations go too far. Should they dislike one another, negotiations would be called off. In more orthodox families, however, the wishes of children count for little, and no premarital meeting will take place. In fact, the whole matter may have been settled years before a child comes of marital age. Prepubertal marriages are now outlawed; but there is still a general prejudice in favor of early marriage.

The wedding ceremony and its attendant feasting and celebration are the final expression of a family's ability to pay. An elaborate ceremony lasting for several days and involving musicians, sound trucks, notables, and hundreds of guests and relatives fed on the finest and most sumptuous foods demonstrates to the whole world that the family has wealth and status. Most families cannot afford such elaborate festivities, but do the best they can. Consequently, marriage ceremonies constitute the largest single expense in most households, consuming not only the hard-won savings of many years, but often plunging the whole family deeply into debt for years to come. In contrast to the elaborate precautions and festivities surrounding it, the wedding ceremony itself is basically simple.

Birth of a Male Child

A woman's status in her husband's household amounts to little until she has given birth to a male child. If a male child is not readily forthcoming, a woman quickly resorts to amulets, charms, vows, and pilgrimages to holy places known for their efficacy in promoting the conception of males. Should she fail to produce a male child, either from barrenness or a perverse tendency to bear only females, her husband will be encouraged to take a second wife and she will be demoted even further in the household ranks. When she has successfully produced a male heir, his arrival is greeted by drumming, singing, and public announcement, but her female children are received without festivity. The comparative desirability of male children is reflected not only in their joyous reception but in differential mortality rates as well. Almost twice as many female children die as infants. Their infant illnesses are not neglected, but they do not receive the frantic concern and immediate attention that is given a male child's slightest gas pain or temper tantrum. After a child is born all the members of the household are ceremonially polluted for at least three days, and in orthodox families up to ten days. Immediately after birth, before the umbilical cord is cut, the birth ceremony (jātakarma) is performed. Sacred mantras are whispered in the child's ear, a mixture of honey and ghī (clarified butter) is placed in its mouth, and a secret name is whispered in its ear.

Within the warm confines of the joint family a child receives its early training and learns the patterns of its language and culture. During most of its infancy and early years it is seldom without human contact. A child is an object of adoration, held and fondled by everyone in the family. Discipline begins only gradually with sweet remonstrances for bad behavior, but eventually stronger measures in the form of scoldings, ear twistings, and arm pinching are brought to bear. As the child acquires language, he is taught by precept and example to be deferential to superiors, and he learns the patterns of hierarchy. When a little older, a child spends long hours in the rote recitation of school lessons. Here, as in earlier training, a child is neither taught nor rewarded for independence or self-reliance. His constant lesson in home or school is the acceptance of authority.

Initiation Rites

In orthodox families of the twice-born castes, a male child reaching adolescence is expected to undergo the upanayana or ceremony of second birth (see p. 87), in which he is invested with the sacred thread and accorded full membership in his caste. Nowadays this ceremony is common only among Brāhmaṇ castes and among the orthodox. There has never been an initiation rite for female children. For them, initiation was and is accomplished by the rites of marriage.

Death Ceremonies

Death, like birth, plunges the family into ceremonial pollution lasting until the funerary rites and purificatory ceremonies are over. As soon after death as possible the deceased is carried to the funeral pyre, followed by mourners made up of his agnatic relatives and sister's son. After circumambulating the funeral pyre in the inauspicious counterclockwise direction, the fire is set alight by the chief mourner (the deceased's son or other male descendant). Three days later the ashes are gathered and thrown in a stream. For ten days following cremation, libations of water and offerings of rice balls (piṇḍa) and milk are made for the dead man by the mourners. During this period the dead man's soul becomes a dangerous ghost (preta) incapable of entering heaven and potentially harmful to its surviving relations. On the tenth day this soul acquires a subtle body and, nourished by the sacrifices of the living, ascends to heaven where it must continue to be sustained by the food offered to it at the annual śrāddha (funerary commemoration) ceremonies. At the end of this ten-day period, the male mourners go to a stream where the chief mourner and a Brāhmaṇ perform a rite of purification. The male agnates then shave their hair and beards which have remained unshaven for ten days. When this ceremony is over, the mourners are ritually purified and may return to their normal activities.

Ancestor Rites

During the first year following the funeral, the chief mourner offers libations and rice balls to the departed on the eleventh day of each lunar period, and on the night of the first Holī festival after the death. After this first year the deceased is honored only once a year in the dark part of the lunar month corresponding to August-September. This is a major ceremony at which the souls of all one's deceased paternal and maternal kin are honored. There is no worse fate than for a man to die without heirs who will perform these śrāddha rites. Without the sustenance derived from these offerings, his soul never attains heaven. It wanders homelessly about the earth working harm on humans. To neglect the souls of the departed is to take a great chance with supernatural vengeance and to place all members of the joint family in jeopardy. Because the ancestors are potentially dangerous, a man would be foolhardy indeed to fail in his obligations to them.

Life Cycle of Joint Family

Like its human members, a joint family has a life cycle of its own. When brothers subdivide their father's estate they establish independent families. In the passage of time these newly independent families acquire new members through birth and marriage, eventually forming a new joint family which in turn will be dissolved by death of the family founder and the subsequent partitioning of the estate by his heirs.

Some researchers have incorrectly concluded from the statistical frequency of joint families that the joint family is in the process of breaking down under the pressures of modern life and urban living. Because a joint family has a life cycle of its own, it is predictable that a percentage of the families in any sample population will be nuclear or nonjoint. What would be significant is evidence of a change in the relative proportions of joint versus nuclear families. As yet, the available evidence does not indicate a change in these proportions. The general conclusion is that the joint family is not deteriorating. This should not be surprising, for the reasons favoring joint families as well as the basic factors influencing their dissolution are no different now than they have ever been.

Family Relations

Relations between most family members are marked by reserve and restraint. From an early age sons must learn to behave circumspectly in the presence of their fathers. Boisterousness, loud talk, sitting on a chair, cot, or stool higher than the father, lying down or sprawling in his presence, smoking, and unseemly behavior of all kinds are forbidden. Sons should be obedient to their father's every command. Argument or "sassiness" meets with immediate punishment. Even though the father is a strict disciplinarian, he often has a real affection for his sons, but it is generally felt to be bad taste to display any feeling of intimacy. Sons are also expected to behave respectfully toward their mothers, but mothers are much more indulgent. They typically accede to every desire of their sons, spoiling them horribly, and interceding for them with their father. Fathers are similarly more indulgent with their daughters while mothers make an effort to teach them household management and proper deportment.

Frequently the paternal grandparents in a joint household undermine the parents' authority. A child who has been disciplined by his parents can count on his doting grandparents to dry his tears and give him a sweet or special tidbit from the kitchen. Children are often entrusted to the care of their grandparents while the parents are working and there is usually a close bond between grandparents and grandchildren.

Importance of the Mother

On the whole a man's most important relative is his mother. Constant in her love and care, a mother entwines her son in a lasting web of dependence that sets up an ambivalence toward other women. Unable to break the pattern of suffocating indulgence, Indian males have difficulty in harmonizing the romanticized view of women fostered by their mothers with the sexual role of a husband. Mothers contribute to their sons' ambivalence toward women even after marriage, for they do not relinquish their authority over their sons when they take a wife. Mothers have been known to regulate their sons' married sexual lives and to constantly blame any illness on sexual overindulgence actively encouraged by the young wife. Young wives are felt to make excessive sexual demands, and, because semen loss is regarded as debilitating, they are often accused of bringing on weakness and susceptibility to other diseases in their husbands. As a competitor for the affections of the mother's jealously guarded son, the young wife may even be accused of practicing sorcery against her husband or his mother.

In general, a wife never replaces a mother in her husband's affections. Even after years of marriage men often feel closer to their mothers than to their wives. This ambivalent attitude toward women is manifested in the general view that women are naturally more libidinous than men. Daughters consequently must be carefully guarded and safely married off as soon as possible before their natural proclivities lead the family into dishonor. Mothers are revered as the epitome of love, affection, and indulgence, but women are dangerous. This twofold aspect of femininity is enshrined in the popular cult of mother goddesses who in their dual aspect are both succoring and fiercely vicious.

The Wife's Status

In view of this ambivalence and jealous animosity, it is not surprising that the position of the young bride in her husband's home is fraught with great tension. She is a stranger among people she hardly knows, in a village far from home, and married to a man she may never before have met. In public she must show not even the slightest sign of affection for her unfamiliar husband, and must defer to and instantly obey her mother-in-law. The mother-in-law criticizes her every action and eagerly blames her evil influence as the source of every minor household mishap. A man should take no public notice of his wife except to display his complete authority over her. She, in turn, must never give any public show of intimacy and must demonstrate to the world that she regards her husband as a god, deferring to him and fulfilling his every desire. Laughter above a demure titter would be a sure sign of frivolousness, and to walk rapidly or unrestrainedly would be a clear indication of boldness or even sexual looseness.

Aside from her husband's younger sisters and the children of the household, the young wife's only ally is her husband's younger brother. With him she may joke and tease even about sexual matters; in some cases this joking relation included sexual relations. Her husband's elder brother must be treated with the same respect and deference as the husband's father. The husband's elder brother must behave with reciprocal circumspection toward his younger brother's wife. Her husband's father may pass an occasional joke at her expense, but she is not permitted to reciprocate. Traditionally, a young wife should cover her face in the presence of her husband's father or elder brother.

A young wife's position in the household remains difficult until she has given birth to a male child. From that time on she is treated more with the respect accorded a mother, but her relations with the mother-in-law are never easy. The mother-in-law will accuse her of spoiling the child or, conversely, of punishing it too severely. With the passage of time the wife may gradually acquire considerable power and authority in the family, badgering her husband and effectively dominating him privately if not publicly. Too, she may publicly embarrass him by taking their quarrels into the street, or privately pollute him by laxness in the observance of ritual purity in the preparation of food.

The worst fate a wife may have to endure is early widowhood, for a widow is an object of scorn, barely tolerated in her deceased husband's home. So low is her status that one of the worst curse words in Telugu is vēdava (widow). Traditionally, even the sight of a widow was inauspicious, and before setting off on any important business men would call out, warning all widows to stay out of sight. A wife who survived her husband was somehow unfaithful—if not in fact, then as a potential source of sexual license. Repugnance for widowhood was expressed in the ancient and now forbidden rite of satī, in which a wife demonstrated her fidelity and devotion to her husband by immolating herself on his burning funeral pyre. Today satī occurs only rarely, but attitudes toward widows have scarcely changed. Although modern law allows widows to remarry, local tradition does not favor it, for a widow should still remain constant to her deceased mate and not take a new husband. Restricted to the inner recesses of the house, widows are expected to be drudges, uncomplainingly performing every household chore in return for economic support. Not only is she suspected of making aggressive sexual advances toward the men of the house, she must be closely watched lest her pent-up sexuality vent itself on outsiders and disgrace the family. Her only security in the household is her children, and for this reason a young childless widow will frequently arrange for her return to her natal household where she may count on her brothers for support. Her status, of course, is mitigated if she is wealthy, or if in her older age she has become the dominant female in the household. Similarly, restrictions on widows are less severe in lower castes, and low-caste widows frequently remarry.

The Husband's Role

A young man's transition to the role of husband is similarly uneasy. During the wedding ceremony he becomes a king bedecked in royal finery and is even treated deferentially by his elders. After the ceremony he must learn to put on a face of determined but easy authority over his new wife, no matter how affectionately he may behave privately. He must also bear a burden of shame, for all in the household suspect him of taking too much sexual pleasure in his wife. He cannot with easy confidence spend time privately with his wife during the day, so the two must get to know one another only in the friendly darkness of their private room. Then, too, he soon realizes the mutual distaste between his wife and mother. He is put in the difficult position of mediating between the two women in his life, favoring both without alienating either. His initial adaptation to his new status is not made easier by the fact that he and his bride are often virtual strangers who in traditional society may never have seen one another until the crucial moment in the wedding ceremony when the veil between them is parted.

In the south where cross-cousin marriage prevails, the transition to the roles of husband and wife are often easier. Because the bride and groom are often close relatives, they are not strangers and their in-laws are familiar, friendly faces.

Brothers and Sisters

The relation between a man and his sister is a close and enduring one. Brothers should protect their sisters, give them gifts, and provide for them in times of disaster. An elder sister is often a boy's chief companion, looking after him when he is small, carryng him about on her hip, and providing him with a watchful, protective playmate. This special bond between brothers and sisters sometimes receives ritual expression in the form of a charm given the brother by his sister. Even after her marriage a brother must look out for his sister's interests, visiting her in her new home, consoling her, and bringing gifts. In the north, the family of his sister's husband regard him as an inferior, for the whole family of the wife is traditionally accorded a status lower than the husband's. They may treat him disrespectfully and even abuse him. In the south, where bilateral cross-cousin marriage is permitted, this pattern of inferiority is less pronounced. When a man's sister gives birth he assumes a new role, becoming mother's brother to his sister's children. The mother's brother is a benevolent and affectionate relative, and in the south he is a potential father-in-law. He is a kind, supportive, and indulgent figure to whom a child may turn for help in distress. He also figures importantly in many of the life-cycle ceremonies, and his nephews have ritual functions to perform at his funeral ceremonies.

Brothers are expected to be mutually supportive, but more often than not they become jealous and quarrelsome, particularly when the father's authority over them declines or ceases with his death. Unless there is a wide age discrepancy between them, brothers can seldom manage to tolerate one another in the close quarters of a joint family. A younger brother is supposed to extend to his elder brother the kind of respect he gives to his father, but he often resents and rebels against this arrogation of his elder brother's status. Conversely, elder brothers quickly take offense at any flippancy or lack of respect from a younger brother. Younger brothers feel that their elder brothers attempt to make them do more than their share of the work, and elder brothers suspect younger brothers of laziness or malingering. Both siblings are quick to suspect the other of receiving a disproportionate share of family income either through paternal preference or skulduggery. As their father becomes older and less active they press him to retire and divide the family property. After the property has been subdivided, they may continue to reside together briefly, but sooner or later one moves out with his wife and children and takes up separate residence. Physical separations do not always put an end to family cooperation, and brothers are expected to assist one another even if they cannot live together. A brother, for example, is expected to support and maintain the widow and children of a deceased brother. Cooperation and mutual responsibility are certainly important aspects of the relations between brothers, but the predominating relation is one of rivalry.

Sisters are often close companions, but the bond between them is less durable. They have no responsibilities toward one another after their marriages, and only if they happen to have married into the same or nearby villages do they maintain close contact after they have married. Technically, the children of sisters are analogous to siblings, but in fact they are usually almost strangers with whom one has little contact. In the south the relation between the children of female siblings is likely to be somewhat closer simply because sisters frequently marry into the same village. Here the mother's sister is a kind of mother, and her children are like brothers and sisters.

Children are expected to behave toward their father's brothers with the same deference and restraint they would give their own father, but if the age difference is slight a father's younger brother may be more of an informal companion and close friend. The spouses of father's brothers are like one's own mother or elder sister, only slightly less indulgent. The children of father's brothers are like one's own siblings, but a child's relations with them are frequently constrained by the father's relations with his brothers.

Rivalry between brothers precludes close relations between their children and spouses, and in fact a man's children often become important pawns in his competition with his brothers. Because small children have the run of the house, they become the eyes and ears of their parents, reporting on the doings of their paternal grandparents, uncles, and their families, and relaying whatever household gossip comes their way. When married brothers reside in the same household, the children sometimes act as messengers between feuding brothers. When they grow older their careers and marriages become extensions of the competition between brothers. A son is urged to do better than the sons of his father's brothers, and, conversely, his failings and inadequacies are compared to the triumphs and prowess of his patrilateral cousins.

EXTENDED KIN GROUPS

Outside the joint family a man's most important relatives in addition to the mother's brother and sister's son are those consanguineous relatives related to him through his father's patriline, his father's relatives by marriage, his own relatives by marriage, and the relatives by marriage of his siblings and children. Very broadly, a man's relatives are divided into consanguineous patrikin (that is, blood relatives related to him by descent through males) and affines (relatives by marriage). The former constitute extended kin groups known as lineages, clans, and jātis. The local lineage consists of families who are descended in the male line from the same ancestor and reside in the same village. All the male members of one's lineage are "grandfathers," "father's brothers," "brothers," "sons," or "brother's sons," and all the women of the lineage are "sisters," "daughters," "father's sisters," or "brother's daughters." Usually, women born into the lineage (father's sisters, sisters, daughters, brother's daughters) cease to be affiliated with their natal lineage at marriage and become affiliated with their husband's lineage.

The members of a local lineage perform rituals together and cooperate in the work of the fields. Lineage members commonly observe the pollution seclusion entailed by the death or birth of a lineage member, participate in the marriage ceremonies of lineage mates, and in some areas join together in the worship of lineage deities. In a sense the lineage is an extension of the joint family deriving from the segmentation of earlier joint families. This process of segmentation is illustrated in Figure 18.

In Figure 18 the lineage was founded by two brothers and now consists of three separate families. One of the founding brothers and his wife are deceased (signified by ∆̸ and ∅). Their two sons have divided the property of their deceased father and now with their spouses and children constitute two separate nuclear families (Families 2 and 3 in the diagram). Family 1, in which one of the founding brothers still lives, continues as a joint family.

Like the joint family, the lineage is also rent by disputes and tensions among its members. In many cases factional groups made up of lineage segments compete with one another and perpetuate old feuds that may have had their origin in some ancient joint-family quarrel.

The clan, a wider and more inclusive group, comprises groupings of lineages who claim descent from the same male ancestor. Unlike lineages, the members of a clan are dispersed over many villages and one usually does not know all of one's clan fellows. Occasionally, the members of a clan congregate in the locality of their traditional origin for worship of the clan goddess, but in most cases the clan merely serves to define the limits of exogamy. Since

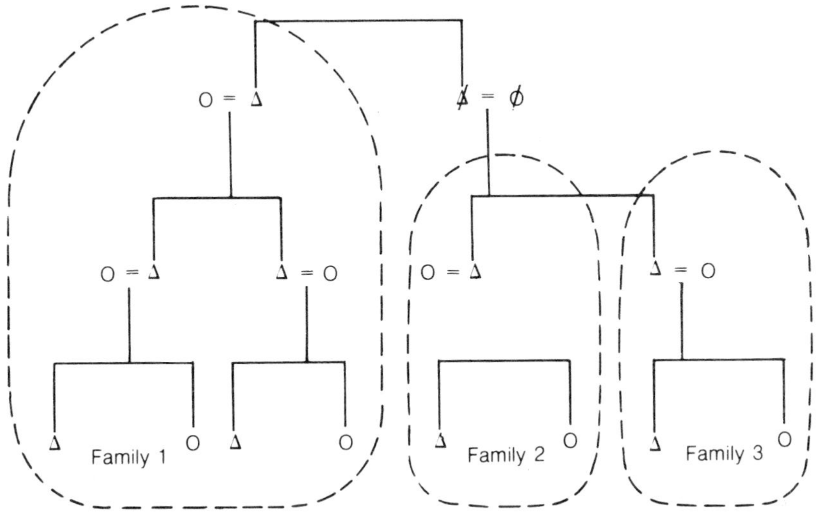

Figure 18. Joint-family segmentation.

all the members of a clan are descended from a common male ancestor, they cannot intermarry. More important than the clan is the jāti, to be discussed in the next chapter.

AFFINALS AND CONSANGUINEALS

It is in the treatment and classification of affinal relatives that the northern and southern patterns of kinship differ most from one another. In general the southern pattern attempts to exploit and intensify existing affinal relations, whereas the northern pattern seeks to establish new and ever-widening affinal links. The southern pattern is postulated on a positive marriage rule which encourages marriages between close relatives, and the northern pattern derives from a negative marriage rule that prohibits marriages between close relatives. Cross-cousin marriage in the south sets up a more-or-less permanent alliance between descent groups or lineages. This is illustrated in Figure 19.

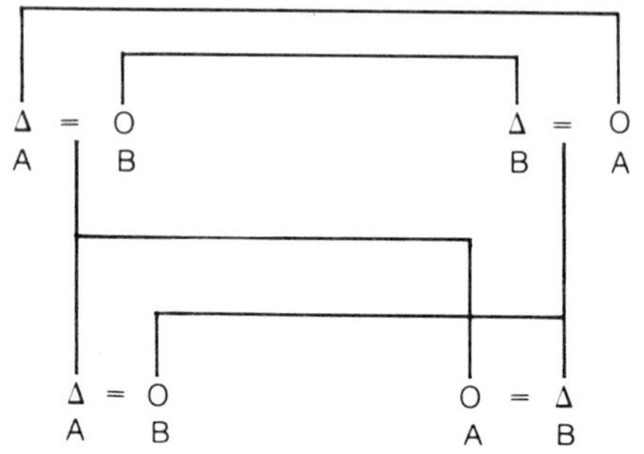

Figure 19. Bilateral cross-cousin marriage.

In Figure 19 there are two patrilineal descent groups, A and B. Men of A marry women of B, and men of B marry women of A. The offspring of these marriages marry their mother's brothers' (or father's sisters') children. Each generation automatically reproduces the relationship of the previous

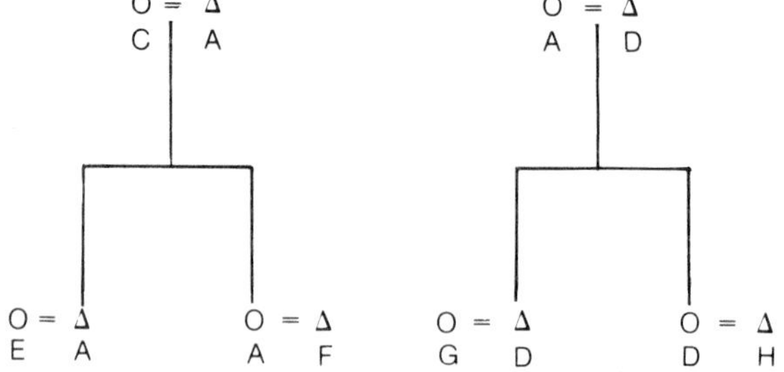

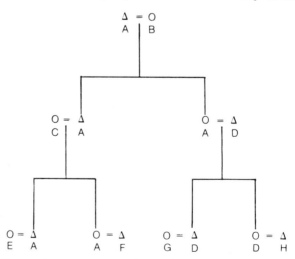

Figure 20. The marriage pattern in northern India.

generation. By contrast, Figure 20 illustrates the northern pattern, in which each marriage establishes a new link between lineages and none of the previous links is repeated in subsequent generations. Where bilateral cross-cousin marriage of the type illustrated in Figure 19 is practiced, it is apparent that affines are merged with consanguines. That is, one's spouse and her parents are consanguineous relatives prior to marriage. This pattern mitigates against the usual status differences between the family of the bride and the family of the groom.

These differences in northern and southern patterns are reflected in the kinship terminologies used in each region. The southern (Dravidian) terminologies class one's relatives into those from whom spouses may be taken (cross-relatives) and those from whom the taking of spouses is prohibited (parallel relatives). It further classifies them according to generation and sex, and in one's own generation differentiates among those who are older and younger than oneself (see Figure 21). Included in the parallel category are all the male members of one's own descent group (father and father's brothers), the spouses of these elder males, one's siblings and parallel cousins (father's brothers' children and mother's sisters' children), one's own children, and the children of male siblings and parallel cousins. The parallel category thus consists of people one calls father, mother, brother, sister, son, and daughter.

		Parallel		Cross	
		Male	Female	Male	Female
	+2	Tāta		Avva	
	+1	Ayya	Amma	Māma	Atta
Generation	Older	Anna	Akka	Bāva	Vodina
	0				
	Younger	Tammuḍu	Cellelu	Bāmaradi	Maradalu
	−1	Koḍuku	Kuturu	Alluḍu	Koḍalu
	−2	Manamaḍu		Manamarālu	

Figure 21. Telugu kinship terminology.

The people one calls father (ayya) are one's own father, father's brothers, and mother's sisters' husbands. Similarly, the people one calls mother (amma) include one's own mother, mother's sisters, and the spouses of father's brothers. In one's own generation elder male siblings and parallel cousins are called anna; elder female siblings and parallel cousins are akka. Younger brothers and male parallel cousins are called tammuḍu, and younger sisters and parallel cousins are called cellelu. In the minus-one generation are one's own son (koḍuku) and daughter (kuturu) and the sons and daughters of one's brothers' children. The cross category includes all of one's own affines, the affines of one's father, and the affines of one's siblings and children. Thus māma is mother's brother, father's sister's husband, and spouse's father; atta is mother's brother's wife, father's sister, and spouse's mother. In one's own generation are one's cross-cousins (children of father's sisters and mother's brothers), among whom are potential spouses, brothers-in-law, and sisters-in-law. The minus-one generation in the cross category includes spouses of children and sister's children. In more remote generations (plus and minus two) the distinction between cross and parallel relatives becomes insignificant and is lost. The classification of relatives into separate parallel/cross categories and the merging of affines with consanguines in the cross category in the Dravidian terminology is thus consistent with the rule of cross-cousin marriage.

By contrast, the northern (Indo-Aryan) kinship terminologies make a clear-cut distinction between consanguineal and affinal relatives and recognize many distinct categories of affinal relationship, providing separate kinship terms for nearly every relative by marriage. There are many variants of the northern terminology, but all of them have a descriptive tendency. That is, there tends to be a separate term describing each genealogical relationship. Thus in Marāthi there are separate terms for father's brother's son, father's sister's son, mother's sister's son, and mother's brother's son, as well as separate terms for the spouses of each of these. The descriptive and particularizing character of the northern terminologies conforms to the diversifying nature of northern marriage alliances. It should be noted that this descriptive pattern is most elaborated among higher castes. Among lower castes, kin terms, particularly for consanguineal relatives, are more classificatory, and in some cases the terminological treatment of affines approaches the Dravidian pattern.

Historically, many of the kin terms for consanguineals in the Indo-Aryan terminologies are recent descriptive compounds built on an earlier more classificatory system. When these relatively recent descriptive accretions are "peeled away," the outline of the Dravidian system of terminology emerges, even though the terms themselves are usually Indo-Aryan. Even the Sanskrit terminology appears to have been affected by Dravidian, for the pattern of Sanskrit terminology departs significantly from the ancient Indo-European system of terminology. In more recent times a reverse process is apparent. Some Brāhmaṇ castes in the south have a terminological structure more similar to the Indo-Aryan pattern, but the terms themselves are Dravidian, or recent compounds of Dravidian stems, and these compound terms reflect an Indo-Aryan rather than Dravidian pattern of compounding. In general, the modern Indo-Aryan terminologies are constructed on a Dravidian base that has been modified by Indo-Aryan terms and logic.

By a controlled intercomparison of regional and caste-specific terminological variants and by paying particular attention to the terminologies of Dravidian tribes bordering Indo-Aryan speech communities, it is possible to reconstruct at least the outlines of the process that transformed this Dravidian base into the modern Indo-Aryan terminologies. In all cases, the first step in this process entails the borrowing of Indo-Aryan terms for certain categories of affines. These borrowed terms do not initially replace the Dravidian terms which denote both affinals and consanguineals, but they come to be used with specific reference to affines, thus restricting the original affinal content of the Dravidian term. The Dravidian term for a male cross-cousin, for example, no longer includes spouse's brother, this relationship having been taken over by an Indo-Aryan term. The first sign of Indo-Aryan influence is thus marked by a proliferation of Indo-Aryan terms for affinal relatives, and the recognition of an affinal category separate from the consanguineal category. Or to put it another way, the Dravidian cross category becomes internally differentiated into separate consanguineal and affinal categories. In many cases, the pattern of influence stops here and the system becomes stabilized, but more frequently other changes are set in motion by these adjustments. Once the initial wedge has been driven between affines and consanguines in the cross category, the cross category becomes further differentiated and is eventually obliterated, bringing about a restructuring of the parallel category. This is often followed by wholesale adoption of Indo-Aryan terms. It is not possible to give more than the barest outline of this complex series of adjustments here, but it is significant that the whole process has its origins in terms for affines. The inescapable conclusion is that these terminological changes are consistent with the imposition of the Indo-Aryan pattern of diversified marriage alliance and the breakdown of the Dravidian pattern of marriage alliance. In short, these changes are consistent with what one would expect of systematic and long-term intermarriage between two different communities when one of the communities dominates the other. Finally, we may note that in kinship, as in all other things Indian, the fundamental, underlying structure is always Dravidian.

One other terminological variant confirming this same general tendency is worthy of note. Among many of the Indo-Aryan tribes on the Afghanistan border, the generalized Middle Eastern pattern of parallel-cousin marriage prevails. That is, a man is expected to marry his father's brother's or mother's sister's daughter. As might be expected, the Brahui, who speak a Dravidian language and for many centuries have lived in close contact with these Indo-Aryan tribes on the border, have adopted a system of terminology that is consistent with parallel-cousin marriage.

SECONDARY PATTERNS

Although the typical pattern of Indian social organization presupposes patrilineal descent, monogamous marriages, and virilocal residence, many castes and tribes are matrilineal, and matrilocal residence is practiced even by groups that are normally virilocal. Similarly, some groups allow polyandry and nearly all permit polygyny as well as other forms of secondary marriage.

Today matrilineality is restricted to the south and Assam, but was once probably more widespread, for some ancient kingdoms and modern princely states like Bhopal are known to have followed matrilineal succession. In these matrilineal groups descent and inheritance are traced through the mother rather than the father. Typically, the husband resides in his wife's joint family which is under the control of his wife's elder female relatives and mother's brother. Men do not directly inherit property, but through their position as mother's brother may have considerable direct control over the allocation of family resources.

As might be expected, these differences in social organization affect patterns of relations between kinsmen. A young bride, for example, faces few of the terrors that her sisters in patrilineal groups must cope with, but the groom may find himself in a more perilous position. He has little authority in his wife's household and must be content with whatever authority he can exert over the household of his sisters. Though his authority is somewhat attenuated, he is still better off than the man in a patrilineal group who resides with his wife's family. Among patrilineal groups it is common practice for a man without male heirs to "adopt" his daughter's husband, and in many castes sons of poor families can only make a good marriage by consenting to such an arrangement. In fact, in many cases a man is agreeing to a form of "bride service," paying for his wife by working a set number of years for his prospective father-in-law. Needless to say, his position in the household hierarchy is low. He should behave like an obedient son and toil like a servant. Bride service is generally held in low esteem, and men enter into it with understandable reluctance and usually as a last resort.

Polyandry, the marriage of one woman to more than one man, is not widely practiced, occurring only among some castes and tribes in the south, in Nepal, and in the border areas between India and Nepal. Its most frequent form is fraternal polyandry—two brothers married to the same woman. Frequently the reason for polyandry is economic. Brothers feel that they are too poor to afford more than one wife between them. The two brothers share sexual access to their joint wife and regard any children as belonging to both. Although polyandry seems strange in the Indian context, it differs but little from the junior levirate (marriage of a younger brother to his deceased elder brother's wife) or from the sexual rights that younger brothers have to their elder brothers' wives in many castes. Then, too, it is structurally similar to the practice, common in many castes, of the younger brother impregnating his elder brother's wife when his elder brother is impotent or sterile. Finally, the whole tali-tying complex formerly characteristic of the Nayar caste of Malabar was a form of polyandry. The rite signaled the sexual availability of a girl to those who stood in the appropriate relation of cross-cousin. There was no expectation that any of her lovers would become permanent husbands, and in a sense all her cross-cousins simply constituted a pool of "brothers," all with equal sexual rights to the girl consecrated at the tali-tying ceremony.

Secondary marriages of various kinds are permitted in most castes. Polygyny, one man married to more than one woman, has always been the privilege of Kṣatriyas, and is common among those of the wealthier landholding castes. A man was also permitted to take another wife in the event of his first wife's death or if the first wife could give him no male heirs. Polygynous marriages consist of two kinds: those entered into for the sake of offspring, and those undertaken for sexual pleasure. Secondary marriages of the first type are solemnized by a brief ritual totally unlike that which celebrated the first union, but all offspring from the marriage are full heirs. Secondary marriage of the second type is actually a form of concubinage unsolemnized by ritual, and producing no legal heirs. Primary marriages and most polygynous marriages for the sake of offspring take place between parties of approximately equal status, but secondary liaisons almost always entail wide status discrepancies between the man and his concubine. The most frequent form of polygynous marriage when heirs are the object is sororal—marriage of a man to two sisters. There is a general feeling that sisters get along better as co-wives, and unless a man can afford to maintain two separate establishments, this is an important consideration. In general, polygyny of whatever form is the privilege of the wealthy. Not many men can afford the expense of an additional wife.

DIVORCE

Modern Indian law permits divorce in the event of desertion, adultery, barrenness, impotence, sexual perversion, and other contingencies, but these modern laws are not consistent with tradition or village custom. The orthodox position taken by the ancient writers on dharma was that marriages between members of the same caste sanctified by appropriate ritual were indissoluble. The husband could take additional wives if necessary for heirs, but a wife could never take a second husband for any reason. Similarly, a man could divest himself of concubines at any time since they were not full wives and their sons had few if any rights of inheritance. Technically, then, marriages entered into according to dharma were permanent for both husband and wife. This is still the predominating attitude among most Indians. Divorces do occur, most of them for childlessness, but divorce is still regarded as a great evil. On the other hand, villagers, and particularly lower castes, have long recognized and accepted *de facto* divorces. Wives sometimes ran away with other men or husbands deserted their families, and these forms of marriage dissolution, though not condoned, were and are common. In fact, such breaches of marital relations constitute one of the most frequent complaints in caste councils. Significantly though, if the culprits are caught they are punished by their caste fellows, and attempts are made to reconcile the stray with his or her spouse rather than undertake divorce proceedings in the courts. Again, punishment and attempted reconciliation are the standard approaches to adultery. In general, the caste councils prefer to punish their own members and effect a reconciliation between defaulting marriage partners rather than have the caste publicly embarrassed in the law courts.

CHANGE

Much has been written about change in Indian society, and many have logically demonstrated that urban life and an industrial economy are inimical to the old ways. The joint family supposedly cannot persist in cities, and the ties of kinship that bind families and other kin groups must necessarily be weakened under the individuating pressures of a market economy. Education, jobs, and separate income for women make them more independent and impatient with their former submissive roles. Western education frees men of their superstitions and is conducive to freedom of choice in marriage. The gap between educated youth and their parents creates new and invidious tensions within the family. Work in a modern factory or office exploits contractual rather than kinship obligations. The list of "structural" inconsistencies between "traditional" and "modern" society is long and impressive, but there is an inconsistency of another kind here. Those who argue in this vein also cite the perverse persistence of the joint family and the "fetters" of kinship as prime impediments to economic "progress" and social change. In this inconsistency they implicitly recognize the fatuousness of their logical demonstrations. Joint families can adapt to urban life and have for several hundred years; close kin groups do not necessarily decline in a market economy, nor do they cease to be important in the context of factory and office. They have assumed new ways of expressing many of their old functions, and one's most effective psychological and economic buffers against the outside world are still close kin. If one wishes to get ahead in the world, the resources of a kin group are still many times greater than anything that can be mustered by mere individual effort. Perhaps educated men do prefer educated wives, but like their American and European couterparts, they still like them submissive. The educated may make a certain pretense to freedom of choice in marriage, but somehow still manage to marry someone in their own caste. Too, the young may feel that their parents are hopelessly mired in senseless tradition, but this makes them neither independent nor innovative. They are not loath to exploit every "traditional" resource in their search for jobs and status, nor are they particularly eager for changes that might threaten the status of their kin group.

Too often, commentators are guilty of a kind of rigid uniformitarianism. The road leading to a modern industrial society is the only road, and it must everywhere be paved with the debris of ancient kin groups and the shattered remnants of former institutions. Only when men fully emerge from the cocoon of kinship, rending its filaments of mutual obligation, can they effectively engage in the "rational" choices of a market economy. Groups based on kinship must be replaced by free associations of men joining together out of common interest and free choice rather than the irrational accidents of birth and blood relationship. Society and its institutions must come to express patterns of "mutual adjustment" between "competing associations," the "countervailing power" of each contributing to a "balance of powers" or "dynamic equilibrium" guided and sustained not by the "unseen hand of God," but by the all too apparent rod of government bureaucracy. "Individualization," "rationalism," "market economy," "urban-industrial society," "free association," "economic plans," these are the shibboleths of those whose minds have been frozen in an archaic "Newtonian" mold. They are the cognitive categories, the articles of faith of a race of men who believe that men and their cultures may be "explained" and ultimately shaped and formed by "scientific" manipulation—if only the appropriate formulas can be found. How different in substance from the ancient *Brāhmaṇas*, but how similar in form.

EIGHT

THE CASTE SYSTEM

No Indian institution has exercised the imagination of foreign observers as fully and completely as the institution of caste. Nor has any other Indian institution been so grossly misunderstood, misrepresented, and maligned. Even the word "caste," deriving as it does from the Portuguese *casta* (color), is a misnomer connoting some specious notion of color difference as the foundation of the system. It is a curious fact of intellectual history that caste has figured so prominently in Western thought. Pressed into the service of nearly every significant social theory from the seventeenth century to the present, this enduringly indigestible kernel of human custom has cast such a persistent spell over the mind of Western man that we can only conclude that caste must strike some deeply discordant note in the Western mind and that its various interpretations reveal more about the categories and presuppositions of Western thought than they do of the Indian scene. This applies equally, of course, to what follows.

PURITY AND POLLUTION

Castes have been likened to medieval guilds, rigidly stratified classes, ossified endogamous descent groups, and their origins attributed to racial conflict, occupational specialization, concepts of mana and taboo—to cite but a few of the various interpretations. While it is true that castes may frequently be associated with such substantive attributes, what is missing here is that *caste is first and foremost a system of social classification*—a means of placing people into named categories. This fundamental classificatory feature is accurately reflected in the native term *jāti*, denoting roughly what Westerners have called *caste*. Jāti primarily denotes species or kind and consequently refers explicitly to a system of classification. To be a member of a particular jāti is thus equivalent to being a special kind or species of human. But classification to what end and in terms of what? Can it be merely one more instance of the play or sport of the human mind exercising its innate capacity for arbitrarily classifying the things of the world? Ultimately, we must admit that it is, but because the system of jāti is consistent with other features of Indian culture, it must reflect some more fundamental attribute of Indian thought. Similarly, because the act of classifying depends upon comparison and differentiation, there must be some set of criteria to provide the salient features in terms of which one thing can be compared to another. That is, x is different from or the same as *y* in terms of something. To understand the system of classification we must understand the underlying criteria that make classification possible. So, too, when we speak of a classificatory system, we imply that the individual classes derived from comparison and differentiation are in some way organized and related to one another. What, then, is the structure of this organization of different classes, and what is the principle of organization that motivates the structure? The position taken here is that the system of jāti is another expression of that universal Indian mode of thought which not only maintains that there is a relativity of human potentiality, but also insists that differences among humans are attributable to inherent degrees of purity and pollution (see pp. 78–81). Thus it is that responses to the question: "Is x more pure than *y*?" permit derivation of a system of hierarchically ranked categories. These categories reflect relative states of hereditary purity and define an hereditary quasi-occupational position in a system of ritual and economic exchange. To put the matter differently, the jāti system consists of named categories that are hierarchically ordered and the hierarchy constrains social relations. The differentiating criterion underlying both the categorization and the hierarchy is the concept of purity and pollution. Thus one classifies according to purity and pollution, and the classifications are ordered in terms of relative purity. The concept of purity not only provides the means of comparison and differentiation, it also makes it possible to organize these differentiated categories into a total system. Just as the differentiation of classes and their systemic organization derive from the criterion of purity and pollution, so do all those incidental features of caste such as exclusive membership, endogamy, exogamy, hypergamy, and occupational specialization.

It is one thing to grasp the notion of purity and pollution, but quite another to understand its application. What, for example, are the indices of purity, and what is the logic of an hierarchical structure? All of the indices of purity which sum up a position in the jāti hierarchy describe a characteristic mode of approach to that which is impure. Consequently, the jāti hierarchy itself presupposes a prior universal classification of things, deeds, and thoughts in terms of their relative purity and impurity. Contact, either directly or indirectly, with anything impure causes pollution which must be removed by various rites of purification. Habitual contact with the impure without purification condemns one to the lowest possible status, and some things are so polluting that habitual contact with them indicates a perversity of nature that is beyond purification. Similarly, some things are so inherently pure that their purificatory value is immense. Because so many functions of daily life are included in the category of the impure, it is not possible to totally avoid all contact with impurity. But pollution incurred from these sources is impermanent and can be removed by purification. What matters is one's habitual relation to those impure things that are not necessarily associated with normal human functioning and one's habitual mode of dealing with the pollution stemming from those that are. In general, the former should be rigorously avoided and the latter immediately removed by purification.

The unitary concept of purity/pollution consists of an ideology which says that all the things of the universe can be classed into categories of pure and impure and that these categories, including those of the jāti system, can be hierarchically ranked. The indices or attributes of purity/pollution thus compose an open set of conceptually discriminable entities. It is an open set because the ideological rule of purity/pollution is capable of generating a theoretically infinite set of attributes. The limits on what can fall under the universal sweep of this general rule are conceivably identical with the conceptual limits of the human mind itself. There is, then, no simple finite list of the indices of purity and pollution. To attempt to list all the possibly relevant indices of purity/pollution would be as hopelessly misguided as an attempt to list all the possible sentences of the English language. This "generative" character of the ideological rule of purity/pollution has important implications both for the local realizations of the jāti system and its persistence—questions to which we shall return subsequently.

THE LOGIC OF HIERARCHY

As for the logic of this hierarchical system, we must first note that several logical operations will produce an hierarchical structure. A taxonomy, for example, employs logical relations of inclusion and exclusion and produces a structure consisting of a series of levels each of which is included in the level that dominates it. The category "dog," for example, includes "cocker spaniel," and is in turn included in the category "animal." Clearly, the jāti system is not this kind of hierarchy. It is instead a semantic "tree," a logical structure consisting of a set of sequential dichotomous contrasts. For expository purposes let us consider a limited and hypothetical jāti system consisting of only five jātis (A, B, C, D, E), and a purity/pollution concept composed of the following four pure criteria: studying the *Vedas*, teaching the *Vedas*, forbidding widow remarriage, and practicing vegetarianism. Let us assume that members of jāti A practice vegetarianism, forbid widow remarriage, study the *Vedas*, and teach the *Vedas*; jāti B is the same as A except that its members do not teach the *Vedas*; members of jāti C neither teach nor study the *Vedas* but practice vegetarianism and forbid widow remarriage; jāti D is the same as C but its members allow widow remarriage; members of jāti E do not perform any of these pure actions. Consider these characteristic modes of relation to the categories of purity as a set of responses to a series of questions like: "Do members of A teach the *Vedas*? Yes or no." That is, each attribute or criterion of purity has only positive and negative components. The resultant structure will be a semantic tree, the sum of positive attributions constituting an index of hierarchic rank. This set of operations is illustrated in Figure 22. In this diagram the sum of positive attributes for A = 4, B = 3, C = 2, D = 1, E = 0. The order of hierarchic rank then is A, B, C, D, E. It is important to note that the position of each jāti in this hierarchy (with the exception of the bottom and the top) is defined in relation to other jātis. It is not defined by reference to an absolute notion of purity. Instead, a given

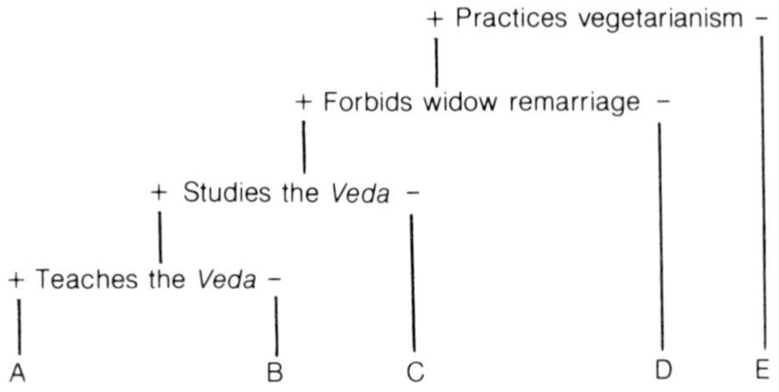

Figure 22. The semantic tree of hierarchic rank. The plus sign (+) indicates "yes"; the minus sign (–) indicates "no."

jāti's purity is relative to the purity of other jātis. It does not make sense to ask if jāti C, for example, is pure or impure. Rather one must ask if jāti C is pure or impure in relation to jātis B and D. The notion of jāti purity is thus relative rather than absolute. In this example jāti C is pure in relation to jāti D, but impure in relation to jāti B.

There are interesting mathematical constraints associated with this type of structure. We have previously noted that certain kinds of scalograms are derived from it (see pp. 82–83), but more important in this context is the fact that each unique discrimination in the bottom row of the diagram requires at least one dichotomous contrast. Furthermore, because the dichotomous contrasts are nonrecursive (that is, cannot occur more than once in the diagram), the number of attributes (given as dichotomous contrasts) will always be one less than the number of uniquely discriminated items in the bottom row. This fact is not interesting in itself, but in the context of potentially large numbers of jātis and criteria it is. No one knows exactly how many jātis there are in India, but let us assume a relatively small number in the neighborhood of 3,000. This would mean that the number of purity/pollution attributes would be 2,999. Given the limited memory capacity of the human mind, it is ridiculous to assume that anyone would have at his fingertips not only the names of 3,000 jātis, but of 2,999 attributes correctly tagged to each jāti. Even when the attributes are recursive as in the case of "Does x take water from *y*?," the absolute number of attributes might conceivably be small, but the very fact of their recursiveness would produce a potentially infinite set of discriminated jātis. In fact, it is primarily because purity/pollution is a recursive function that it must be identified as the underlying motivation of the hierarchy. That is, each individual attribute, whether of marriage practices, the taking of water or food, or the giving of services, is ultimately but part of a response to the question of whether x is more pure than *y*. All of the attributes acquire their legitimacy from their reference to purity/pollution. Purity/pollution is thus the fundamental recursive function.

Here then is the clue to the variability of local jāti hierarchies. Many writers have emphasized the fact that there is no universal, all-India system of jāti hierarchy. Each village or local region has its own often unique configuration of jātis, but this is not inconsistent with the underlying system of hierarchy. It is, in fact, precisely what one would expect. The mistake too often made is to assume that a consistent set of jāti rankings should be present.

What is consistent in the system is not a substantive set of jātis or jāti ranks, nor even a consistent set of ranking criteria, but a purely formal logical principle of ordering. This underlying logical system provides not only the element of universal consistency, but also makes possible an infinite variety of substantive realizations at the local level.

What has been said applies not only to the local rankings, but also to the criteria or indices of ranking. Again, it is a mistake to search for a universal and immutable set of ranking criteria that would be expressed in each local hierarchy. Different collocations of criteria or even totally unique criteria may be used in each village setting or by different jātis, or even by different individuals, but as long as these criteria are indices of purity/pollution and as long as they fit into the pattern of dichotomous contrasts, they are still consistent with the underlying logic of the system. They are, in effect, variable substantive realizations of the same formal principle.

Here, too, is the secret to the persistence of the jāti system. Numerous authors have descried the downfall of the system in changing patterns of occupational specialization, attitudes toward widow remarriage, child marriage, the challenge of Western education to the Brāhmaṇ's position, or to changes in the distribution of wealth and political power. While it is true that there have been substantial changes in all these features, what remains to be demonstrated is that these changes in any way impinge on the underlying logical system of ranking or on the ideology of purity/pollution. So long as these two remain intact, changes in other areas of Indian society are mere epiphenomenal fluctuations. What must be emphasized is the fact that the constituent components of the jāti system can be changed, altered, or rearranged, the number of components can be increased or decreased, or positions of various groups in the hierarchy may be altered, but none of these effect any change in the parameters of the system. Only if the underlying ideology of purity/pollution and the logical structure of hierarchic ranking are changed can we speak of any real change in the jāti system. In fact, the future of the jāti system will probably see some transformation in the ideology of purity/pollution, but the notion of hierarchic ranking will probably simply be allied to some new ideological principle. When this happens, of course, it will no longer be a jāti system.

VARNA AND JĀTI

At this point it is useful to point out that the underlying logic of the jāti system is identical to that of the varṇa system described earlier (see p. 81). The formal properties of the jāti system were already present in the earlier varṇa system. What makes the jāti system different from the varṇa system is the fact that this principle of logical ordering is directly geared to the ideology of purity/pollution in the jāti system, whereas it was not so related in the varṇa system. As we have seen, the jāti system that emerged in medieval India was the result of combining the ideology of purity/pollution with the logical structure of the system of social classes expressed in the varṇa system.

Aside from its formative role in the development of the jāti system, the varṇa system supports the jāti hierarchy in one other respect. Because it presents a simplified picture of any local jāti hierarchy and because it embodies the same logical principles as the jāti hierarchy, the varṇa system provides a simple and convenient model of the jāti system. Moreover, it has sound scriptural authority behind it. In this sense the varṇa system is a kind of mnemonic device providing both a ready-made scheme of classification and a set of indices to which individual jātis may be homologized. It is not so much the case that some particular jāti is in fact a member of the Kṣatriya varṇa, for example, but rather that its traditional mode of approach to the impure can be in some respect equated with that of a purely idealized Kṣatriya varṇa. Here again is a persistent pattern of Indian thought: the microcosm can always be understood in terms of the macrocosm. The microcosm is infinitely variable, fluctuating, impermanent, but it falls into order when seen in the light of the immanent macrocosm. Just so, local jāti hierarchies are impermanent, constantly shifting, changing, but the varṇa system is a fixed point in the "natural" order.

THE "INTERACTIONAL" THEORY

It is sometimes argued that the jāti system should not be understood in terms of the kind of attributional notions outlined above. Instead, jāti rank is to be explained by "interactional" patterns involving such decisions as which jāti will accept food or water from which other jāti, and which jātis perform what kinds of service for other jātis (cf. Marriott, 1959). While it is true that characteristic patterns of giving and receiving food, water, and services will provide a statistical distribution indicative of status rank, it must be emphasized that such a distribution is neither "explanation" nor "understanding." It neither explains why a particular distribution prevails nor enables us to understand why there should be a distribution at all. In other words, the so-called "interactional" theory makes no sense except in terms of an attributional theory. The interaction patterns in fact are mere expressions of the underlying ideology of purity/pollution. In this respect it is interesting to note that the interaction patterns also "scale" hierarchically in exactly the same logical pattern as other kinds of attributes. In fine, the interaction patterns themselves are attributes in exactly the same sense as occupational specialization, widow remarriage, and the like. The interaction patterns are mere artifacts of the rules that underlie them and give them their meaning. Thus, while we may agree that any particular local hierarchy is an emergent phenomenon, that it arises as a more or less consensual structure as the end-product of the relations between jātis, *we must insist on the priority of rules that initially constrain the very relations between jātis which eventually produce a local hierarchy.* That is, the relations between jātis are not anarchic; they are always constrained by previous rules. Even though the substance of some of the rules also emerges or is negotiated in the context of social relations, the notion of rules and, I would add, the underlying form of rules must precede the negotiation, else there is nothing to negotiate. To argue that the form of the rules of hierarchy could only emerge from statistical patterns of negotiation is to fall into the error of creation *ex nihilo.* It is like believing that people regularly negotiate the rules of grammar in the process of speaking before they know how to speak grammatically. Consequently, we may say that patterns of relationship do not determine hierarchy, rather they express it; and if hierarchy were not expressed in social relations, the whole jāti hierarchy would simply be a sterile classification. To employ an Indian metaphor, the jāti hierarchy, like puruṣa, is powerless to act; its concrete realization in the world of affairs is manifested through the prakṛti of social relations. We must now turn to a discussion of how social relations are both constrained by and express the principle of hierarchy.

THE A-PRIORI GROUND OF HIERARCHY

Thus far we have denied the existence of a single all-India jāti hierarchy, demonstrating instead the necessity of looking for what constitutes the grounds of Indian hierarchy. We have argued that hierarchy presupposes three notions: the concept of purity/pollution, a system of logic, and a generalized model of hierarchic arrangement (the varṇa system). We have also emphasized the idea of hierarchy itself as constitutive of the grounds of Indian experience. That is, the Indian lives in a world that presupposes the idea of hierarchy. He not only assumes that human groups can be hierarchically classified, he also believes they should be. Taking our cue from the Jainist logicians who argued that reality is relative to the standpoint of the viewer (p. 59), we will now demonstrate that just as there is no single all-India jāti hierarchy, the same logic forces us to accept that there is no such thing as a single local hierarchy. There are instead many local hierarchies, all arrived at by means of the three principles cited at the beginning of this paragraph.

What should by now be apparent from numerous cognitive studies is the fact that human classification answers to pragmatic concerns. Humans classify more thoroughly those things that interest them, and as their interests or purposes change so do their classifications. In an Indian village are many situational dependencies that entail different hierarchies. First of all, who does the classifying makes a difference. A local hierarchy does not look the same to a Brāhmaṇ and a blacksmith. To a Brāhmaṇ a blacksmith is simply one of a large group of undifferentiated Śūdras, but to a blacksmith the class of Śūdras breaks down into numerous significantly differentiated groups. Conversely, from the blacksmith's point of view all Brāhmaṇs are much alike, but what the blacksmith lumps together, the Brāhmaṇ differentiates. Similarly, the kind of hierarchy that emerges in any setting will be a function of associated activities. For example, the number and kind of classificatory discriminations will not be the same when men of different jātis work together in the fields as they would be when they participate in common festivals, dine, cook, perform religious rites, or answer an anthropologist's questions about ranking.

Villagers live in a world where hierarchy constitutes a fundamental part of routine activities, and they do not (unlike anthropologists) constantly engage in working out the precise dimensions of *the hierarchy* any more than an anthropologist forever engages in determining the probabilities of his body moving to the right or left when he wants it to. Both of these features constitute

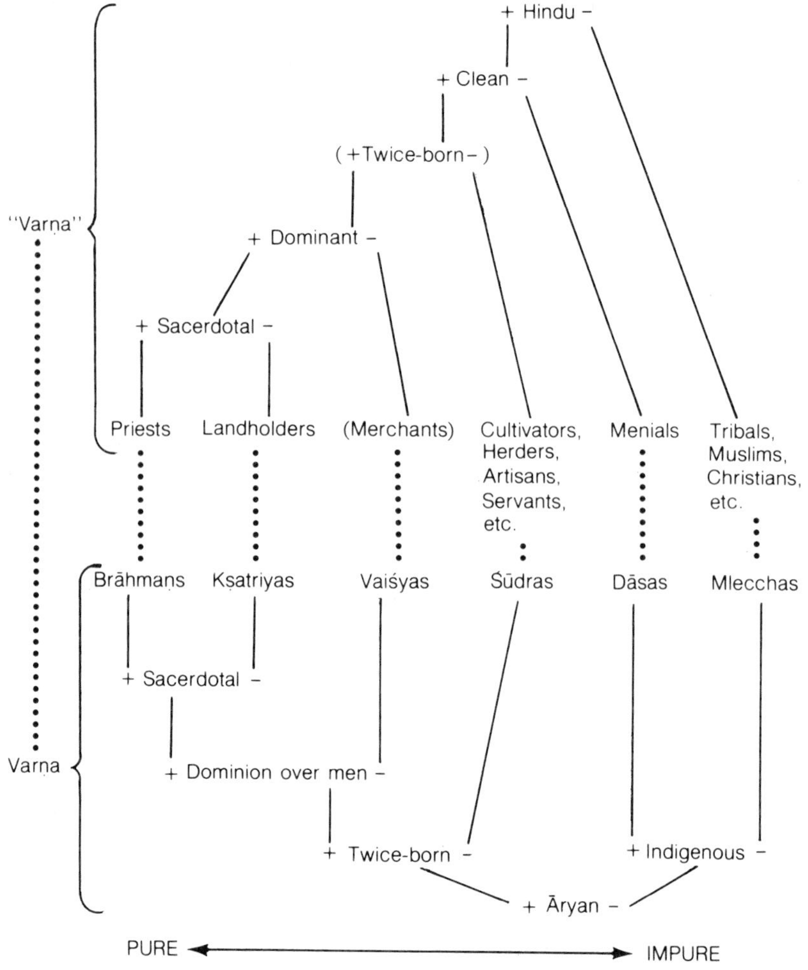

Figure 23. Generalized varṇa homology. Dotted lines represent the relation of homology; parentheses indicate optional distinctive features and categories in a village setting. "Varṇa" (in quotes) represents the local homology, and Varṇa (without quotes) the classical scheme.

a part of what is taken for granted. They are some of the "givens" of human experience. Hierarchy comes to the surface of the Indian's awareness only when there is some necessity for it to. In the absence of prying anthropologists, questions of hierarchic rank arise from uncertainty or potential for conflict. Villagers then initiate a complex series of covert and overt negotiations, and from these negotiations a temporary consensual hierarchy emerges—or the situation degenerates into open conflict.

The character of these negotiations exemplifies the underlying principles of hierarchy. First, the villagers must presuppose the necessity of hierarchy itself. Second, they arrive at a determination of the pertinent purity/pollution attributes. Third, they work out the logical relations of these attributes. Finally, their model for this whole process is a generalized varṇa system homologized with the varṇa system of sacred literature (see pp. 81–85). This model is illustrated in Figure 23. For variations in these homologies, see the discussion in Appendix II. On the use of homologies in anthropology, see Lévi-Strauss (1966).

In the actual jāti classifications founded on this model, the terminal node denoting a "varṇa" category is in theory infinitely expandable as suggested by the node labeled: cultivators, herders, artisans, servants, etc. The same is true for the category formed from an expanded node. Thus, for example, the herder category may be expanded as illustrated in Figure 24.

The hierarchic rank of each of the segments in Figure 24 will usually be under constant negotiation, but will normally be a matter of small concern to anyone other than the herders themselves. This same general picture is true of the entire Śūdra category and accounts for the often-reported hierarchical indeterminancy among members of this category. In fact, the jāti representatives of the same local "varṇa" category will be in competition with one another more than with the jātis of different local "varṇa" categories. The hierarchic constellations that emerge within "varṇa" categories are consequently typified by their impermanent, shifting character. A hierarchy may momentarily emerge from complex negotiation only to be negated by the potential for new alignments in changed circumstances.

There is then no single local jāti hierarchy any more than there is a single all-India hierarchy. There is merely a potential for numerous hierarchical expressions—a kind of hierarchical "becoming." In this view villagers constantly engage in what might be called "constructive metaphysics." Their categories of interpretation, their logical methods, and their general model of the world of social relations are part of a culturally constituted *a priori* method, and though their specific results are constrained by these a-priori factors, they are not determined by them. Indian social groups must be hierarchically ordered in terms of purity and pollution, but the place of any group in the hierarchy is not uniquely and finally determined.

THE EXPLOITATIVE ARGUMENT

Some authors, reversing the relation outlined above, have maintained that the jāti system must be understood as a product of an exploitative organization of political and economic power (Gough, 1959; Rosser, 1966). In this view the jāti system is merely the social expression of differential access to the

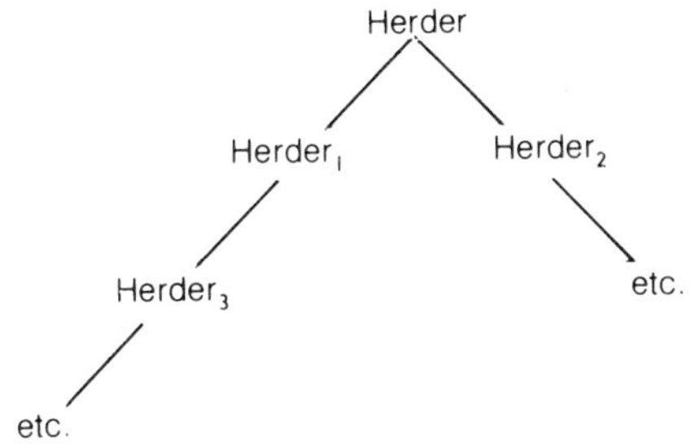

Figure 24. Theoretical expansion of the herder category. (See also pp. 200–201 in Appendix II.)

sources of political and economic power. This notion is attractive from the point of view of rigid materialism, but it founders on the question "Why this particular form of social organization?" That is, differential access to the sources of political and economic power is a fact not only of Indian society, but of practically every other society as well. The question that remains unanswered is "What is there about the political and economic structure of India that not only differs from other societies, but also differs in such a way as to produce a jāti system?" In effect, it is impossible to locate any particularly Indian genius of economic and political organization that could possibly account for a jāti system. In fact, those very things that do make the Indian political and economic system radically different from that of any other society can be traced to the jāti system itself. In other words, it is not a case of the political and economic system producing the jāti system, but rather of the jāti system affecting the structure of political and economic power. Consequently, it is a mistake to think of politics and economy independent of the jāti system.

POWER AND HIERARCHY

Although we cannot accept either the notion that political and economic power determine the form of the jāti system or even that economics and politics can be thought of apart from the jāti system, this still leaves unanswered the question of how the distribution of power relates to the jāti structure. To be more precise, we are interested not only in how power is distributed, but also in what kind of authority or sanction holds the jāti system together. What prevents those who are disadvantaged in the hierarchy from overturning it? It would be the simplest of all possible worlds, of course, if the distribution of political and economic power exactly paralleled the status rankings of the jāti hierarchy—that is, the highest jātis would always be the most powerful. That the distribution of power does not work this way is evident first of all in the very nature of the underlying ideology of the jāti hierarchy. The concept of purity/pollution does not derive from or refer for its justification to economic and political criteria. Its ultimate reference and derivation is always sacerdotal and ritualistic. This is not to say that considerations of relative power are entirely disregarded in the determination of jāti rank—quite the contrary. Aside from the Brāhmaṇ and the untouchable, the status rank of a particular jāti is often a function of its relative power, but the legitimization of its position in the hierarchy is couched in terms of its relative purity. If it were otherwise, the acquisition of power and its consequent exercise would have to be revolutionary. In other words, the acquisition and use of power is not dedicated to the overthrow of hierarchy but rather to the enhancement or protection of one's position in the hierarchy. Note that it is precisely those like the untouchables who are either prevented from acquiring economic power or a level in the hierarchy consonant with their economic position who agitate for an end to the hierarchy based on purity/pollution—but not necessarily for an end to hierarchy (cf. Lynch, 1969). The fundamental fact is that *jockeying for position in the hierarchy and the consequent reshuffling of jāti ranks does reflect the changing distribution of power, but it does not reflect either a change in the system or the determinism of power.*

It must be borne in mind that this struggle for power and attendant enhancement of jāti rank applies only to the middle ranks in the hierarchy, not to the Brāhmaṇ or the untouchable. Both are excluded from the struggle. The Brāhmaṇ's position is independent of the vicissitudes of secular power, and the untouchable is either not permitted to participate in the power quest or his participation is effectively circumscribed. This unalterable position of the Brāhmaṇ and the untouchable is criterial to the persistence of the purity/pollution hierarchy and its subordination of power. So long as these two remain the upper and nether anchors of the hierarchy, their relative positions in the hierarchy unaffected by changes in the distribution of power, just that long will the jāti fluctuations in the middle ranks of the hierarchy be what they have always been—inconsequential realignments of components in a fixed and unchanging structure. The hierarchic position of the Brāhmaṇ and the untouchable remains stable in the face of changing power distributions because the Brāhmaṇ and the untouchable embody the two poles of purity/pollution, and their unalterable positions reflect more clearly than anything else the persistence and primary importance of purity/pollution to the whole jāti system. Should the hierarchic position of these two become subject to the secular vagaries of power, it would be a sure indication that the force motivating hierarchic ranking was no longer purity/pollution, and it would signal the demise of the jāti system. Thus, although the distribution of power does not correspond to the distribution of status rank in the jāti hierarchy, the distribution of and the quest for power are both constrained by and reenforcing to the jāti hierarchy. Paradoxically, the quest for political and economic power itself provides the sanctions and legitimate force that hold together a sacerdotal hierarchy. And it does so because it willingly acquiesces in and operates within the ideological constraints of the sacerdotal hierarchy.

THE JAJMĀNĪ SYSTEM

This rather depressing picture of unremitting competition for power and status is thankfully somewhat misleading, for it emphasizes conflict at the expense of cooperation. Conflict there certainly is (cf. Beals and Siegel, 1966), but its complement, cooperation, has always been present in both the theoretical and actual economic interdependence of jātis. Traditional accounts of the varṇa system emphasized the functional interdependence of classes. Hereditary occupational specialties associated with each varṇa come to be interpreted as overt symbols of the functional interdependence of varṇas. Each class performed essential services for the other, and each contributed to the moral order of society by proper performance of its hereditary occupational specialty. This theoretical exposition of interdependence achieved concrete expression in a system of reciprocal economic exchange. Widely known as the jajmānī system, this method of economic exchange is postulated on the notion of reciprocal exchange of goods and services among hereditary occupational groups (jātis). Theoretically, the division of labor corresponds to jāti categories

Division of Labor		Jāti Category									
		Brāhmaṇ	Kāpu	Golla	Kummari	Kammari	Vaḍla	Sākali	Mangali	Māla	Mādiga
	Priest	+									
	Landholder		+								
	Herder			+							
	Potter				+						
	Blacksmith					+					
	Carpenter						+				
	Washerman							+			
	Barber								+		
	Laborer									+	
	Servant										+

Figure 25. Jāti categories and the division of labor. The plus sign (+) indicates the appropriate traditional occupation associated with each jāti; the Brāhmaṇ is a priest, the Kāpu a farmer, and so on. The jāti names used are widespread in Āndhra Pradesh—different names for these specialties occur in other regions.

and each jāti is associated with a traditional hereditary occupation. This theoretical correspondence between jāti categories and the division of labor is illustrated in Figure 25.

Payment for services should be made either in the form of other services or in traditional noncontractual payments of grain. The Brāhmaṇ, for example, should perform rituals for other jātis and receive payment from them in other services or in a fixed amount of grain. Similarly, the blacksmith should make implements for the landholder and receive a share of the landholder's grain at harvest time. Ideally, then, each jāti should have a traditional occupation, the performance of which entitles it to services from other jātis or to a share in the village produce. The occupational specialty of each jāti thus contributes to the interdependence of jātis and the cohesiveness of the whole group. The pattern of reciprocities understood in this interpretation is indicated in Figure 26. Thus jāti A performs services for (or gives goods to) B and C; B and C perform services for A; B performs services for C; C performs services for

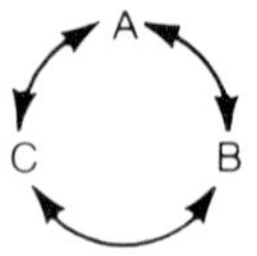

Figure 26. Hypothetical jajmānī reciprocities.

B. The pattern of relations is symmetrical, transitive, and connected. The reciprocities are direct and presumed to be equal.

Although this idealized picture of the jājmanī system makes clear the means by which the economic factors of production and distribution could be made subservient to the jāti system, it omits or oversimplifies several crucial points. In the first place, there is nothing here that corresponds to hierarchy. The implicit notion is that this is a system of symmetrical exchange. Each jāti plays, in turn and in equal proportion, the role of giver and receiver of goods or services. Such a symmetrical system of reciprocity is inconsistent with the asymmetry of hierarchy, and would imply that the economic system is, at least in part, unconstrained by hierarchy. Second, inasmuch as it implies an equal redistribution of goods among cooperating groups, it is inconsistent both with the accumulation of wealth and its unequal distribution. Third, it seems to entail the notion that each group has equal access to the sources of economic power and is thus inconsonant with the struggle for power. Finally, it assumes a substantive rigidity in jāti occupational specialization.

We must initially recognize that the jajmānī system encodes a distinction between two relations, namely: "gives services to" and "gives goods to." The distribution of these two relations over the set of jātis is given in Figure 27.

"Gives services to"	"Gives goods to"
Brāhmaṇ	Landholder
Artisan	
Untouchable	

Figure 27. Distribution of relations "gives services to" and "gives goods to."

Thus while the Brāhmaṇ, artisan, and untouchable jātis "give services to" other jātis, only the landholder "gives goods to" other jātis. Next, we must note that the hierarchical principle manifests itself again in the asymmetric distribution of services. Not all jātis perform services directly for all other jātis. Consider the following case. There are four jātis: A, B, C, D. Priestly jāti A performs services for artisan jāti B and landholding jāti D. Jāti B performs services for jāti A and jāti D. Jāti C, an untouchable jāti, performs services for jātis A and D, but not for B. Neither A nor B performs services for C, and D performs services for none of the others. The pattern of reciprocity resulting from this distribution of the relation "gives services to" is illustrated in Figure 28. Here the relation "gives services to" is obviously asymmetric except between A and B. Further, the relation is not fully transitive in the whole set

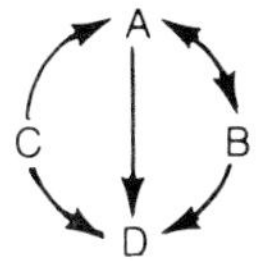

Figure 28. Distribution of the relation "gives services to."

because D does not give services. This is, in fact, the pattern for the relation "gives services to" in the jajmānī system. The pattern is basically asymmetric, and it should be noted that this asymmetry is consistent with the principle of hierarchy and the concept of purity/pollution, whereas the pattern of symmetry in Figure 26 is not.

Given this pattern of reciprocity, can we still speak of the mutual interdependence of jātis? Because the jātis are still logically though asymmetrically connected by the relation "gives services to," they are still interdependent but they are not directly or symmetrically connected. Yet it is possible to salvage the notion of direct and symmetric interdependence if we speak of something other than the jātis themselves—something to which the jātis and relations between jātis comprise a part-whole relationship. In more concrete terms we must think of the Brāhmaṇ's performance of ritual as somehow beneficial to the untouchable even though it is not performed explicitly for him. And this relationship is reciprocated by the untouchable not only in the menial tasks he performs for the Brāhmaṇ, but more importantly in his own ritual performances dedicated to the propitiation of unclean demons and spirits. Here, too, the untouchabe does not perform the ritual for the Brāhmaṇ, but the Brāhmaṇ benefits from it anyway. In both cases the ritual performance benefits the whole group whether it is performed explicitly for each of its constituents or not. I think we must admit the rightness of Hocart's (1950) contention that the jāti categories and the jajmānī system have reference to a ritual system. Underlying both is a conception of society as a ritual order. Each jāti's traditional occupation is consequently transformed from a mere division of labor to a position in a ritual. Performance of its traditional task contributes to the whole ritual and consequently benefits the whole society. This still does not account for the fact that the landholder does not enter into the system as a giver of services, but this hiatus in the system is only apparent, for the landholder is the one for whom services are performed. His position as receiver of services is thus pivotal to the whole system. Here we must recognize the homologies between the performance of service in general and the performance of ritual service, between the landholder and the king, between occupational specialists and ritual specialists, between village and kingdom, and between the king's traditional role of "giving protection to" and the landholder's role of "giving goods to," and finally between the Brāhmaṇ and the deity. This suggests the pattern of homologies represented in Figure 29. In this respect it should be remembered that the word *jajmānī* is derived from the Sanskrit root *yaj-* (to sacrifice) and first referred to a ritual context. Its original denotation was "the one for whom a sacrifice is performed," and its extension of usage to denote the person for whom services are performed (jajmān) clearly indicates a homology between ritual service and the giving of service in general. Similarly, the use of royal titles in addressing the landholder reflects the homology between the landholder and the king.

Thus, one way to salvage symmetric interdependence is to think of it in ritual rather than economic terms. On the whole I think this is the correct view and, I would submit, the one that has motivated Indian conceptions of social order from the days of Mohenjo-daro to the present. There is, howev-

Microcosm		Macrocosm
Jajmānī	:	State ritual
Giving service	:	Ritual performance
Landholder	:	King
Brāhmaṇ	:	Deity
Occupational specialists	:	Ritual specialists
Village	:	Kingdom
Giving goods	:	Giving protection

Figure 29. *Homologies between ritual categories in the jajmānī system and the system of state ritual.*

er, another conception of interdependence which opposes this. Instead of transforming economic relations into ritual relations, it transforms the latter into the former. In this view one focuses on the relation "gives goods to" and assesses the Brāhmaṇ as a giver of goods rather than a giver of ritual service. As a giver of goods it becomes possible to say that the Brāhmaṇ and the untouchable enter into a direct reciprocal exchange. The untouchable gives service to the Brāhmaṇ and the Brāhmaṇ gives goods to the untouchable. In order for this transformation to work it is necessary to relax the rigidity of occupational specialization and allow the Brāhmaṇ to engage in activities other than priesthood. In short, he must become a landholder who has traditional goods (grain) to distribute to those who perform services for him. Here it is important to recognize the central position of the landholder as the preeminent giver of goods in the jajmānī system. In a sense all the other economic specialists are defined in relation to the grain heap produced by the landholder. It is, after all, the produce of the land that supports all of them. Thus, if we postulate a set of jātis A, B, C, D where A is a priestly jāti, B an artisan jāti, C an untouchable jāti, and D a class of landholding jātis, the relation "gives goods to" is asymmetric and intransitive in this set—as illustrated in Figure 30. In this interpretation each specialist has a right to a share of the produce by virtue of his economic specialty. All the jātis thus depend on the landholder, and each landholder is a petty king who has at his disposal a retinue of servants compensated primarily in grain at harvest time. Here again, Hocart's (1950) description of the system as a degradation of the royal style is apt. In fact, the individual landholder is the last in a series of increasingly inclusive homologies. Just as the king's court is a homology of cosmic

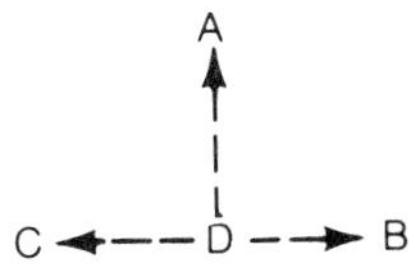

Figure 30. *Distribution of the relation "gives goods to."*

order, the individual landholder's role in the jajmānī system is a homology of the king's role; and at various times in Indian history local chiefs and holders of grants to land or rights to revenue have been interposed between the individual landholder and the king, but each was simply a homology of the king's role. At this point we see the difficulty in interpreting the relation between the jajmānī system and the jāti system as an economic rather than a ritual one. It requires us to ascribe a role to the Brāhmaṇ which has traditionally been reserved to the king or to those who govern. In effect it makes necessary an interpretation of the Brāhmaṇ's position in the jāti hierarchy as one based on economic power, and this we have seen (pp. 155–157) is incorrect. This is not to deny that Brāhmaṇs are not sometimes landholders, but it does deny that the Brāhmaṇ's position can be properly understood if it is thought to be based on the landholding function. Consequently, it is improper to attribute the interdependence of jātis to their economic role.

The centrality of the landholder's position clearly illustrates the economic dominance of the landholding jātis and the dependence of all the other jātis. The locus of power in the jajmānī system is predicatable from the distribution of the relation "gives goods to," but does this imply that the interdependence of the system can be traced entirely to the relation "gives goods to"? The answer is no, because this relation does not constitute an ordering of the set of jāti occupational categories. Formally, it does not constitute an ordering because the logical relation "gives goods to" is not transitive in the set of jāti categories. That is, D gives goods to A, but since A gives no goods to anyone, the relation is not transitive. For the set of jāti occupational categories to be ordered it is necessary that the relations between jātis be transitive. What is it then that provides the ordering?

To get a complete view of the jajmānī system and its role in fostering interdependence, it is necessary at this point to introduce further distinctions. Having established the pivotal position of the landholder, it is evident that the relations "gives goods to" and "gives services to" are unevenly distributed among jāti categories. That is, all jātis do not give both goods and services to all other jātis, nor do they receive both goods and services from all other jātis. In part, this is determined by the nature of the occupational specialty. Some occupational specialties, like the laundryman, do not have goods to give; others, like the farmer, do not have services to give. Here we can speak of a "natural" constraint on the relations of giving goods and services, but more important are the purely cultural constraints on these relations. There is, for example, no "natural" constraint against the Brāhmaṇ's giving services to the untouchable. In this respect, it is important to note that the Brāhmaṇ is not the only jāti to refuse services to the untouchable. The clean artisan jātis and the untouchables similarly refuse to reciprocate goods and services. In respect of their occupational specialties, then, we should recognize a category of jāti specialists who have only services to give and no goods; another category that has goods but no services. These "natural" restrictions must then be plotted against the cultural constraints that interdict the giving of goods and services even when they are potentially available. We should then conceptually distinguish among those who give only services: a category of jātis engaged in priestly activities (A), a category of clean artisan jātis (B), and finally a category of untouchable jātis (C). Next, we should recognize a category of jātis having only goods to give. This category should be designated primarily as a group of landholding jātis (D). Simultaneously mapping the distribution of the relations "gives services to" and "gives goods to" onto these jāti categories produces Figure 31.

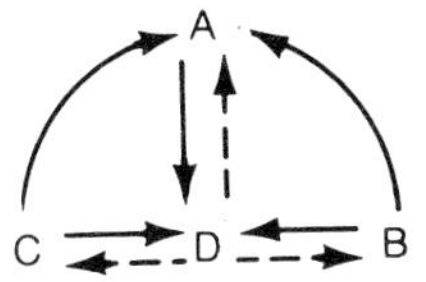

Figure 31. Mapping of relations "gives goods to" and "gives services to." Solid arrow indicates "services"; broken arrow indicates "goods."

In this diagram the pivotal position of the landholder is clear. Only the landholding jātis engage in reciprocal relations with all other jātis. But it is apparent that the nature of this reciprocity requires a complementarity in the relations "gives goods to" and "gives services to." That is, only the landholding jātis give goods and receive services. All other jātis, where they are related, rely exclusively on the reciprocity of the same relation—that is, jāti A both gives and receives services from B. The essential character of jāti interdependence, then, derives from the combination of the relations "gives services to" and "gives goods to," and cannot be attributed to one apart from the other. They are necessarily complementary. The relation "gives services to" provides the requisite transitivity that permits the system to be ordered, and the relation "gives goods to" is the means by which the landholder is incorporated into the system. That is, by combining these two relations we derive a single relation "gives to," which logically connects each jāti to the other. It will be remembered that the relation "gives services to" was not reciprocally connected because landholders gave services to no one. The set of jātis is connected by the relation "gives to," and it is this relation that defines its boundaries. That is, the local scope of the jajmānī system is defined by the domain of the relation "gives to." But the resulting pattern of relations is not entirely symmetrical. C gives to A, but A does not give to C, and B does not give to C nor does C give to B. By contrast, the relation "gives to" is symmetrical between A, B, and D. Thus, just as we recognized a distinction between givers of goods and givers of service (see p. 159), we must also accept a similar distinction in the complement of these relations—that is, between receivers of goods and receivers of service. The distribution of these two relations is given in Figure 32. Only the Brāhmaṇ and the artisan jātis both "receive services from" and "receive goods from." The landholder receives only services, and the untouchable only goods. These two relations then segregate out the untouchable on the one hand and the landholder on the other. As for the untouchable, this distribution parallels the asymmetry of the relation "gives to."

Now it should be noted that this distribution of symmetry and asymmetry in the relations "gives to" and "receives from" corresponds to the varṇa division between the twice-born and the Śūdras. Similarly, if we consider jāti

"Receives services from"	"Receives goods from"
(A) Brāhmaṇ	(A) Brāhmaṇ
(D) Landholder	(B) Artisan
(B) Artisan	(C) Untouchable

Figure 32. Distribution of the relations "receives services from" and "receives goods from."

A homologous with the Brāhmaṇ varṇa, jāti D homologous with the Kṣatriya, jāti B homologous with the Vaiśya, and jāti C with the Śūdra, other significant correspondences emerge. A, B, and D are segregated from C by the symmetry of the relation "gives to," A and D are segregated from B by the fact that only A and D "receive from" all others, and finally A is segregated from D by the fact that A "receives goods" and D does not. To put it differently, both A and D receive services from all others, but A receives both goods and services from all others and D does not. The distribution of these relations exactly replicates the hierarchy of the varṇa system as illustrated in Figure 33 (cf. Figure 9). Here again the logical pattern of hierarchy prevails. Defined by the asymmetry, transitivity, and connectedness of the relations "gives to/receives from," it is the same logical pattern that occurs in the varṇa/jāti hierarchy, and it segregates out the varṇa/jāti categories in exactly the same order of rank as the varṇa/jāti hierarchy. In sum, the domain of the relations "gives to/receives from" defines participation in the jajmānī system, and the pattern of constraints on the occurrence of these relations among participants provides its structure. And finally, the source of these constraints lies outside the system, not within it. That is, the pattern of constraints derives from the hierarchy of the varṇa system. The hierarchic pattern does not emerge from the relations between participants, but is expressed in the pattern of relations.

The character of the relations in Figure 33 reveals that the underlying assumption of the jajmānī system is the giving and receiving of "gifts." The inclusion of groups is defined by their participation in a system of exchange, the Brāhmaṇ standing at the apex of the system as the chief recipient of "gifts." We can thus understand why the ancient law books placed such an

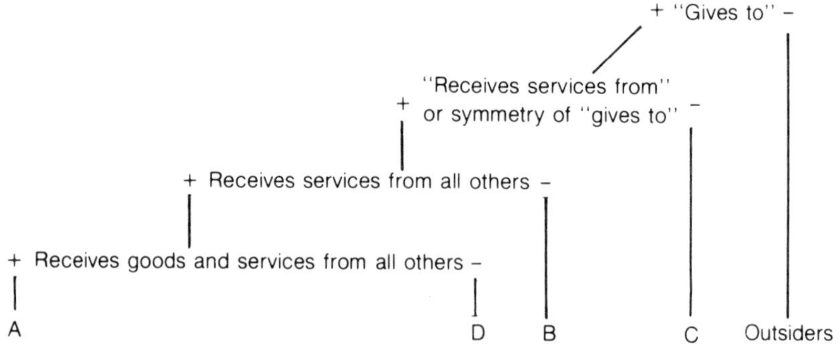

Figure 33. The hierarchy of the relations "gives to" and "receives from."

emphasis on the act of giving gifts to Brāhmaṇs and why the best of any kind of gift was a "Brāhmaṇ gift." Here, too (see p. 160), we see the precise nature of the homology between Brāhmaṇs and deities—a homology that all the traditional sources insist upon. The Brāhmaṇ is a god, and his position as the primary receiver of gifts exactly parallels that of the gods in the ritual. Because the relation "gives to" defines the boundaries of the jajmānī system, we must also recognize that the jajmānī system is itself simply a structure for the giving of gifts. Thus we are in a position to understand why it is inappropriate to think of the jajmānī system as an economic system. That it has economic implications is undeniable, but economic relations neither motivate nor structure the system. Instead, the motivations of ritual and hierarchy structure the economic aspects of the system.

Because the position of the landholder is uniquely defined by the relations "gives goods to" and "receives services from," the homology between the king and the landholder is apparent. Both have effective command over services by virtue of their unrestricted access to the primary sources of goods—the produce of the land. Just as the king was the supreme landholder in the kingdom, the landholder is the preeminent landholder in the village; and just as the king exercised the power of ultimate jurisdiction over the jātis in his kingdom, the landholder enjoys a similar power over his village realm—his local power tempered only by the superordinate power of the king. Finally, just as the principal royal function was to maintain social order, in particular the order of castes, the landholder is arbiter of village disputes. Here his ultimate authority is constrained only by jāti councils, the village council (panchāyat), and, of course, the king's authority.

Although each jāti traditionally has a council which adjudicates intra-jāti disputes and punishes infractions of jāti rules, both inter-jāti and irreconcilable intra-jāti disputes are referred to the landholder or, in extreme cases, to the central authority. Local sentiment still favors remission of disputes to the landholder despite the importance of modern courts of law. Here the villager expresses his preference for the traditional mode of Indian adjudication which is particularistic and based on arbitration and reconciliation rather than punishment through rigid enforcement of impersonal legal codes or the purely secular workings of a universalistic abstract justice.

The traditional village council of elders supposedly consisting of five members representing different jātis is largely a democratic myth. None of the traditional sources precisely describes the mechanism for selecting council members beyond specifying that they should be "important men." In all likelihood, the council did not represent different jātis, but represented instead those who had economic wealth and prestige—in short, the landholders. The elected and theoretically representative village council is a creation as modern as it is ineffective. Numerous observers have reported that the modern village council is powerless and ineffective because it does not accurately reflect existing power relationships. Villagers bypass the village council and persist in taking their disputes to the landholders. We may add that they persist in this not out of perversity or irrationality, but because they realistically appreciate the realities of village power and the pervasiveness of hierarchy.

Since the ubiquitous notion of hierarchy structures the rank of social groups and their "economic" and "political" relations, it should not be surprising to find that it similarly structures other kinds of relations among groups. Here we will only mention briefly the giving of food and water (commensality) and the giving of women (connubiality). Hierarchy constrains the rules of commensality and connubiality.

Food and Water

The rules governing the giving and receiving of water and food are affected by such contextual constraints as the kind of food or water and the social occasion on which food or water are given and received. Food, for example, is classified as kachchā (ordinary) or pakkā (pure), and the latter has fewer constraints than the former (see p. 79). Similarly, purely ritual occasions or those involving ascetics have fewer constraints on the giving and receiving of food and water than do ordinary occasions and personnel. Although the pattern of constraints entailed by these contextual features is complex, it is possible to perceive a basic or underlying form. In general the relations "gives food and water to" and "accepts food and water from" are reflexive, transitive, asymmetric, and connected in the set of jātis. The generalized distribution of these relations over the set of jātis is given in Figure 34. Thus the Brāhmaṇ gives food and water to all the other jātis, but accepts food and water only from his own jāti. The untouchable accepts food and water from all other jātis, but gives to no others (that is, they do not accept from him). Here the hierarchical pattern is clear: the giving and accepting of food and water is constrained by jāti rank.

Women

It is generally held that castes (jātis) are endogamous. One must marry a person who is a member of one's own jāti. Yet, if the giving of women were to follow the pattern of other gifts, jāti endogamy would be inconsistent because it would not fit into a pattern of asymmetric exchanges between jātis. The rela-

"Accepts food and water from" \ "Gives food and water to"	Brāhmaṇ	Landholder	Artisan	Untouchable
Brāhmaṇ	+	+	+	+
Landholder		+	+	+
Artisan			+	+
Untouchable				+

Figure 34. Distribution of the relations "gives/accepts food and water to/from."

	Brāhmaṇ	Landholder	Artisan	Untouchable
Brāhmaṇ	+	+	+	+
Landholder		+	+	+
Artisan			+	+
Untouchable				+

Figure 35. Distribution of the relation "has access to women of."

tion "gives women to" thus would not have the logical property of connectedness, and the giving of women would not serve to interrelate jātis. Unlike the exchange of goods and services, the exchange of women would be restricted to members of the same jāti. This state of affairs is generally the case, but there are numerous exceptions to jāti endogamy which must be taken into account. Here we must distinguish between primary marriages and secondary marriages (cf. Dumont, 1970a, 111) or between rights to sexual relations for the sake of progeny and rights to sexual relations simply for sexual gratification. Similarly, we must distinguish marriage between jātis of approximately the same rank from marriage between jātis of widely separated ranks.

Primary marriages are almost universally between partners of equivalent rank or who are members of the same jāti, but secondary marriages typically involve partners of unequal rank. In every case the man is higher than the woman and this reflects a widespread hierarchic distinction. Men are universally higher status than women. Similarly, the old are higher status than the young. Consequently, a primary marriage is always between a man who is older than his bride, and a secondary marriage is always between a man who is higher status than his sexual partner. If we consider the giving of women in secondary marriages in terms of who has access to women as sexual objects, we can derive a theoretical hierarchic pattern of relations between jātis (Figure 35). The Brāhmaṇ has access to the women of every other category, and in general the women of every jāti lower than one's own are available as more-or-less permanent sexual partners, but those of jātis higher than one's own are not.

This same pattern is present even in primary marriages between members of the same jāti or of equally ranked jātis. The exogamous lineages or clans that compose a single jāti, or groupings of lineages and clans within the same jāti, are also often hierarchically ranked, repeating the pattern of hierarchic ranking obtaining between jātis. In these cases a man's wife comes from a lineage lower than his own. Hypergamy (marrying upward) is thus often a characteristic of primary marriages between members of the same jāti. If jāti A consists of ranked jātis A_1, A_2, A_3, A_4, the pattern of giving women in primary marriage appears as shown in Figure 36. Men of A_1 can marry women of A_1, A_2, A_3, A_4, but men of A_2 cannot marry women of A_1, and so on.

	A_1	A_2	A_3	A_4
A_1	+	+	+	+
A_2		+	+	+
A_3			+	+
A_4				+

Figure 36. Distribution of the relation "marries women of."

Except for the character of the groups involved, this is the same hierarchic pattern of marriage as that revealed in Figure 35. Assuming a constant and equal sex ratio, this is an interesting pattern because if such exchanges were statistically general they would entail an overaccumulation of women in the higher jātis or lineages and a scarcity of women in the lower jātis and lineages. Excess women in the higher ranks would have to be accommodated through polygyny or doomed to female infanticide or a lifelong maidenhood. Some men in the lower ranks would have to engage in polyandry or lifelong abstinence. Although Indians at various times and places have systematically expolited all of these techniques, it is difficult to say that they did so out of an awareness of the structural complexities of hierarchic marriage. Nonetheless, it is a fact that the principle of hierarchy, though undeniably and expectably present in marriage relations, is subordinated to the rule of endogamy in primary marriages. It is only in secondary marriages that the hierarchic principle is fully realized.

ASYMMETRY AND CHANGE

Having traced the implications of purity/pollution and hierarchic ordering from the ranking of social groups through the various relations between social groups, it is necessary now to emphasize the importance of the logical relation of asymmetry which we have seen most often expresses the character of hierarchic relations. It is apparent that the relations between those of equal rank in whatever context should be symmetrical, and that relations between those of unequal rank should be asymmetrical. Consequently, the first indication of segmentation in the formation of new jātis (subcastes) or of a change in a jāti's hierarchic position is the expungement of a previously symmetric relation between those who were formerly equal, and an attempt to similarly obliterate an asymmetric relation with superiors. For example, a group of lineages within a jāti may begin to assert their independence from other lineages in the jāti by refusing to give women to them. Because a jāti's position in the hierarchy is expressed by its particular pattern of asymmetric relations with other jātis, any change in jāti rank involves a change in the pattern of those relations. To move up in rank requires abrogation of former patterns of asymmetry and formation of new ones.

Such changes in rank require more than a change in patterns of asymmetric relations; they also require, as an absolute minimum, the ability to make the change stick. In order to enforce its new position in the hierarchy, a jāti must have both religious and secular authority. Its religious authority derives from a form of status emulation known as Sanskritization (cf. Srinivas, 1956). In this process a low caste arrogates to itself elements of the manners and way of life of the Brāhmaṇ or local dominant landholding jāti. By emulating the mode of life of purer jātis, an ambitious jāti declares to the world that its own mode of approach to purity/pollution corresponds to that of the higher, purer jātis and therefore justifies its enhanced position in the hierarchy. But acquisition of the appropriate attributes of purity would remain an empty gesture if a jāti lacked the economic resources to free itself from its former asymmetrical economic obligations. Thus both economic and religious authority are necessary to a jāti's successful change of status.

Here it must be noted that this whole discussion of relations has been postulated on their occurrence in a restricted context. We have assumed a context consisting of people living in villages and participating in a peasant economy in which rights to land constitute the major source of wealth. What are the implications for jāti relations when these contextual features are changed? What happens in an urban setting or in a market economy where goods and services are bought and sold for a contracted price, and land is no longer the principal source of wealth? In short, what are the effects of the whole panoply of features associated with Westernization or moderization?

It is popularly assumed that the Westernization of Indian society initiated by the British and subsequent programs of modernization set in motion by the Indian government not only have abolished caste, but also have created a social and economic context antithetical to the old patterns of asymmetry. In this view Indian social life has undergone or is undergoing an enormous transformation which involves something far more serious than the age-old circulation of jātis within a fixed and unalterable hierarchic structure. Such notions have even prompted some Western-educated Indians to assert that "caste is dead"—outlawed in fact by the Indian constitution. Preliminary to a discussion of the effects of change we may note that caste indeed is dead, except in those academic discussions where it was born and lived most robustly, but jātis are very much alive and well not only in their original village and peasant setting but equally in the modern milieu.

Much of the popular assessment of change in Indian society foresees the emergence of an egalitarian, individualistic society in which interpersonal relations are rationally constrained by a purely secular ("Western"), socialistic, industrial economy, and Westerners and Indians alike excoriate the existing state of affairs for its retention of "irrational" characteristics (cf. Myrdal, 1968). Motivating this assessment is the naive assumption that the forces of Westernization will not only overthrow the bad old asymmetric pattern of relations, but will replace it with good, healthy symmetric ones. In short, it forecasts a transformation from asymmetry to symmetry, as if the symmetry that formerly animated only intra-jāti relations had burst its bounds and engulfed the whole society. It is apparent, both from the indignant fulminations of those who are intellectually frustrated by the "irrationality" of Indian society and from the facts, that nothing of the sort has occurred or is apt to.

Despite all the changes wrought by modernization, hierarchy and asymmetry persist. It is true that rules regarding pollution have been relaxed. The interdependence of village jātis has been partially supplanted by a market economy, primary marriages occur between persons of unequally ranked jātis, the authority of the Brāhmaṇ has been challenged by anti-Brāhmaṇ movements, untouchables may enter temples or get an education and have frequently refused to perform their traditional polluting tasks, and jātis have entered the state and national political arena as vociferous pressure groups. Except for the last, there is nothing new in all this, nor is there anything in this list that is solely attributable to the processes of Westernization. Rules regarding pollution have always been a matter for negotiation and variable interpretation, the jajmānī system has probably always coexisted with a market economy, some primary marriages have always occurred between persons of inequivalent rank, the authority of the Brāhmaṇ has been challenged by anti-Brāhmaṇ movements at least since the fifth century B.C. advent of Buddhism, and untouchables have frequently abandoned their masters and acquired kingdoms or fame. Even political pressure groups organized on jāti lines were not totally unknown in the past. Jātis frequently petitioned kings to recognize and enforce their new status in the hierarchy. Those who so presciently perceive harbingers of total change in these insignificant epiphenomenal fluctuations confuse substance with form, the expression of a relation with the form of the relation. What is there in all these manifestations that constitutes a real threat to asymmetry, to hierarchy, or to the ideology of purity/pollution? It is useless or worse to persist in cataloging substantive transformations in the expressions of these underlying themes unless it can be demonstrated that some item in the catalog cannot be incorporated as yet another manifestation of the same thing in new form. Here it is important to note that even the most determined legislative attacks on asymmetry, hierarchy, and purity/pollution often merely serve to express and intensify these themes. Legislation reserving positions in the universities or bureaucracy to untouchables or "scheduled castes," for example, does not threaten hierarchy, it exploits it. Even if the ideology of purity/pollution were to disappear, we must ask what would be the effect of its disappearance on asymmetry and hierarchy? It is doubtful that they would be much affected. After all, asymmetry and hierarchy are not unknown in societies that do not enshrine an ideology of purity/pollution. Even the angels in heaven constitute a hierarchy. Seraphim, cherubim, thrones, dominations, virtues, powers, principalities, archangels, and angels (in descending order) are ranked according to divine perfection, not purity/pollution. What right have we to expect any better from mere human societies?

APPENDIX

I LANGUAGE FAMILIES

Languages are grouped into families on the basis of similarities in phonology, syntax, and semantics. The major principle in assigning individual languages to families is lexical comparison. Vocabularies of different languages are compared and those that have a significant proportion of words with similar phonological shape and meaning are assigned to the same family. The following example illustrates this technique:

Telugu	Tamil
anna (elder brother)	*aṇṇan*
tala (head)	*talai*
mūḍu (three)	*muṉṟu*

Although there are only three items in this list, the similarities between Telugu and Tamil are evident. Within any family some languages are more closely related than others. Closeness of relationship is assessed by the number of similarities and shared innovations. These differences in closeness of relationship create subgroups within a family. Once the subgroups are known, it is usually possible to construct a purely hypothetical proto-language—that is, a more ancient form of the language from which each subgroup is descended. The construction of proto-languages is a highly technical process involving the invention of consistent rules which account for the phonological differences occurring in each daughter language. Thus, in the series Telugu mūḍu, Kui mūnji, and Koya mūṇḍu (all meaning "three"), we postulate the cluster *-ṉṟ- as the most ancient form (proto-forms are indicated by *), and establish a rule which says that *-ṉṟ- will be realized as -ḍ- in Telugu, -nj- in Kui, and -ṇḍ- in Koya. If the rule expresses a genuine tendency in the languages, then a significant number of the instances of -ḍ- in Telugu, -nj- in Kui, and -ṇḍ- in Koya should be derivable from *-ṉṟ-. The relationships of daughter languages to proto-languages derived from these techniques of comparison and historical reconstruction are often represented in branching diagrams (stemma) rather like a tree or genealogical diagram.

The Indo-European languages of India belong to the Indo-Iranian branch of Indo-European. This branch consists of two subgroups: Indo-Aryan and Proto-Iranian. The Indo-Aryan group consists of an inner branch and an outer branch, with the latter divided into eastern, western, and southern branches. The inner branch consists of the following languages: Hindī, Urdu, Gujarātī, Rājasthāni, Eastern Panjābī, and Pahāṛī. Sinhalese, spoken in Ceylon, is frequently assigned to this branch, and some authors place Eastern Hindī in a category intermediate between the inner and outer branches. The eastern outer branch consists of: Oriya (Oḍiā), Bengāli (Bāṅglā), Assamese (Asamīyā), and Bihāri. The southern outer branch consists of Marāthi. The western outer branch consists of Western Panjābī and Sindhi.

The Proto-Iranian branch is divided into Dardic and Iranian subbranches. The latter is divided into eastern and western branches. The Dardic branch

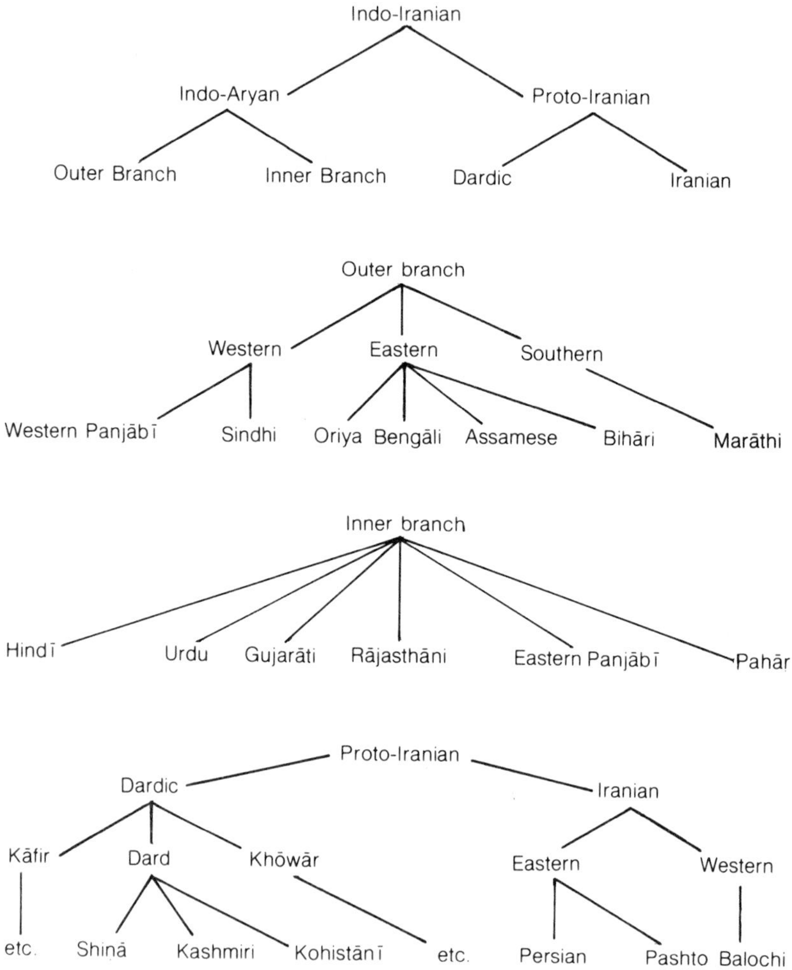

Figure 37. The Indo-Iranian language family.

consists of the Kāfir, Dard, and Khōwār language groups. The Kāfir and Khōwār groups contain a number of relatively unknown languages and dialects. The Dard languages are: Shiṇā, Kashmiri, and Kohistānī. Of the Iranian languages spoken in India, the western branch of Iranian consists of Persian and Pashto, the eastern of Balochi. These relationships are summarized in Figure 37.

With the exception of Persian, all the Proto-Iranian languages are spoken in the far northwest on the borderlands between India and Afghanistan. The position of the Dardic group is in dispute. Some authors do not accord it separate status, placing it instead under the Indo-Aryan branch. Most admit, however, that the Kāfir group should be accorded special status. Similarly, there is some evidence to suggest that Assamese, Bengali, and Marāthi in the outer branch of Indo-Aryan are derived from the same proto-language.

Historically, the Indo-Aryan and Iranian languages separated from one another more than three millennia ago. The Dardic group may represent an early wave of invaders, followed later by the Indo-Aryans who spoke several dialects of a language similar to Vedic Sanskrit. Vedic Sanskrit or a related dialect later developed into classical Sanskrit, which was replaced in turn by the more popular speech forms known as Prākṛts. The spoken language continued to change, resulting in "corrupt" or "decayed" forms known as Apabrahṃśas. Sometime around 900 A.D.there developed from these Apabrahṃśas the current modern languages. All the modern Indo-Aryan languages thus derive from Vedic Sanskrit by a series of complex linguistic changes. These developments are summarized in simplified form in Figure 38.

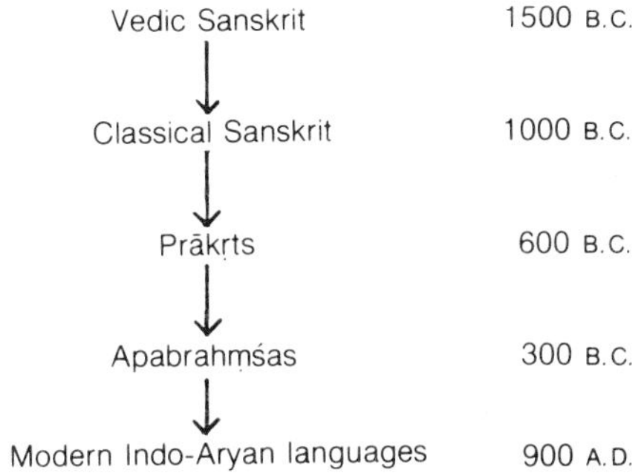

Figure 38. Development of modern Indo-Aryan languages.

The most important aspect of these changes involved what might be called the "Dravidianization" of Indo-Aryan. There is evidence of Dravidian loan words even in Vedic Sanskrit, but more important are Dravidian influences on phonology and syntax. The presence of cerebral (retroflex) consonants in Sanskrit is the most apparent evidence of Dravidian phonological influence. Somewhat later, the extensive use of noun compounds in Indo-Aryan languages attests to a more pervasive Dravidian syntactic influence. Finally, the use of post positions and noun-noun predications in modern Indo-Aryan corresponds closely to Dravidian syntax. In later times a similar process of language change occurred within the Indo-Iranian family. When the Islamic invaders came into contact with the Indo-Aryans of north India, they learned a regional dialect

(Khaṛī Bōlī) which was first a soldier's and trader's patois, but gradually became a *lingua franca* in the north. This language, though derived from an Indo-Aryan dialect, contained a large number of Persian loan words and eventually came to be written in the Arabic script. Subsequently, it developed a highly stylized literary form and eventually replaced Persian as the official language in lower administrative levels. This "Persianized" language, known as Urdu, was also written in the Devanagari script derived from Sanskrit, and in the nineteenth century developed a "Sanskritized" literature. This "Sanskritized" version came to be known as Hindī.

DRAVIDIAN

The Dravidian family of languages is divided into three groupings all deriving from Proto-Dravidian. The three groups are: South Dravidian, Central Dravidian, and North Dravidian. The major South Dravidian languages are Tamil, Malayālam, Koḍagu, Kota, Toda, Baḍaga, and Kannaḍa. Central Dravidian consists of Tuḷu, Telugu, Kui, Kuvi, Pengo, Manḍa, Konḍa, Gondi, Kolami, Naiki, Ollari, and Parji. Gondi is actually a cover term for a number of related languages. The North Dravidian group comprises Malto, Kuruḵẖ, and Brahui. Koraga, a recently discovered language spoken in South India, has also been assigned to this group. The relationships among these groups are represented in Figure 39.

In these diagrams the position of Tuḷu is doubtful, and the relation of

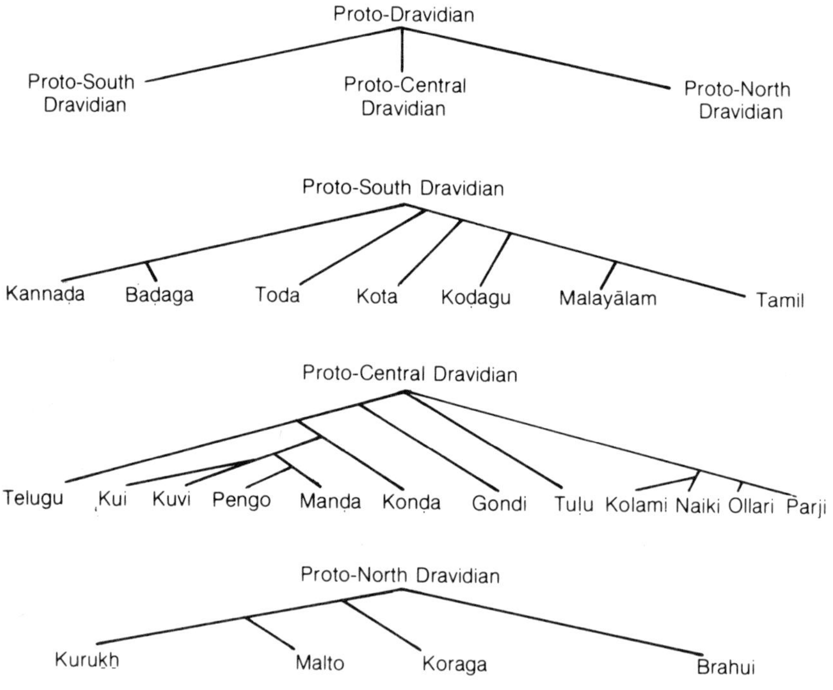

Figure 39. The Dravidian language family.

Telugu to the Kui/Kuvi group is tentative. Telugu may have separated off first from the Kui/Kuvi and Gondi groups. Similarly, the position of Koraga is purely speculative. Of the Dravidian languages, Tamil, Malayālam, Kannaḍa, and Telugu have significant literary traditions dating in the case of Tamil probably from the second century B.C. This early literary activity was inspired by Sanskrit models, and all the early grammatical work was based on the Sanskritic literature. Although Sanskrit loan words abound in much of the Dravidian literature, most of the modern Dravidian languages were not structurally influenced by Indo-Aryan. In this respect the North Dravidian languages show more influence than the others. Brahui, in particular, has been significantly modified by its neighboring Indo-Aryan languages. In general, the pattern of mutual influence between Dravidian and Indo-Aryan confirms an essentially Dravidian substratum in the modern Indo-Aryan languages. Thus the modern Indo-Aryan languages were built on a Dravidian base which was superficially modified by the Sanskritic and Prākṛtic dialects of the Indo-Aryan invaders. In previous chapters it has been seen that this same pattern prevails in other aspects of culture. All of Indian civilization is built on an underlying base of Dravidian language and culture.

AUSTRO-ASIATIC

The Austro-Asiatic family of languages is divided into two major groupings, an eastern and western. The western group comprises the Munda languages and the eastern group includes the Nicobarese and Palaung-Khmer subgroups. Some authorities include Nahālī (Kalṭo) as a separate subgroup in the eastern division, but recent evidence indicates that Nahālī is not an Austro-Asiatic language. As yet there is no convincing case for its genetic affiliation to any other language group. Like Burushaski in the northwest, it remains anomalous. The Munda group is subdivided into northern and southern subbranches. The southern subbranch comprises Sora (Saora, Savara), Gorum (Parenga), Gutob (Gadba), Remo (Boṇḍo), Gata? (Dire), Khaṛia, and Juang. The northern subbranch consists of Korku and the Kherwarian languages. The latter include Santali, Muṇḍari, Ho, and Korwa. The Nicobarese division of eastern Austro-Asiatic consists of Car and Nancowry, languages spoken in the Nicobar Islands. The Palaung-Khmer division of eastern Austro-Asiatic is represented in India by Khasi, a language spoken in the Shillong plateau of Assam. Other languages of the Palaung-Khmer division are spoken in southeast Asia. The relationship between these language groups is outlined in Figure 40.

Until recent times none of the Indian Austro-Asiatic languages had a literary tradition or writing system. Under the influence of regional Indo-Aryan languages and Christian missionaries, various scripts have been devised and a small body of literature created. With two exceptions, these scripts are adaptations of one or another Indo-Aryan script or are Romanizations. The two exceptions are the Ho script for the Ho language, and the Ol Cemet' script for Santali. The former is actually a complex adaptation of the Devanāgarī alphabet, but the latter is a purely indigenous invention combining some features of the Devanāgarī script with the principles of the Roman model.

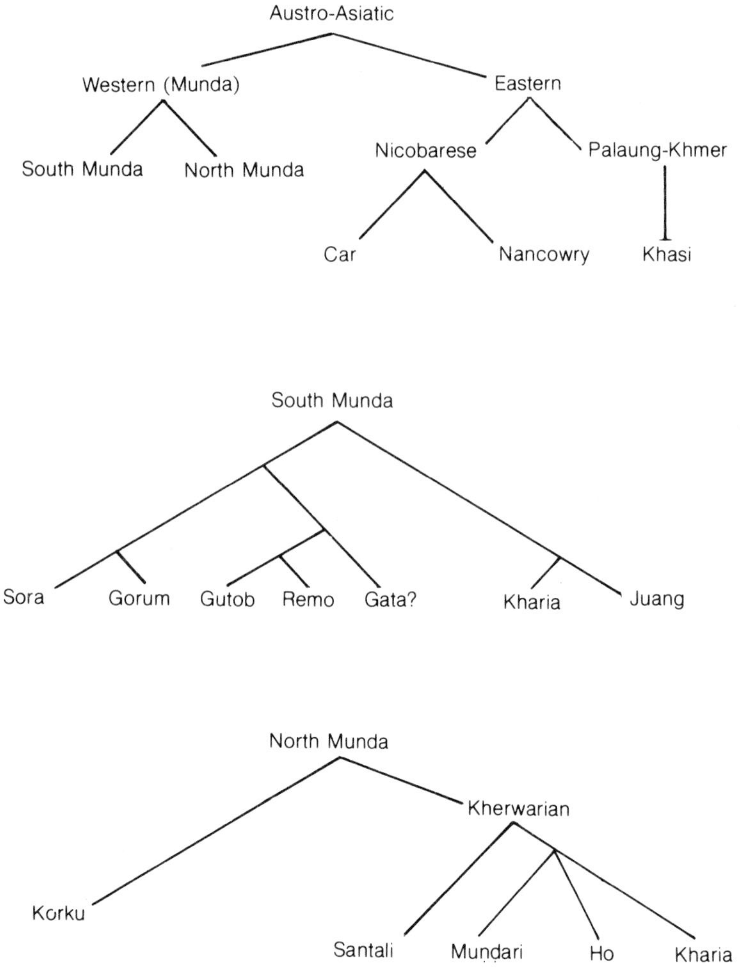

Figure 40. The Austro-Asiatic language family.

TIBETO-BURMAN

Relationships among the Tibeto-Burman languages are quite complex, and much of the work of comparison and reconstruction has been hampered by lack of data. What follows then is a rather sketchy and simplified outline. As the name implies, Tibeto-Burman is divided into a Tibetan and a Burmese branch. The Tibetan branch contains Tibetan, Rgyarung, Gurung, and Himālayan branches. Tibetan is further subdivided into western, central, southern, and northeastern subgroups. Among the western Tibetan languages are Western Tibetan itself, Balti, Ladak, and others spoken on the India–Tibet borderlands. Central Tibetan comprises Central Tibetan spoken from west Bengal to Tibet proper, Lhasa, standard Tibetan, and others. Southern Tibetan consists of Sherpa, Lhoke, and others spoken in northern Nepal. None of the northeastern Tibetan languages are spoken in India. This is also true of the Rgyarung languages. The Gurung branch consists of Gurung and Murmi, both spoken in Nepal. The Himālayan branch is subdivided into western and eastern sections, the latter again divided into western and eastern subsections. Included in the former are Vayu and Magari, both spoken in central Nepal. The western subsection contains Bahing, Sunwari, and Dumi. The eastern subsection comprises Rodong, Waling, and Limbu, all spoken in the Himālayas. Reported as separate subgroupings coordinate with the Himālayan branch are the following: Newari, spoken in Nepal and one of the most important languages in the group; Taying; Midźuish; Hurso; Dhimal; Toto; Abor; and Dafla, all spoken in northern and northeastern Assam.

The Burmese branch consists of a Lolo section and a Kuki section. The former is unimportant in India, but the latter includes a majority of the tribal languages of Assam. In India it is represented by a Lakher branch, a Kuki branch, a central branch, a northern branch, a Naga branch, a Mikir branch, and a Bodo branch. The Lakher branch consists of Mara and Luce. Kuki contains Aimol and Purum. The central branch comprises Lushai, Haka, and Pankhu. The northern branch has Thado. The Naga branch is divided into northern and eastern sections. Northern Naga is represented by Lhota, Mongsen, and Rong (Lepcha); Eastern Naga by Rengma, Sema, and Angami. The Mikir branch is represented by Mikir. The Bodo branch consists of Kachari, Garo, and Koch. Much is purely speculative about these relationships, and consequently I will not attempt to represent them diagrammatically.

Some of the Tibeto-Burman languages—for example, Tibetan and Burmese—have ancient and respectable literary traditions, but most of the Tibeto-Burman languages represented in India are spoken by tribals who have no literary tradition. In modern times Christian missionaries have promoted literacy projects among the tribals and there is now a certain amount of literature, most of which is written in a Romanized script.

Appendix II

ETHNOGRAPHIC SURVEY

From ancient times the diverse inhabitants of India have been organized into exclusive groupings, separated from one another by differences of origin, custom, and religious belief. The residue of every migration, religious sect, economic specialization, or military conquest is reflected in compartmentalized or segmentary units known variously as tribes, castes, and religious sects. The difference between a tribe and caste or between a caste and a religious sect is usually only a matter of arbitrary designation indicating no substantial difference in organization. For all practical purposes, many groups commonly called tribes are hardly different from other groups called castes, and many religious sects cannot be differentiated from castes. In part this ambiguity is only definitional, but more importantly, it accurately reflects the segmentary character of Indian society. Each minor difference between peoples has been seized upon as an indication of inherent difference justifying rigorous separation through denial of intermarriage, interdining, common residence, common occupation, and common worship.

Whether known as tribes, castes, or sects, each of these groups participates in a hierarchic pattern of ranking based on concepts of ritual purity, and each is homologized to the traditional ranked varṇa categories of Brāhmaṇ (priest), Kṣatriya (warrior), Vaiśya (merchant), Śūdra (servant), and untouchable specified in Hindu sacred literature. Because they participate in this ranking system, each distinctive Indian group is, in a sense, a caste or, more specifically, a jāti. This usage accords with the Indian practice of recognizing each jāti as a separate species of human, inherently different from every other, but it is contrary to general anthropological usage.

Anthropologists like to think of castes and tribes as different forms of social organization. In general, a tribe should be an endogamous group whose members are related, even if vaguely. The tribe should have a common territory and its constituent groups should have minimal internal functional diversification. A caste, by contrast, should be but one of the constituent groups of a society. Minimally then, tribes might have internally differentiated groups corresponding to castes, but a caste should have no internal divisions corresponding to tribes. Similarly, tribes ought to be independent, castes interdependent. In fact, none of these criteria can effectively differentiate tribes from castes in India. The situation is similar with respect to sects. Muslims, Christians, and Jews are all recognized religious sects, but they tend to be endogamous and have developed internal subdivisions corresponding to castes and subcastes. Even though many sects may originally have recruited members openly by initiation or credal avowal rather than by birth, the historical tendency has been in the direction of recruitment by birth. Similarly, many sects began by disavowing caste distinctions, but in time were encapsulated within the hierarchic pattern, becoming endogamous groups. The general pattern is clear: one becomes a member of a tribe, caste, or sect largely by birth; one marries within one's own tribe, caste, or sect; one's most important personal relationships are with members of one's own group; and one's characteristic relations with other groups are defined by the pattern of relations attributed to one's own group. Finally, one's categorical membership in a group defines one's inherent and unchangeable personal character.

Castes, tribes, and sects thus reflect the same set of logical principles: each is defined by the twin processes of *separation* and *inclusion*. Each is rigorously separated into distinctive social categories, and each is included within a system of hierarchic ranking. This system of *folk classification* permits variable regional patterns of classification and hierarchic arrangement, but its underlying logical principles are everywhere the same. Furthermore, the classification and hierarchic arrangement of these groups is not necessarily dependent on consensus even in a common region or village setting. People may (and do) disagree on the number and names of different groups, and they may disagree even more on the precise position of each group in the hierarchy or even over the relevant features of classification and hierarchic assignment, but what they do not disagree on is the fact that groups *ought to be rigorously classified and assigned positions in a hierarchy.* From the Indian point of view, castes, tribes, and sects are simply jātis, species of humans, and the *anthropological classification* not only is pointless but is nonsensical in its own terms, for designation as a caste, tribe, or sect is based on no effective principles of structural differentiation. But, although the anthropological distinctions are pointless, certain groups have come to be known as tribes, castes, and sects in the literature and we will adhere to this tradition, noting only one further point. Groups traditionally called tribes almost always live in relatively isolated hill or jungle areas, follow a form of shifting cultivation, hunting and gathering, or pastoralism, quite frequently speak a language that is different from that spoken in the surrounding plains, and participate less completely in the higher forms of Hindu religious ceremonial. This, it seems, is the real basis for the anthropological tradition of calling some Indian groups tribes rather than castes.

MAJOR CULTURAL ZONES

The survey that follows recognizes four major cultural zones: southern zone, central transition zone, northern zone, and the borderlands. Except for broad regions where differences are minimal, the survey proceeds state by state listing and briefly describing linguistic, sectarian, caste, and tribal divisions.

Southern Zone

The southern zone comprises a solid block of groups speaking Dravidian languages and corresponds to the modern political divisions of Kerala, Madras, Mysore, and Āndhra Pradesh. Ethnologically this zone is defined by a roughly common pattern of kinship and marriage, and a similar caste structure. The system of kinship and marriage entails a rule of cross-cousin marriage, and the caste structure displays a fivefold classification requiring strict separation between Brāhmaṇs and non-Brāhmaṇs, and a similarly rigid distinction between clean non-Brāhmaṇs and unclean non-Brāhmaṇs, and between unclean non-Brāhmaṇs and untouchables. Over much of the region there is a general tendency toward dual hierarchy reflecting sectarian affiliation among the Brāhmaṇ and some non-Brāhmaṇ castes, and division into right and left factions among low castes and untouchables. There is also a distinctive group of affiliated artisan castes in the middle ranges of the hierarchy.

Kerala (Travancore-Cochin, Malabar)

Language:	Malayālam
Sects:	Hindu, Christian, Muslim, Jew
Castes:	Nambūtiri Brāhmaṇ, Nair (Nāyar), Iṟavaṉ, Tiyyaṉ, Māppilla, Pulayaṉ, Ceṟumaṉ, Pānaṉ, Parayaṉ
Tribes:	Kadaṉ, Malapantaram, Paliyaṉ Urali, Malavetaṉ

Kerala has the most rigid caste system in India. Here rules of pollution attained their most elaborate form with the lowest untouchables regarded as polluting even from a distance. The Nambūtiri Brāhmaṇs are one of the most conservative and orthodox Brāhmaṇ castes in India. Originally deriving from the north, they are patrilineal and once followed a rigid rule of primogeniture which not only excluded younger sons from inheriting, but also forbade them to marry. These younger sons were permitted to form informal liaisons with Nāyar women, but the offspring of these unions were not accorded Brāhmaṇ status; they belonged to the caste of their mothers.

The Nāyars, by contrast, were matrilineal, excluding sons from inheriting family property. With an aristocratic and martial tradition, the Nāyars were the dominant, ruling caste of Malabar. Under the British they readily assimilated Western education and now constitute one of the most Westernized and politically influential groups in India. Nāyar women have traditionally had greater freedom than most other Indian women, and female education is higher among Nāyars than among almost any other Indian caste.

Christians fall into two groups: Roman Catholics and Syrian Christians. The Roman Catholics, largely recruited from the lower castes by European missionaries, are now a highly literate and politically active group. The Syrian Christians trace their church from St. Thomas, who is believed to have come to India to propagate the faith. Except for a brief period of enforced unity, the two Christian communities have kept apart and the earlier Syrian Christians have merged more completely into the caste system.

Cochin Jews are divided into three jātis: Black Jews, White Jews, and Brown Jews. The White Jews, supposedly fairer than the Black Jews, are ranked highest and refuse to intermarry or interdine with the other Jewish jātis. The Brown Jews are supposedly local converts to Judaism. Today the Jewish community has dwindled to a handful of faithful who still maintain a synagogue and Judaic ritual.

Descendants of Arab traders, the Māppillas are the predominant Muslim jāti in Kerala. They have a reputation for religious fanaticism and have often attempted to convert Hindus to Islam by force.

Until recently the majority of Hindu castes in Kerala were matrilineal, following the dominant Nāyar pattern, and today many of the tribals still adhere to this arrangement. Many of the lower castes are polyandrous. Among the lower Hindu castes are the Tiyyaṉ whose traditional occupation was the extraction of wine (toddy) from palm trees. The Iṟavaṉs are a former toddy-tapping caste which has given up its traditional occupation, adopted Nāyar customs, and acquired a higher status in the caste hierarchy. Cerumaṉs and Pulayaṉs are both castes of agricultural serfs. In former times they were slaves, capable of polluting a high-caste person from a distance of thirty feet. The Pānaṉ caste is known for its striking "devil dances." Dancers mask as demons and dance about the body of a sick person, driving the illness from his body. Parayaṉs are among the lowest untouchable castes, their name in its anglicized form, "pariah," has come to denote every kind of outcast. In Cochin they practice oti, a kind of magical cult that enables them to possess great magical powers.

The nontribal population of Kerala is densely settled along the coast, but the interior mountains are inhabited by tribal peoples. Many of these tribals hunt and gather, others practice slash-and-burn (swidden) agriculture, and still others have become settled cultivators and are in the process of being transformed into castes. Kadaṉs, Malapantarams, and Paliyaṉs are nomadic hunters and gatherers who subsist on the produce of the jungle and live in caves or rude leaf huts. Uralis and Malavetaṉs are shifting cultivators. The former live in tree houses where they are safe from marauding elephant herds and other wild animals. Many Kerala tribes have customs, such as filing the teeth, that have been interpreted as evidence for affiliation with Negrito tribes in Southeast Asia.

Politically, Kerala is a Communist stronghold, but the political divisions are only superficially Communist versus Congress. In large part, the current political parties are really the contemporary vehicles of the traditional competition between Nambūtiris and Nāyars, and between Hindus and Christians.

Madras (Tamilnad)

Language:	Tamil
Sects:	Hindu, Christian
Castes:	Brāhmaṉ, Cettiyar, Kalla, Vellāla, Kammālaṉ, Nādar, Kallar, Maravar, Palla
Tribes:	Toda, Kota, Baḍaga, Kurumba

Tamilnad is the heart of Dravidian India and the center of the movement for a separate Dravidian nation. The Tamils are proud of their ancient culture and resentful of Indo-Aryan domination. This resentment is expressed in their refusal to accept Hindī as the official language of India, in their agitation for separate nationhood, and in their vigorous anti-Brāhmaṇ movements. Stereotypically, the Tamil is hardheaded, practical, and crafty. Tamil Brāhmaṇs are split along sectarian lines between followers of Viṣṇu (Śrī Vaiṣṇava Brāhmaṇs) and followers of Śiva (Smārtha Brāhmaṇs). In the past Brāhmaṇs have generally dominated the government, but in recent years their power has been effectively challenged by non-Brāhmaṇ castes. Cettiyars are a caste of shopkeepers and moneylenders widespread throughout southern India and parts of Southeast Asia. The Kallas and Vellālas are the principal cultivating and landowning castes. Kammālaṉ is a general term for several artisan castes (blacksmith, carpenter, goldsmith, stone mason, brazier). The Nādars are a populous Christian caste. Kallars and Maravars are former criminal tribes, known for their cattle stealing and for their bullfights. The Pallas are a numerous low-caste group who have recently engaged in dramatic attempts to raise their status.

In Tamilnad, Brāhmaṇs are identified with the north and are considered to be part of the pattern of northern domination. Low-caste groups are identified as the original Dravidians (ādi Drāvidas). In their struggle against Brāhmaṇ domination, the low castes are led by the Vellālas and other landowning castes. This conflict is expressed in communal political parties. The DMK (Dravidian First Association), the major anti-Brāhmaṇ party, controls most of Tamilnad.

The Nilgiri Hills on the border between Madras and Kerala are inhabited by tribals. Most distinctive of the tribal groups are the Todas, a cattle-keeping people whose striking appearance and sacred dairy complex set them off from surrounding populations. Neighboring the Todas are the Kotas, artisans for the Todas and Baḍagas, a Hinduized tribe of cultivators. Kurumbas are hunters and gatherers. Relations among these Nilgiri tribes replicated the caste structure of the plains. At the top of the hierarchy were the Todas, who provided buffalo carcasses and dairy products in return for Kota implements and music. From the Kurumbas the Kotas received forest products and magical charms, and from the Baḍagas, grain. In recent years the Baḍagas have abrogated their traditional relations with the Kotas, buying their tools from the plains, and the Kotas have taken to cultivation. At one time the Todas were near extinction, but now seem to be recovering.

Mysore (Karnāṭak)

Language:	Kanarese (Kannaḍa)
Sects:	Hindu, Lingāyat, Muslim, Jain
Castes:	Brāhmaṇ, Okkalīga, Pancāla, Holeya
Tribes:	Koḍagu, Tulu

Prior to the Indian States reorganization act of 1956, Mysore was a princely state, and one of the most progressive and advanced of the princely states.

The caste structure of Mysore parallels that of Madras with the same antagonism between Brāhmaṇs and non-Brāhmaṇs. The Brāhmaṇs are in the forefront of all political and intellectual movements in Mysore and still control much of the political power. Like the Tamil Brāhmaṇs they are divided into Smārtha and Śrī Vaiṣṇava sects. The two most influential Brāhmaṇ castes are the Saraswat and Havik Brāhmaṇs. The latter are agriculturalists largely localized in the northwest part of the state. Saraswat Brāhmaṇs are a merchant group prominent in banking, commerce, and newspapers.

Lingāyats are unique to the Karnāṭak. Followers of Vīrśaivism, their sect began as a protest movement against the Brāhmaṇs. They denied caste distinctions, disavowed the authority of the Brāhmaṇs, and developed their own priesthood (Jangama) and monastic organization. Their monastic organization (math) has considerable temporal as well as spiritual authority. As the name implies, Lingāyats are worshipers of Śiva, particularly revering him in the form of a lingam (phallus) worn on the body or installed in the Temple. In addition to the Jangamas, each math has a guru (religious leader) who is even more sanctified than the Jangama. Although the Lingāyats recognize the authority of the Vedas, they dispense with the whole apparatus of Hindu ritual pertaining to purification and ancestor worship. One who has become a Lingāyat is purified and will be totally united with the deity at death, and consequently has no need of purificatory and ancestor rites. Because the Lingāyats have freely recruited from many different castes which did not in fact lose their status as castes, the sect now contains a number of different castes who do not intermarry. Today the pattern of competition between Brāhmaṇs and Lingāyats continues in the political realm.

Primarily cultivators, Lingāyats also contest for power with the Okkalīgas, the largest cultivating caste in the state. The Pancālas of Mysore comprise an artisan group roughly equivalent to the Kammālaṇs of Madras. Traditionally shepherds, the Kurubas have become landholders in some parts of Mysore. The Holeyas constitute the most numerous and widespread untouchable caste. Like the ādi Drāvidas of Madras, the lower castes of Mysore are sometimes referred to as ādi Karnāṭakas (original inhabitants of Karnāṭak). The Muslims of Mysore are remnants of invading Mogul armies and converts from the local population. The major merchant castes of Mysore are the Balijas (Banajigas) and Kōmaṭis originally deriving from Āndhra Pradesh.

In the southern part of the state in the hilly plateaus bordering Kerala live the Coorgs (Koḍagus). Formerly a fierce, martial tribe, they are now peasant cultivators. Residing in the uplands of southern Mysore is another formerly martial tribe, the Tulus or Bants. Unlike the Koḍagus, the Tulus are matrilineal, their social organization in many ways paralleling that of the Nāyars of Kerala. Most of the Tuluvars are Hindus and have a separate Brāhmaṇ caste (Śivalli), but a fairly large number are Jains. Today, the Tulus, like the Koḍagus, are peasant cultivators.

Āndhra Pradesh

Language: Telugu
Sects: Hindu, Muslim

Castes: Brāhmaṇ, Kamma, Reḍḍi, Balija (Naiḍu), Kāomati, Panc-Brāhma, Māla, Mādiga
Tribes: Chenchu, Koṇḍa Reḍḍi, Gond, Koya, Koṇḍa, Kolām

Āndhra, the first Indian state constituted on linguistic grounds, set the pattern for all the subsequent linguistic states. Modern Āndhra consists of the northern divisions of the old Madras Presidency and the former dominions of the Nizam of Hyderabad. Hyderabad city and much of its surrounding region is still dominated by Muslims. Popular stereotype regards the Telugus as volatile and short-tempered. The Brāhmaṇ castes of Āndhra are divided into two major groups: Vaidiki Brāhmaṇs and Niyogi Brāhmaṇs. Vaidiki Brāhmaṇs are most populous in Telangana (the Nizam's former domain), but their relative power is less than that of the dominant cultivating caste of Kammas. Traditionally, Niyogi Brāhmaṇs are ranked lower than Vaidiki Brāhmaṇs.

Reḍḍis, the dominant cultivating caste of the coastal and riverine areas of Āndhra, claim kinship with the Rājpūts of north India. Both the Reḍḍis and the Kammas are ancient martial peoples who have traditionally competed with one another for dominance, and today this competition is expressed through the medium of modern politics. The Kammas control the powerful Āndhra Communist party, and the Reḍḍis control the Congress party. As in Kerala, political competition is only superficially Communist versus Congress —it is primarily Kamma versus Reḍḍi. Modern political organization merely provides a new vehicle for an old conflict.

Balijas (Naiḍus) and Kōmaṭis are the merchant castes of Āndhra. Although the Balijas claim Kṣatriya status, they are probably an offshoot of the Reḍḍis. Primarily shopkeepers, merchants, and pedlars, they are also often small cultivators and public servants. Kōmaṭis are widespread throughout southern and central India. As merchants, moneylenders, and traders, they are shrewd, industrious, and thrifty, and they are often accused of sharp practices. Like many other merchant castes, they reportedly have a secret language which they use in commercial affairs. The Panc-Brāhma group, consisting of artisan castes, resembles the Kammālaṉ and Pancāla groups of Madras and Mysore. In Āndhra the Panc-Brāhma castes wear the sacred thread of the twice-born and refuse to accept food even from Brāhmaṇs. Mālas and Mādigas are untouchable castes and like many low castes in other parts of the south are divided into left- and righthand factions. The two factions refuse to intermarry or interdine and frequently feud with each other.

In the Nallamallai Hills of eastern Āndhra are the Chenchus, a hunting and gathering tribe. Though some sections of the tribe practice shifting cultivation on the lower slopes, most prefer to keep to the higher hills to avoid contact with the plains people. In the heavily forested region near the Godavari gorge are the Hill (Koṇḍa) Reḍḍis. Most are now settled agriculturalists, but until recently they were practically enslaved by Hindu timber merchants. In the hills and plains farther up the Godavari River are the Koyas. Most Koyas are now permanent field cultivators, but some still practice shifting cultivation in the hills. Living in the hills of northeastern Āndhra are other shifting cultivators known as Koṇḍas or Kūbis. On the northern borders of Āndhra are Gonds and Kolāms. The Gonds of Adilabad refer to themselves as Rāj

Gonds and claim high rank as a martial group. Most of the Kolāms are shifting cultivators, while the majority of Gonds practice permanent field cultivation.

Central Transition Zone

The central transition zone consists roughly of the modern Indian states of Orissa, Madhya Pradesh, southern Bihār, southeastern Bengāl, and Mahārāshtra. In general, forms of social organization and cultural orientation in the central zone are a mixture of northern and southern patterns. Very broadly, social organization among tribals and lower castes corresponds to southern configurations, while social organization among higher castes conforms to northern patterns. Thus, for example, many lower castes practice cross-cousin marriage and have kinship terminologies reminiscent of the south. On the other hand, the Brāhmaṇ/non-Brāhmaṇ opposition so characteristic of the south is absent in the central zone, and this corresponds to the northern pattern of caste structure. All the states in this zone and Āndhra Pradesh in the southern zone are important frontiers between Hindu civilization and tribal cultures. Before independence much of this zone was made up of numerous backward and generally authoritarian princely states.

Orissa (Utkal)

Language:	Oriya (Odiā)
Sects:	Hindu, Muslim
Castes:	Brāhmaṇ, Khandait, Kalta, Kāran, Ghasia, Pano
Tribes:	Khond, Sāvara

Orissa is a land of fabled temples and religious shrines, the most famous being the temple complex at Puri where Viṣṇu is worshiped as Jagannath (lord of the world). Puri is famous, or infamous, for the erotic sculpture of its temples and for the festival of Jagannath which attracts thousands of pilgrims. Most of Orissa's Hindu population live in the coastal districts and along the fertile valley of the Mahānadi River. The hilly, forested inland regions are occupied by tribals. Orissa, Bengāl, and Assam were once a common cultural area, but Bengāl developed along independent lines and drove a wedge between Assam and Orissa. Today Assam and Orissa still share many common traits.

Orissa's caste structure lacks both the polarization of high and low castes characteristic of the south, and the proliferation of middle-ranked castes found in the north. The Brāhmaṇs of Orissa, generally classed as Utkal Brāhmaṇs, are numerous and important only near the famous temples and in the coastal districts. Elsewhere the most important caste is the former warrior group known as Khandait. The Khandaits now claim the rank of Kṣatriya, but this status is only very recent. Like most other castes in Orissa, the Khandaits are made up at least partly of local aborigines. With the Kaltas, the Khandaits are the principal landowners of Orissa. Kārans were traditionally scribes. Often recruited into the British civil service, they benefited from contact with their rulers and since independence have emerged as one of the most powerful political groups in the state. Ghasias, a low caste, were traditionally occupied as grass gatherers and grooms. More recently they have become general laborers and small cultivators. The Panos are a widespread untouchable caste.

The tribal groups of Orissa speak Dravidian or Munda languages. Tribals known as Khonds actually consist of two closely related tribes (Kuvis and Kuis) of shifting cultivators. Once infamous for their practice of human sacrifice (the meriah sacrifice), the Khonds are now pressed on every side by Hindu castes moving into their tribal territory. This is a common story in India. For centuries tribals have been persecuted and deprived of their lands by greedy Hindus. The Sāvaras are one of the numerous Munda tribes. Some Sāvaras are reputed to be hunters and gatherers, but most practice either a form of shifting cultivation or permanent field agriculture.

Madhya Pradesh (Central Provinces)

Language:	Hindī, Gondi, Halbi
Sects:	Hindu, Muslim
Castes:	Brāhmaṇ, Rājpūt, Marāthā, Kunbi, Kāyastha, Gūjar, Halba, Ahīr, Camār
Tribes:	Gond, Baiga, Birhor, Korku, Juang, Parji, Ollari

Madhya Pradesh encompasses a very jungly area with a preponderantly tribal population. Most of the state has been only partially colonized by Hindus and still represents a kind of frontier area. Its frontier status is reflected by the fact that nearly every Hindu caste now resident in Madhya Pradesh originally came from somewhere else, and rather recently at that. Marāthā Brāhmaṇs, Marāthās, Kunbis, and Gūjars all migrated from the west; Rājputs and Chamārs came from the northwest. Only the tribal population can claim ancient occupance. The long-term Marāthā influence is reflected not only in the presence of numerous Mahārāshtrian castes, but also in the distinctive language, Halbi, derived from Marāthi. Because it is a frontier area inhabited by a large and varied aboriginal population and recent Hindu and Muslim immigrants, Madhya Pradesh lacks any real unity. Its caste structure and kinship organization vary widely from group to group and region to region. Higher-caste Hindus and Muslims and many of the Munda tribes adhere to northern patterns of social organization, while low castes and Dravidian tribes follow southern patterns which have been partially influenced by northern traits. The Rājpūts in Madhya Pradesh, as elsewhere, are a landowning aristocratic military caste. So, too, are the Marāthās. Kāyasthas are former scribes and, along with Kunbis, Gūjars, and Halbas, they make up the principal cultivating and landholding castes. The Ahīrs are traditionally herdsmen, and the Camārs are an untouchable caste whose traditional occupation is leatherworking. Kunbis and Camārs are the most numerous Hindu castes.

The tribals of Madhya Pradesh speak Dravidian or Munda languages. The premier tribal group are the Gonds. In medieval times the Gonds, developing their own kingdoms with fortified capitals, constituted a powerful force. They fought against invaders and formed alliances with kingdoms on their borders. Many of the princely states of Madhya Pradesh derived from conquered Gond kingdoms. Because of their martial background, many Gonds claim Rājput status, and in some areas are still the principal landowners. In other areas they are shifting cultivators living in isolation from the Hindus of the plains.

Like the Gonds, the Parjis and Ollaris speak Dravidian languages. Primarily shifting cultivators, they live in remote hill areas. The Baigas, Birhors, Korkus, and Juangs are Munda tribes. The Baigas have adopted Hindi and no longer speak a Munda language. The Birhors and Juangs are still hunters and gatherers, but many have turned to agriculture. The Baigas and Korkus are shifting cultivators.

Southern Bihār and Southeastern Bengāl

This region is largely a continuation of Madhya Pradesh. The hilly country of Chota Nagpur and the Rajmahal Hills is the home of numerous Dravidian and Munda tribes. The Dravidian tribes, represented by the Malers and Oraons (Kurukẖs), are shifting cultivators who have been considerably influenced by Hinduism and the surrounding Munda tribals. For example, both Dravidian and Munda tribes hold a ceremonial spring hunt and have the institution of bachelor houses in which the young men of the tribe live until they marry. Among the more important Munda tribes are the Santals, Mundas, and Hos. Most are shifting cultivators, but many have become settled cultivators and laborers. Both the Santals and the Mundas have been strongly influenced by Christian missionaries.

Mahārāshtra:

Language:	Marāthi
Sects:	Hindu, Parsee (Pārsī), Muslim
Castes:	Brāhmaṇ, Rājpūt, Marāthā, Kunbi, Pancāla, Koḷi, Camār, Mahār
Tribes:	Bhil, Gond

Of the numerous Brāhmaṇ castes in Mahārāshtra, the most important are the Konkanasthas (from the Konkan) and the Deśasthas ("countryside"). Among the Konkanasthas, the Citpāvan Brāhmaṇs make up one of the highest ranking castes in India. They are typically Westernized, educated, and cosmopolitan. On the other hand, they are religiously conservative. The center of Citpāvan population is Poona, but their influence reaches beyond Mahārāshtra into Madhya Pradesh as well. Marāthās are a warrior group who claim Rājput origin. Their culture hero, Śivāji, welded the Marāthās into a skillful and dedicated army. With the Kunbis, the Marāthās are the most important landholding caste in the state. Significantly, many regions of Mahārāshtra have the peculiarly southern group of affiliated artisan castes known as Pancāla. Though they are somewhat less organized than in the south, their very presence indicates a basically southern pattern in the Mahārāshtrian caste structure. Similarly, the broad division between Konkanastha and Deśastha Brāhmaṇs has elements of the southern tendency toward dual hierarchy. Koḷis, originally a caste of fishermen, have been agricultural laborers for many years, and tradition attributes to them the derivation of the word "coolie" (laborer). The Mahārs are untouchables, but have been one of the first untouchable groups to respond to reforms. Ambedkhar, founder of the scheduled castes federation devoted to improving the status of untouchables, was a Mahār. The Mahārs are now a politically active reform group.

Parsees descended from immigrants from Persia. They are Zoroastrians or, as they are commonly known, fire worshipers. Their sacred text, the *Zend Avesta*, is written in Avestan, an ancient Iranian language. Both the language and the content of the *Avesta* are closely related to Vedic Sanskrit. The *Avesta* teaches a dual principle of good and evil. Ahura Mazda is the supreme deity and upholder of good. His constant foe is Ahriman, who is assisted by six fiends and hosts of evil spirits (devas). Ahura Mazda will eventually triumph in a final contest with the forces of evil. A virgin will then give birth to a second Zoroaster who will cause the resurrection of the dead. The world will be purified by a general conflagration and all of humanity will unite in adoration of Ahura Mazda. The visible symbol of Ahura Mazda is fire, and in the Avesta he is referred to as luminous and shining. He created fire and the light of day. Ahriman is represented by darkness and night. Ahura Mazda also created the sun, symbolized by the god Mithra. Because of its association with Ahura Mazda, the Parsees worship fire, and most of their rituals center around the sacred fire. Their fire temples contain a separate room in which a fire is constantly tended by white-robed priests. These priests form an hereditary caste. Parsees expose their dead on dakhmas, or towers of silence, where they are devoured by vultures. At the ages of seven and nine respectively, Parsee boys and girls are received into the faith. After being purified and bathed they are invested with a sacred shirt and cord which they must never remove. Unlike Hindus, Parsees have no objection to alcohol, but regard smoking as a crime against fire. Most Parsees live in Bombay city where they form one of the most progressive, best-educated, and influential groups in India. Known for their business acumen, they dominate all forms of commerce and industry.

The Bhils are a tribal people who occupy the northern section of Mahārāshtra. They also extend into parts of Gujarāt, Rājasthān, and Madhya Pradesh. Tradition accords them status as great hunters, but popular prejudice brands them as a gang of lawless brigands, given to witchcraft. In fact, they are largely peaceful small cultivators and laborers. Although they currently speak an Indo-Aryan language, many have speculated that they originally spoke a Dravidian or Munda language.

Northern Zone

The northern zone consists of Gujarāt, Rājasthān, the Panjāb and Sindh, the lowlands of Kashmir, Uttar Pradesh and northern Bihār, and Bengāl and the riverine plain of Assam. Over much of this area there is not only a common caste structure, but a fairly consistent set of dominant castes. Brāhmaṇs, Rājpūts, Jats, and Camārs constitute the basis of the caste structure. The northern system of kinship, unlike the southern, forbids marriage between close relatives. The caste structure over much of the area normally entails only a threefold classification: clean high castes, clean low castes, and untouchables. The middle category of clean low castes makes up the majority of the population. Clean low castes consist of numerous occupational and artisan groups who are divided into several competing, but more-or-less equivalently ranked, hierarchic divisions. In Bengāl and much of the hill country north of the plains, the caste structure tends to be simplified into two basic groups, but with different criteria in each case.

Gujarāt:

Language:	Gujarāti
Sects:	Hindu, Muslim, Jain
Castes:	Brāhmaṇ, Rājpūt, Bania, Kunbi (Pattidar), Camār, Bhangi
Tribes:	Bhil

Gujarāt has the most complex caste system in India, with more than a hundred different Brāhmaṇ castes alone. As the home of Indian business, Gujarāt's dominant ethos and dominant groups center around business. Gujarātis not only dominate Indian business at home, but are also active throughout Africa and Southeast Asia. Noted for their hardheadedness, Gujarātis are extremely influential in Indian politics. Nagar Brāhmaṇs, the most important Brāhmaṇ caste, include in their ranks many politicians and bankers. Banias are found in both Hindu and Jain communities. They are businessmen par excellence, controlling most of the commerce, banking, and moneylending. In fact, Bania is a term widespread in India for moneylenders and shopkeepers in general. Among many, it is a derogatory term connoting sharp practice and rapaciousness. Rājpūts are most populous in Saurāshtra and the northern parts of the state. The Kunbis here, as in Mahārashtra, are a populous cultivating and landholding caste. They often refer to themselves by the more honorific title pattidar (landowner) in order to raise their status. Bhangis, traditionally sweepers, constitute the largest untouchable group in the state. They are commonly employed as agricultural menials, garbage collectors, and the like. Muslims are found in Gujarāt in fairly heavy proportions. Some, like the Khojah caste, are Bania groups converted to Islam by Muslim pirs (saints). Bohras and Memons are similar converts and, with the Khojahs, were among the more wealthy and powerful commercial castes. When India and Pakistan were partitioned at independence, many from these castes migrated to West Pakistan and now dominate much of the business life there. Gujarāt has the largest number of Jains in India. For centuries the Jains have been successful merchants, moneylenders, and traders conducting far-flung enterprises. In Gujarāt they are a highly Westernized, educated group, important not only in business and commerce, but dominant in many of the professions as well. The Jain saintly tradition has exerted great influence in Indian political life. For example, Gandhi, a Gujarāti, acknowledged his debt to the Jain tradition in formulating his doctrine of nonviolent protest.

Rājasthān

Language:	Rājasthāni
Sects:	Hindu, Jain, Muslim
Castes:	Brāhmaṇ, Rājpūt, Daroga, Bania, Jat, Gadri, Camār, Bhangi

Rājasthān, or Rājpūtāna, as it is sometimes called, is the homeland of the Rājpūt caste. Rājpūts are the premier aristocratic, warrior caste of India, conforming most closely to the traditional Kṣatriya or warrior and ruling class of sacred literature. The name Rājpūt itself means "son of the king." At one time the Rājpūts ruled the whole of Rājasthān as well as large portions of Madhya Pradesh. Their traditions and style of clan organization have been copied by many other martial castes and tribes who now claim Rājpūt status. In their time of greatness the Rājpūts developed a feudal form of organization. The best lands (khālisa) were held by the ruler, and less desirable portions of land were meted out to local chiefs. The chiefs were ranked into four classes with different rights to land and obligations to the ruler. The court and household organization of chiefs were miniature replicas of the sovereign's. Under the chiefs were fighting men holding grants to land from the chief's estate. Beneath all these were the peasant cultivators and other Hindu castes.

Rājpūts are traditionally divided into 36 exogamous patrilineal clans, each of which belongs either to the solar or lunar branch. Each of the clans was subdivided into numerous branches. The clans and their subdivisions were ranked, and precedence was jealously guarded. Associated with the chief's courts, castes of bards (Mīrāsis) and genealogists (Bhāts) recorded genealogies and recited important events in clan history, eulogizing the great heroes among the chief's ancestors. Genealogists were essential in maintaining the ranking of clans and in establishing rights of inheritance. The Brāhmaṇ castes of Rājasthān are extremely conservative and orthodox. In some parts of Rājasthān, Rājpūts rank higher than Brāhmaṇs.

Darogas descended from unions between Rājpūt men and non-Rājpūt women. They were traditionally servants of the great Rājpūt lords, but many have now become cultivators and claim Rājpūt rank. Jats are an important agricultural caste from the Panjāb. Gadris are traditionally shepherds. Bania, Camār, and Bhangi castes are equivalent to similarly named groups of other regions, but one group of Banias, known as Mārwāri (from Mārwār in northeast Mahārāshtra), are particularly noted for their extortions and unscrupulous rapacity. So bad is their reputation that the word Mārwāri has become a pejorative term the length and breadth of India.

Panjāb, Haryana, Sindh, and Himāchal Pradesh

Language:	Panjābi, Sindhi
Sects:	Hindu, Muslim, Sikh, Jain, Ārya Samāj
Castes:	Brāhmaṇ, Rājpūt, Khatri, Bania, Jat, Gūjar, Chuchra, Camār

Under the British Rāj, Panjāb was a favored area, treated with deference. The best civil administrators were sent to the Panjāb and Panjābis were favorite recruits for the native army. The caste structure of the Panjāb is much more fluid than other areas, and though this has sometimes been attributed to the influence of Islam, it is more likely due to the absence of any significant and influential Brāhmaṇ group. The Khatris are a mercantile caste who claim direct descendence from the ancient Kṣatriyas of sacred tradition. Khatris have always been important in government administration, and have also provided many of the priests and teachers of the Sikh religion. Although traditionally associated with Sikhism, they are primarily Hindus. Before partition they monopolized the trade of Panjāb, Sindh, and much of Afghanistan. In addition to the Khatris, the principal Bania castes of Panjāb are the Aggarwāls, Āswāls (Oswāls), Mahesris, Saralias, and Mahājans. The Aggarwāls are the most numerous Bania caste. A few are Jains, but most are Hindu. The Āswāls come from Gujarāt and are predominantly Jain. Mahājans are Brāhmaṇs who have taken to commerce. Not very numerous in the Panjāb, they dominate trade and commerce in the hills, particularly of the Pahāri region.

The Jats are the most advanced agriculturalists not only of the Panjāb but probably of the whole of India. With the Rājpūts they are the dominant landholding caste. Like the Rājpūts, the Jats are a great military aristocracy and the "sturdy" Jat was a great favorite of British administrators. The majority of Jats follow Sikhism, a syncretistic faith incorporating elements of Hinduism and Islam. The Sikh religion was founded by Bāba Nānak, a Khatri, in the fifteenth century. He preached the unity of god, abolition of idols, and disregard of caste, but one of his gurus later transformed Sikhism into a powerful military organization that eventually threw off Muslim rule in the Panjāb. Guru Govind Singh stipulated unshorn hair, abstinence from tobacco, and the title Singh (lion) for all male initiates. The distinguishing marks of a Sikh are the five K's: kes (unshaven hair and beard), kacch (short drawers), kasa (iron bangle), khanda (steel knife), and kanga (comb). Sikhs should wear blue clothes, eat only the flesh of decapitated animals, observe personal cleanliness, abstain from worshiping saints or idols, eat with the head covered, revere the one God, and pray and recite passages from the Granth (their sacred text) morning, evening, and before all meals. Their military organization consisted of a great council, at which all the chiefs elected a general to lead them against the enemy, and an army called Dal Khālsa (army of God). Recently, Sikhs have agitated for a separate state.

Gūjars are a prominent landholding caste allied to the Jats, but most populous in hillier tracts. They have a reputation of fondness for other people's cattle and are generally regarded as much inferior to the Jats. Chuhras and Camārs are outcastes. The Chuhras are the equivalent of the scavenging Bhangi caste in other parts of northern India.

Founded in the latter part of the nineteenth century by Pandit Dayanand Sāraswati, a Gujarāti Brāhmaṇ, the Ārya Samāj is a reforming Hindu sect attractive to political conservatives and the educated. The tenets of the Ārya Samāj include abandonment of caste, purification of ritual, abolition of lavish wedding ceremonies, and encouragement of widow remarriage. Its basic doctrine is "back to the *Veda*." Everything in Hinduism that is not specified in the *Vedas* should be expunged. The *Vedas* are the only source of authority, and in their attempts to justify the authority of the *Vedas*, some Ārya Samājists have taken rather wide liberties in interpreting the texts. They find, for example, airplanes and atomic bombs in these ancient texts. The basic rite of the Ārya Samāj is the old Vedic sacrifice of offering clarified butter and grain in the sacrificial fire.

Kashmir Lowlands

The lowlands of Kashmir are partially an ethnological extension of the Panjāb.

The local language is Kashmiri and the majority of the population are Muslims. The principal Hindu castes are Kashmiri Brāhmaṇs, Puribs (Purbis, eastern), Dogras, and Bohras. The Bohras are Brāhmaṇs from Mahārāshtra who have become merchants and moneylenders. The Dogras are the Rājpūts of Kashmir. The Puribs or Purbis are an immigrant Brāhmaṇ caste. Brāhmaṇs of Kashmir rank among the highest Brāhmaṇ castes in India. Renowned for their scholarship, they are known as Kashmiri pandits (learned men) in all parts of India. The Muslims of Kashmir are natives descended from converts, and more recent immigrants. The native Muslims make up the majority of peasant proprietors, village artisans, and occupational specialists. The immigrants are mainly semi-nomadic herdsmen.

Uttar Pradesh (United Provinces of Agra and Oudh) and Bihār

Language:	Hindī and Bihāri
Sects:	Hindu, Muslim, Ārya Samāj
Castes:	Brāhmaṇ, Rājpūt, Ṭhākur, Kāyastha, Kurmi, Camār, Bhangi, Ḍom

The highest-ranking Brāhmaṇs of the U. P. are the Sarwaria branch of Kaṅkubja (Kanauji) Brāhmaṇs. They are an orthodox and conservative group who look down on other Kankubja Brāhmaṇs such as the Sanādhya as well as the Gaur Brāhmaṇs of Delhi. All of these groups regard as low those Brāhmaṇs who live near sacred rivers and temples and earn their living by conducting pilgrims through the ceremonies and acts of worship at these sites. Prominent among these are the Gayawāls of Gaya, and the Gangaputras of Benares. Their status equals that of similar Brāhmaṇ groups in other areas such as the Pantārams of southern India, the Prayāgwāls of Allahabad, the Chaubes of Mathura, and the Naramdeo Brāhmaṇs on the Narbada River. Even more degraded is the widespread Mahā-Brāhmaṇ caste whose members accept gifts from the relatives of the deceased and eat the food offered to benefit the soul of the departed. Less low are the Bhāts and Charans, professional Brāhmaṇ genealogists attached to royal houses or wealthy families. Those who limit their practice to temples and pilgrimage sites rank lower, and in general Brāhmaṇ rank is determined by the rank of those they serve. Genealogists for Brāhmaṇs or Rājpūts rank high, genealogists for lower castes rank low. In Bihār the most influential Brāhmaṇ caste is the Maithili Brāhmaṇ, but they are regarded as degraded by many other Brāhmaṇs because of their adherence to the Śakti cult, and because they eat meat and fish.

Rājpūts, Ṭhākurs, and Kāyasthas are the principal landholding castes. Ṭhākurs claim Rājpūt status, but are generally agreed to be inferior. Kāyasthas were formerly scribes who became landowners. In Bihār the Kurmi are also large landholders. Camārs, Bhangis, and Doms are all untouchables. These Harijans (people of god) are highly organized and politically powerful. In recent years, speakers of Maithili have pressed for a separate state corresponding to the linguistic boundaries of Maithili. The Muslims of the U. P. and Bihār, as elsewhere, are landowners, artisans, and occupational specialists. In the sub-Himālayan regions (Pahāṛi), the caste structure is simpler than in the plains. In contrast to the threefold division of the plains, Pahāṛi villages are characterized by a twofold division of castes: high caste and untouchable. The plains castes also maintain greater social distance between groups and have a greater proliferation of subcastes.

Bengāl and Assam Plain

Language:	Bengāli, Assamese
Sects:	Hindu, Muslim, Brahmo Samāj
Castes:	Brāhmaṇ, Kāyastha, Baidya, Māhishya, Bagdi, Dom, Caṇḍāla, Nāma Śūdra

Bengālis have long held a special position as interpreters of India to the West. Among the first to benefit from Western education, they filled the ranks of British administration with clerks, interpreters, and minor officials. Educated Bengālis produced the first flowering of modern Indian literature in the works of Rabindranath Tagore and Bankim Chandra Chatterjee. Avid businessmen, the Bengālis transformed Calcutta into the financial capital of India. Calcutta's Clive Street is the Wall Street of India.

Caste divisions in Bengāl are not so finely graduated as in other parts of India, and in some respects Bengāl has a class structure. The Brāhmaṇs and Kāyasthas compose the Bengāli upper class (Bhadralok). The caste system seems never to have been strong in Bengāl, and castes are now largely divided into two groups: Brāhmaṇ and Śūdra. The Śūdras were classed as clean, unclean, and untouchable. British administration destroyed the power of Muslim officeholders and landowners, and the new Bengāli upper class emerged from the imposed British revenue system, the new opportunities for trade, and increasingly from professional groups. Bengāli Brāhmaṇs are mainly Kanauji Brāhmaṇs augmented by immigrants from other areas. One subcaste of the Rarhi Brāhmaṇs, the Kulīn Brāhmaṇs, was widely known for its marriage system. The practice of hypergamy among Kulīn subcastes created a superfluity of women in some subcastes. This was resolved by allowing a Kulīn Brāhmaṇ to marry a large number of women whom he never intended to support or live with. But, because they had undergone the marriage sacrament, the women were legally married and their fathers had fulfilled their obligation of finding suitable mates for them. With the Brāhmaṇs, the Kāyasthas and the Baidyas are the principal landowners and also monopolize the educational system and most of the administrative posts. As elsewhere, Brāhmaṇs are ranked among themselves on the basis of whom they serve—those who serve Brāhmaṇs being higher than those who serve non-Brāhmaṇs and so on. The Māhishyas, claiming to be the original farmers of Bengāl, are a caste of small cultivators ranked considerably below Kāyasthas and Baidyas. Bagdis also claim to be farmers by tradition, but they have a history of thievery and brigandage and are generally ranked with the impure castes. Doms along with the Caṇḍālas and other untouchable groups compose the Nāma Śūdra class. Traditionally, Doms are watchers of burning funeral ghats and Caṇḍālas are sweepers. Muslims in Bengāl, before partition, were administrative officials, cultivators, artisans, and various other occupational specialists. Many Muslims were originally immigrants who held important administrative positions under the Moguls, but were reduced to small landholders under the British administration. The bulk of the Muslim population are converts from low castes and aboriginals.

The riverine plain of Assam is a continuation of the social system of Bengāl augmented by immigrants. Laborers in the tea gardens of Assam, for example, are recruited from every Indian region, and many have settled permanently in Assam. Assam was conquered in the thirteenth century by the Shans of Burma. Known as Ahoms, the Shans gave their name to the country and their descendants still constitute a significant proportion of the population.

The Brahmo Samāj is a syncretistic cult founded by Rām Mohun Roy, a Brāhmaṇ, in the late nineteenth century. Roy studied under Muslim teachers, received Vedic instruction in Benares, studied Buddhism in Tibet, and later studied the Bible with English missionaries. Held in high esteem by the British for his reforming efforts, he was sent to England. The first Brāhmaṇ to cross the sea, he made a great impression in England. In 1830 he founded the Brahmo Samāj (Society of God). A monotheistic sect, the Brahmos worshiped the deity by "none of the names known to men." Brahmo services consisted of Vedic recitations and readings from the *Upaniṣads*. The society flourished under Debendra Nath Tagore, spreading among the villages of Bengāl. Under Keshub Chandar Sen (a Baidya), the society came out against caste and was instrumental in the passage of the Native Marriage Act of 1872, which for the first time legalized civil marriage in Hindu society. These progressive moves created a split in the Brahmo movement, and when Sen permitted his own daughter to marry below the legal age (he had also been partly responsible for legislation banning infant marriage), the progressive branch, or New Dispensation as it was called, began to crumble. Sen eventually lapsed into a form of pantheistic mysticism and proclaimed himself an inspired prophet. With his death the movement more or less returned to its earlier theistic doctrine. The Brahmo Samāj was the first attempt at reconciliation between Hinduism and Christianity, but it never gained large numbers of adherents. Even so it had enormous influence and many of the reforms it sponsored were adopted.

Borderlands Zone

Defined more by diversity than similarity of features, the borderlands zone is largely a residual category. Its geographic boundaries extend in a northward arc from the Arabian Sea to the Bay of Bengāl, enclosing in their sweep the entire mountainous region that defines the northern borders of modern India and Pakistan and includes Nepal, Sikkim, and Bhutan. For reasons of space I do not include the outlying island areas of Ceylon, the Andamans, and Nicorbars. This zone is further subdivided into three regions: northwest frontier, central Himālayas, and northeast frontier.

Northwest Frontier

Historically an unstable area through which most of India's invaders passed, the northwest frontier was a romantic and strategic spot under the British Rāj. Fearful of Russian aggression and French and German plotting in the Middle East, the British directed their most elaborate supply lines, and sent their best troops, to the northwest frontier. Then as today, it was the habitat of turbulent Islamic tribal nomads.

The principal tribes along the southern and central border between Pakistan and Afghanistan (that is, Baluchistan, Swat, and the Northwest Frontier Provinces) are the Balochs, Brahuis, and Pathans. The Balochs and Pathans speak Indo-Iranian languages (Balochi and Pashto), but the Brahuis speak a Dravidian language (Brahui). Despite their linguistic differences, all share in a common pastoral way of life. Their wealth consists of the camels, cattle, sheep, and goats which they graze in the sparse upland pastures. By habit and inclination all are warlike and treacherous, feuding among themselves, raiding the agriculturists of the plains, and constantly on the lookout for herds ripe for lifting, or rich caravans to plunder. They are all subdivided into separate tribes, each having a traditional tribal territory. Each tribe is under the authority of a chief (Khān), and the chiefs of the separate tribal divisions make up a council of elders. The tribes are in turn subdivided into exogamous clans and lineages. Most groups follow the Middle Eastern pattern of parallel-cousin marriage. Throughout this entire region the distinctions of caste society, though attenuated, are present. The Pathans, for example, have hierarchically ranked lineages known as *qoum,* and artisan subdivisions ranked beneath the landowning lineages. All groups also come into contact with castes from the plains, particularly Gūjars and various trading castes of Banias from the Panjāb.

Farther north, bordering on the Pathan country in an area known as Dardistan, are the Red and Black Kāfir tribes. Speaking archaic Indo-Aryan languages, the Kāfirs may represent an early wave of Indo-Aryan invaders. Until recently they were headhunters. Primarily pastoralists, they do some farming in narrow side valleys of the mountains. Farther eastward in Gilgit and Baltisthan are the Muslim Khos, Baltis, and Burushos. For the most part these are little-known tribes. To the south is Ladakh, home of the Buddhist Ladakhis. Ladakhis are settled agriculturalists and, like their brethren to the east, polyandrous. Farther south are the Hindu Kanets of the Kulu Valley. Except for the Kulus, caste distinctions are practically absent in this whole region. The twofold Kulu caste structure approximates that of the so-called Khasa tribe farther east and is generally consistent with the caste structure of the whole Pahāri region. The area from Ladakh eastward to Assam, and including the Pahāri region, is characterized by polyandry, practiced not only by Buddhists but by many Hindu castes as well.

Central Himālayas

The central Himālayan region includes Nepal, Sikkim, and Bhutan. Nepal is divided into three physical-cultural regions: valley, mountain, and terai. The mountainous areas are inhabited by various tribes, among which are the Bhotiya, Gurkha (Gurung), Magar, Sherpa, Tamang, Rai, and Limbu tribes. The Bhotiyas are traders and pastoralists who follow a seasonal migration from the valleys to the high, Alpine pastures during the summer. The rest of the year they are cultivators living in valleys. Both the Gurungs and the Magars are proud, martial groups. The former conquered the whole of Nepal in the eighteenth century. They were favorite recruits in the British army and many still follow the tradition of military service. The Gurungs are divided into two endogamous units of unequal status. The Magars, particularly in the valleys, are on the point of being accepted into the caste system of the valley. They employ Brāhmaṇ priests and observe prohibitions on intermarriage and interdining with other castes and tribes. Aside from their well-publicized mountaineering skills, the Sherpas are traders and pastoralists similar to the Bhotiyas. Sherpas in general do not observe caste restrictions, eating and intermarrying with other Nepal groups, but they do regard one class of recent Tibetan immigrants as polluting and similarly prohibit close intercourse with the Kami caste of blacksmiths from the plains. The Tamangs are peasant cultivators and landowners, and the Rais and Limbus are primarily pastoralists, though a few of the two latter groups have taken up residence in the valley where they are government servants. All of these tribes speak Tibeto-Burman languages and follow the Lamaist form of Tibetan Buddhism.

The terai is a jungly rainforest on the Nepal-India border. In the hot weather and the rains it is practically uninhabitable. Its climate coupled with the absolute certainty of malaria have kept the terai relatively free of human occupance. Brief stopovers by traders and an occasional royal hunting party characterize the transience of the human population. Only the Thārus (a caste claiming Rājpūt status) and a few allied castes seem to be inured to the heat and fever. These groups of settled cultivators are Hindu immigrants from the plains. Historically the terai has played an important role in the isolation of Nepal. For centuries it served as an effective barrier to Hindu colonization.

Most of Nepal's inhabitants are concentrated in the narrow, densely populated Nepal Valley, the cultural and political heart of the Kingdom of Nepal. The people of the valley are divided into two general groups: Parbatiyās (hill men) and Newars. The Parbatiyās comprise immigrant Hindu groups who speak Nepali, an Indo-Aryan language. Newars speak Newari (a Tibeto-Burman language), and are the ancient inhabitants of the valley, ruling it until overthrown by the Parbatiyā and Gurung confederation in the eighteenth century. Some authorities have connected the Newars with the Nāyars of southern India, and although the linguistic correspondence between the names of the two groups is dubious, there are certain striking parallels between Newar social organization and the Dravidian south. A Dravidian element in the Nepal Valley would not be surprising since there are Dravidian tribes practically on the Nepal-India border.

In addition to the Newar-Parbatiyā distinction, the peoples of the valley are further divided along sectarian lines into Buddhists and Hindus. Although the mass of Newars were traditionally Buddhist, their kings, the Mallas, were Hindu. Thus Hinduism enjoyed royal patronage and protection. Although Buddhism was tolerated, it began to decline and was further hastened in decline by the Hindu fanaticism of the Rānās, the ruling clan among the conquering Parbatiyās. Both the Newars and the Parbatiyās are caste societies and each community is subdivided into a full range of castes. Thus two separate caste systems exist side by side in a common territory. The major Newar castes are: Brāhmaṇ, Gubhāju, Śreṣtha, Uray, Jyāpu, Nay, Pore, and Chami. The first five are clean castes, the others unclean. Brāhmaṇs and Gubhāju are priestly castes—Hindu and Buddhist, respectively. The Śreṣthas and Urays are merchant castes, again respectively Hindu and Buddhist. The Jyāpus are the dominant agricultural caste, and although predominantly Buddhist, many attempt to raise their status by adopting Hinduism and calling themselves Sreṣthas. Traditionally butchers and musicians, the Nays are Buddhists. Pores and Chamis are untouchable sweepers. Fundamentally, the Newar caste structure with its basic division into clean castes and unclean castes corresponds to the generalized Pahāṛi twofold division, but its cleavage along sectarian lines, producing a dual hierarchy among the higher castes, is reminiscent of the Dravidian pattern.

From the Parbatiyā point of view, Nepal society is divided into "drunkards" (Matwalis) and those who wear the sacred thread. The Matwalis include all of the Tibeto-Burman groups, and the appellation refers to their habit of drinking alcoholic beverages. The major Parbatiyā castes are: Brāhman, ṭhākuri, Chetri (Khas), Sārki, Kāmi, and Damai. Here again, the basic division is twofold, separating the twice-born Brāhmaṇs, Thākuris, and Chetris from the untouchable Sārkis, Kāmis, and Damais. The major Brāhmaṇ caste is the Upādhyāya or Purbi (eastern). Both ṭhākuris and Chetris claim Kṣatriya status and both have shared in the political dominance of Nepal. The royal house of Saha comes from the ṭhākuri caste, and the once all-powerful Rānās were Chetris. The Sārkis are shoemakers, the Kāmis blacksmiths, and the Damais tailors.

The major ethnic groups of Sikkim are Bhotiyas, Lepchas, and various Nepalese immigrants. Lepchas are Tibeto-Burman and constitute the chief aboriginal and tribal element in the population. Formerly swidden cultivators, they now cultivate wet rice on irrigated hillside terraces. The Bhotiyas are not the same as the Bhotiyas of Nepal, though both groups derive from Tibet. Bhotiya, Bhot, and Bhotya are common names for Tibetans throughout Nepal and northern India. Bhotiyas migrated to Sikkim and Bhutan sometime in the seventeenth century. In both states they played a major role in the formation of central political power, welding the Lepcha and other tribes into a feudal system. The tribal chiefs retained their lands and were transformed into an aristocracy. In the nineteenth and twentieth centuries Nepalese castes and tribes began migrating into Sikkim where marginal cultivable lands were unoccupied. Today these Hindu immigrants outnumber both the Lepchas and the Bhotiyas. Intermarriage, a common language (Sikkimese), a common faith (Buddhism), and more-or-less equal participation in government administration have leveled the differences between Bhotiyas and Lepchas, but the Nepalese constitute a segmented group, do not intermarry with Lepchas or Bhotiyas, and maintain their adherence to Hinduism. Because the Nepalese have not established economic or political dominance, Sikkim still remains relatively free of caste.

In the foothills and valley plains of the Assam-Bhutan border are the Mech and Kachari tribes belonging to the Bodo branch of Tibeto-Burman. Other sections of the Kacharis or Kochs are scattered throughout the Assam highlands. The Kacharis on the Bhutan border have been largely Hinduized and are now part of the caste structure of the Assam Valley, but the more remote Kacharis still persist as independent swidden cultivators.

A horseshoe curve running eastward from Bhutan along the Assam-Tibet frontier and then south along the Assam-Burma border encloses a remote mountainous area inhabited by tribals. It includes the Northeast Frontier Agency, the Naga Hills (Nagaland), Manipur, the Shillong Plateau, the Lushai Hills, and the Chittagong hill tracts. Despite the determined efforts of Hindus, Ahoms, Muslims, Tibetans, British, and Japanese, the tribes of the northeast frontier have never been completely subjugated. Although there is much variability among the tribes of this region, they do share some common features. Nearly all are Tibeto-Burman and the majority are swidden cultivators. Many incorporated headhunting, ritual feasting, and distribution of wealth into a system for the achievement of individual status, and nearly all erect memorial stones or pillars commemorating these feasts. Most are divided into exogamous patrilineal clans and have little or no political unity above the village or clan level. Except in the more accessible areas, they have been little influenced by Hinduism and Buddhism, adhering instead to their tribal cults. Their easy-going gaiety, independence, and individualism contrasts sharply with the dour, subdued, and downtrodden Hindu peasant.

Akas, Daflas, Apa Tanis, Abors, Miris, and Mishmis are among the more important tribes of the Northeast Frontier Agency. All are Tibeto-Burman and, except for the Apa Tanis, all are swidden cultivators. The Apa Tanis follow a pattern of intensive wet-rice cultivation. Since the Chinese border incident in 1962, the Northeast Frontier Agency has become a highly strategic area. New military roads and fortifications have been built and new attempts to bring these tribes under effective administrative control have been initiated. If these efforts are successful, the old, independent tribal way of life may be extinguished.

The Naga Hills are inhabited by a congeries of Tibeto-Burman Naga tribes. Fiercely independent, the Nagas have thwarted every effort to bring them to heel. Even today they mount occasional harassing raids on the Indian police and railways. The Nagas desire complete independence from India and have even attempted to present their case in the United Nations. Like many other Assam tribes, the Nagas were formerly infamous headhunters. With few exceptions they are primarily swidden cultivators.

Just south of the Naga Hills is the tiny principality of Manipur, inhabited by Hindus and Naga and Kuki tribes. Hindu peasants occupy the fertile valley floor while the Tibeto-Burman tribals live in the surrounding hills where they practice swidden cultivation. Famous for its distinctive dance form and the origin of polo, Manipur is the most densely populated region in the whole northeast frontier.

Directly west of Manipur is the Shillong Plateau, home of the Mikir, Khasi, Garo, and Kachari tribes. Garos, Mikirs, and Kacharis are Tibeto-Burmans, but the Khasis are Khmers. Most are swidden cultivators. Unlike the majority of Assam tribes, the Khasis and Garos have matrilineal descent and inheritance.

South of Manipur are the the Lushai Hills and the Chittagong hill tracts. The Lushai Hills are occupied by the Tiberto-Burman-Lushai and Lakher tribes. Moghs and Chakmas are among the principal tribes of Chittagong.

Brāhmaṇs

Unlike most other castes, Brāhmaṇs are found throughout India. They are the main purveyors and protectors of Hindu ritualism and the Sanskritic tradition. Historically, the Brāhmaṇs played a major role in the formulation and dissemination of sacred tradition, and no upstart ruler could legitimately claim Kṣatriya status or have a respectable court without a resident Brāhmaṇ advisor. Throughout Indian history parvenue kings and petty rājahs sent off for Brāhmaṇs often before the corpses of the previous palace occupants had been decently disposed of. Kings built elaborate temples endowed with lands for their Brāhmaṇ guests and supported them with gifts and outright grants of land.

In the *Puruṣa Sūkta* of the *Ṛg Veda*, the Brāhmaṇ varṇa originates from the sacrifice of the divine being Prajāpati, but all Brāhmaṇs are also traditionally descended from seven (in some cases, eight) great sages (ṛsis). The patrilineal descendants of each sage constitute a gotra. Each gotra is divided into gaṇas and each gaṇa is defined by the names of its founders (pravaras). There are exceptions, but each gaṇa should have one pravara name in common. For example, the Āgastya gotra, founded by the sage Āgastya, would have the name Āgastya in the pravara of each of its gaṇas. The system is actually based on a segmentary patrilineage and can best be illustrated diagrammatically as in Figure 41 (see Karve, 1953, 60–61). In Figure 41 the gotra name is Āgastya, named for its founding sage. The gotra is divided into 18 gaṇas—Idmavāha, Sāmbhāva, Māyobhuva, and so on. The pravara is found by reading up from the bottom name to the top. Thus one pravara is: Idmavāha, Dṛḍacyuta, Āgastya; another is: Sāmbhavāha, Dṛḍacyuta, Āgastya, and so on. The general rule is that any two persons sharing one pravara name are related and therefore forbidden to marry. In fact, the Brāhmaṇ gotra is a mythical charter and not all Brāhmaṇs are descended from the seven sages. Historically, the non-Brāhmaṇ priests of many different castes have become Brāhmaṇs.

In addition to the gotra divisions which regulate marriage, Brāhmaṇs are divided into three groups (śākhās) for ritual purposes. Each Brāhmaṇ caste follows a set of ritual procedures set forth in one of three Vedic schools: Ṛg, Yajus, Sāman. Each school has a set (or several different sets) of ritual

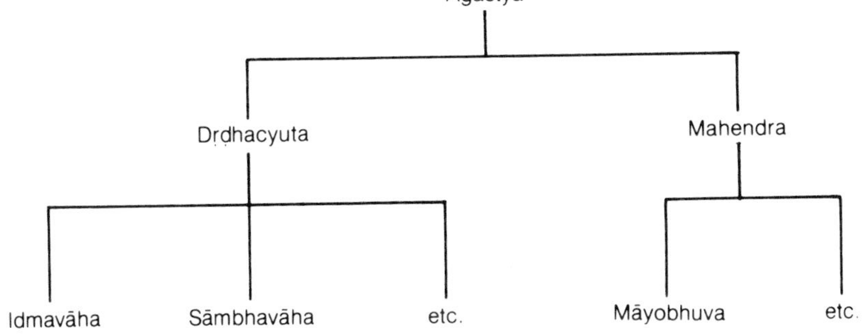

Figure 41. Āgastya gotra.

books *(Gṛhya Sūtras)* specifying the rules of ritual performance. A part of every Brāhmaṇ's religious duty is the salutation of his ancestors at the close of his prayers. This salutation includes recitation of his own name, gotra name, pravara names, sūtra name, and śāka name.

Brāhmaṇs are also classified by region and dietary prohibitions. The southern or Panc Drāvida Brāhmaṇs are pure vegetarians while the northern or Panc Gauda Brāhmaṇs may eat fish. As the names imply, each division traditionally contains five sections. Included in the Panc Drāvida division are: Drāvida Brāhmaṇs of Tamilnad and Kerala; Āndhra Brāhmaṇs of Āndhra Pradesh; Karnāṭaka Brāhmaṇs of Mysore; Mahārāshtra Brāhmaṇs of Mahārāshtra; and Gurjara Brāhmaṇs of Gujarāt. The Panc Gauda division includes: Sāraswat Brāhmaṇs of the Panjāb; Gaur Brāhmaṇs near Delhi; Kānakubja or Kanaujia Brāhmaṇs from the Ganges in eastern Uttar Pradesh; Maithil Brāhmaṇs of Bihār; and Utkal Brāhmaṇs of Orissa.

Sectarian differences further divide Brāhmaṇs. In the broadest terms they are either Vaiṣṇavas or Śaivites, but both of these sects are broken into numerous subsects. In the south, Vaiṣṇavas are divided into Mādhavas and Śrī Vaiṣṇavas; the latter again are subdivided into northern (vaṭakalai) and southern (teṅkalai) sects. In the north, Vaiṣṇavas are divided into followers of Rāma and followers of Kṛṣṇa. The former are subdivided into Mādhavas, Rāmanandis, Kabīrpanthīs, and so on. Followers of Kṛṣṇa are similarly divided into subsects, the most important being Chaitanyas and Rādhā-Vallabhas. Śaivites are either Śaivites proper or Smārthas.

Brāhmaṇs are sometimes classified on the basis of occupation. Those who follow the traditional Brāhmaṇ occupations of studying and teaching the Vedas and performing rituals are frequently called Vaidika or Ved Brāhmaṇs. Those who follow clean, secular occupations are called Laukikas. Theoretically, many occupations are closed to Brāhmaṇs except in times of dire necessity. Brāhmaṇs, for example, should not till the soil nor should they traffic in unclean things. Those who follow traditional occupations are classed as priests, teachers (gurus), or pandits (scholars). Priests are either temple priests (pūjāri) or family priests (purohitas). The latter are attached to a family or group of families and serve the family altar through rituals or the keeping of genealogies.

Finally, Brāhmaṇs are divided into a multitude of named endogamous patrilineal groups. These in turn are often divided into smaller subsections. Thus, for example, the Smārtha Brahacharanam Brāhmaṇs of Tamilnad are divided into nine sections, most of which refuse to intermarry.

Not all Brāhmaṇs are of equal rank. Although there is no all-India hierarchy and specific Brāhmaṇ ranks are always determined at the local level, some general criteria have universal application. Those who follow traditional occupations and observe orthodox rules of ritual purity are higher than those who do not. Among the orthodox who follow traditional occupations, scholars and family priests are higher than temple priests. Finally, priests who serve high-ranking families are higher than those who serve low-ranking families. Among those who no longer follow traditional occupations, government employment is higher ranking than other forms of work. The overall ranking

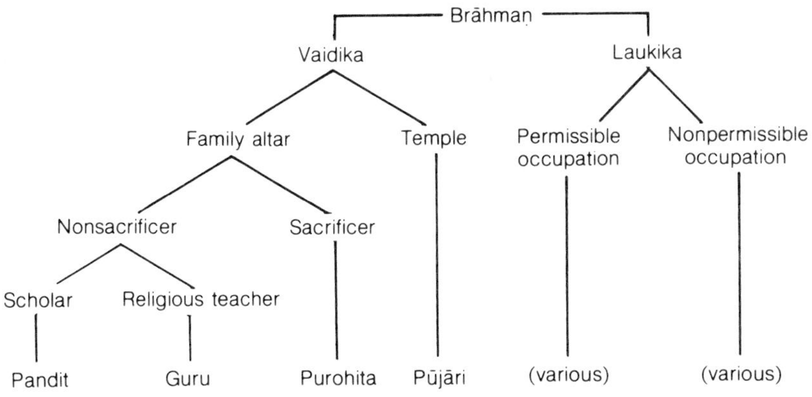

Figure 42. Ranking criteria among Brāhmaṇs.

system is illustrated in Figure 42, where ranking is from left to right. The pandit is higher than the nonmonastic guru and so on. This is a very generalized picture of a complex process that is more fully treated in Chapter 8.

Ascetics

Sacred literature prescribes that a man who has fulfilled his obligations to this world through Vedic study, household sacrifices, and progeny should spend his remaining years as a homeless ascetic seeking spiritual perfection. Although most men do not become wandering ascetics (sannyāsi), preferring instead a more comfortable symbolic gesture, ascetics are a ubiquitous part of the Indian scene and the ascetic and the model of asceticism are held in high esteem. In the broadest terms these homeless seekers are either cenobitic swāmis (monks) who are members of a monastic order or simply anchoritic private individuals unaffiliated with any religious order. The latter are often called sādhus, but this term is also used in a wider sense for all ascetics.

Under the influence of Buddhist and Jain monasticism, Hindu reformers established monastic orders, and today each Hindu sect is divided into a community of celibates and a community of lay members. Patterns vary from sect to sect, but in general each monastic order is led by a guru (teacher, spiritual advisor) and contains a group of initiates and a group of novitiates. Training of novitiates entails not only religious instruction and the practice of a form of meditation (yoga) designed to bring about spiritual enlightenment, it also includes a year-long period of wandering as a homeless beggar. Originally the monastic orders seem to have accepted only Brāhmaṇs as members, but caste restrictions were later dropped, at least in theory. In fact, one who becomes an ascetic is outside the caste system and the system of values and rules governing ordinary life. He has given up all desire for wealth and progeny, and has no need of ritual or of the gods. He is living his last incarnation and will not be reborn.

It is commonly believed that the ascetic has acquired enormous holy power through meditation, and that one acquires merit merely from beholding a holy man. A holy man communicates power not only by sight (darśan), but equally by touch, and anything that has come into contact with a holy man becomes prasād, a divine gift imbued with holiness. In addition to darśan and prasād, a holy man also communicates directly with the laity through instruction (upadeś). An ascetic is believed to have direct access to both spiritual and secular knowledge, and though he is not usually a permanent family advisor, he can be called on for both spiritual and secular advice. Unlike the priest, an ascetic is not a ritualist. He is above family rituals and does not perform them. Similarly, he is above the gods, blesses them, does not worship them, and takes no part in temple rituals devoted to them.

What the laity thinks an ascetic should be conforms to a well-defined model with scriptural authority. An ascetic has certain signs: he seldom smiles, eats little, is celibate, and always speaks the truth. His appearance accords with the iconographic representation of all great Indian religious teachers with their rather severe, remote, and slightly bored facial expressions. An ascetic's continence and abstention from excessive eating are not necessarily indicated by outward signs, for an ascetic is technically a corpse. Thus it is not the ascetic who eats, excessively or otherwise, or who possibly fornicates, it is only his gross body. Consequently, an ascetic is endowed with a cosmic appetite and enormous sexual powers. In fact, most ascetics are abstinent and continent, but the general belief is that their mind control is such that if they were inabstinent and incontinent, their appetites would be superhuman.

In part, the mendicant aspect of the ascetic's life constitutes a mission, the transmission of spiritual values to villagers, and is one of the main links between the great tradition of Hinduism and village Hinduism. When a monk arrives in a village he is preceded by a drummer boy who announces his arrival. After bathing and meditating outside the temple (inside would be beneath him), he begs food from seven different houses. When he has dined, the villagers gather around while he reads and explains scriptures. Then, following his lead, all join in singing devotional songs (bhajans). Next morning the monk rises before the villagers and proceeds to the next village.

In the formative period of monasticism, mendicant monks wandered from place to place engaging in religious debate with monks and the learned of other sects, championing and spreading the doctrine of their own particular sect. Today, disputation between orders takes place mainly at an assembly of monks (khumba mela) held every six years at such auspicious localities as Hardwar, Allahabad, or Nasik. The central feature of the assembly is a dip in the Ganges accompanied by chanting. The ranking of monastic orders is determined by the order of entering the river. The 91 different orders are led by the Nāga monks from the Himālayas. With their matted hair, bodies smeared with sandalwood ash, and trisul (three-pronged fork), the Nāgas most closely approximate the iconographic Śiva, patron of all ascetics. They are followed by the Dasanāmī (ten names), founded by the great religious teacher Saṅkarācārya. His four disciples founded monasteries in the four corners of India and set the original pattern for monastic life. They wear the classic ochre robe, speak Sanskrit among themselves, and are regarded as the most scholastic order. Next come the Udāsins and Vairāgis. The latter carry a cinta (two iron rods fastened together by iron rings and festooned with bells) for fighting the Nāgas. In the past the khumba mela seems to have been a kind of wrestling match between different orders and the Vairāgis continue this tradition, contesting with the Nāgas for the first dip. All the other orders, including the spectacular Aghoris who carry a bleached human skull as their drinking vessel, follow in turn. Each order is assigned a camping ground on the river bank where they set up large tents for audiences. After the dip in the Ganges, they return to their camps and engage in debate and discussion. They discuss not only sectarian differences, but also deliberate any pending government legislation that might have religious implications. Laymen from all walks of life attend their sessions for darśan and instruction.

Modern Indian intellectuals are divided in their attitudes toward ascetics. Some, like the late Pandit Nehru, argue that the ascetic has had his day; his ideas are redundant and no longer necessary. The ascetic is a parasite who makes no contribution to social and economic change, but instead opposes it. Others feel that the ascetic is the truest expression of India's "spiritualism," and that even if most cannot follow the ascetic pattern, it represents a tradition worthy of emulation. On the whole, these are squabbles among intellectuals of little or no relevance to the great mass of Indians who revere ascetics as living deities.

Muslims

Like the Brāhmans, Muslims are widely distributed in India, residing in nearly every state and district. Many of India's Muslims are descendants of Islamic invaders and Arab traders, but the vast majority are converts from Hindu castes and tribes. Muslims in India are traditionally divided into four classes: Shaikh, Sayyid, Mughal, and Pathān. The term Shaikh is properly restricted to the descendants of Muhammed's two fathers-in-law (Abu Bakr Siddīk and Umar ul Fārūk) and uncle (Abbās). Sayyids descended from the prophet's son-in-law Ali and daughter Fātimah. Sayyids are often Pīrs (spiritual guides) to other Muslim families. The Mughals are either Persian (Irāni) or Turkish (Turāni) converts to Islam. The Pathāns, originally descendants of Afghān invaders, now form an important tribe on the Pakistan-Afghānistan border.

Muslims are also divided into sects and subsects. The most important division is between Sunnis and Shiahs. Shiahs hold that the spiritual leadership of Islam (the caliphate) should have descended to Ali and his sons Hassan and Hussein. Consequently, they reject all the caliphs and maintain that there are twelve Imāms (spiritual leaders), the last of which will return as a Messiah (Mahdi). Shiahs also reject the four great schools of Sunni tradition and have developed their own. Shiahs are further subdivided on points of succession in the Imamate into Zaidiyah and Ismaili subsects. The major event in Shiah history is the slaughter and martyrdom of Hussein by the second caliph. This event is commemorated in the festival of Muharram. Shiahs are supposedly more liberal than Sunnis, who are by reputation orthodox and conservative. They adhere to the succession of caliphs and claim to be followers of the "one way."

All Muslims of whatever sect acknowledge observance of the five pillars of faith: belief in Allah as the one god and Muhammed as his prophet, five daily prayers, the fast of Ramazān, the giving of alms, and pilgrimage to Mecca. In addition to the Muharrram festival celebrated by the Shiahs, Muslims also observe two Id festivals, one at the end of the fast of Ramazān and the other on the tenth of the last month of the Islamic year. The Muslim temple is the mosque in which weekly services are held on Fridays. In charge of the mosque is the Mulla, a priest who proclaims the call to prayers, leads prayers, and often runs a small religious school in the mosque courtyard. More important than the Mulla is the Maulvi who is versed in Islamic law and acts as a preceptor and preacher. Another officiant, the Kāzi, was once an important civil functionary, but is now only a leader of public prayers at the Id festival and keeper of a register of marriages and divorces.

The sacred text of Islam is the *Korān*, the direct word of Allah revealed to Muhammed through the angel Gabriel. Written in Arabic, the *Korān* is held in great reverence, protected from contamination, and, as the word of God, regarded as the repository of law. Supplementing the *Korān* are the traditions and sayings of the prophet, known as Hadis or Sunnah. Next in importance to the traditions are the schools of law. Each major sect has its own collections of law, differing from one another.

Although Islam does not recognize caste, most Muslims in India belong to castes, prohibit intermarriage between castes, and follow restrictions on giving and receiving food between different castes. On the whole, Muslims follow most of the patterns of social organization prevalent in the area where they live, but there are some features common to Muslims in all areas. Parallel-cousin marriage (marriage with a father's brother's or mother's sister's child) is the preferred form of marriage, and there are rituals for both male and female initiation and for circumcision. In orthodox tradition, women should be kept in rigorous seclusion (pardah), hidden away in a back part of the house known as the zenāna, or deeply veiled when seen in public. Contrary to Hindu practice, divorce is recognized and both the husband and the wife may exercise this right. Muslims and Hindus similarly disagree over questions of diet. Orthodox Hinduism enjoins vegetarianism, but Islam permits meat-eating if the animal has been slain according to custom. Pork is forbidden. Both Muslims and Hindus are supposedly teetotalers. Theoretically, a Muslim should not eat with Hindus or eat food prepared by Hindus, for they are idolators; in practice, however, this restriction is rarely observed.

Muslims are found in every occupation and profession, and their status in the caste hierarchy varies from family to family, caste to caste, village to village, and region to region. In some places they are homologized with the Kṣatriya varṇa, in others with the Vaiśya varṇa, but most often their status is roughly equivalent to that of various artisan and specialist castes in the middle ranges of the hierarchy.

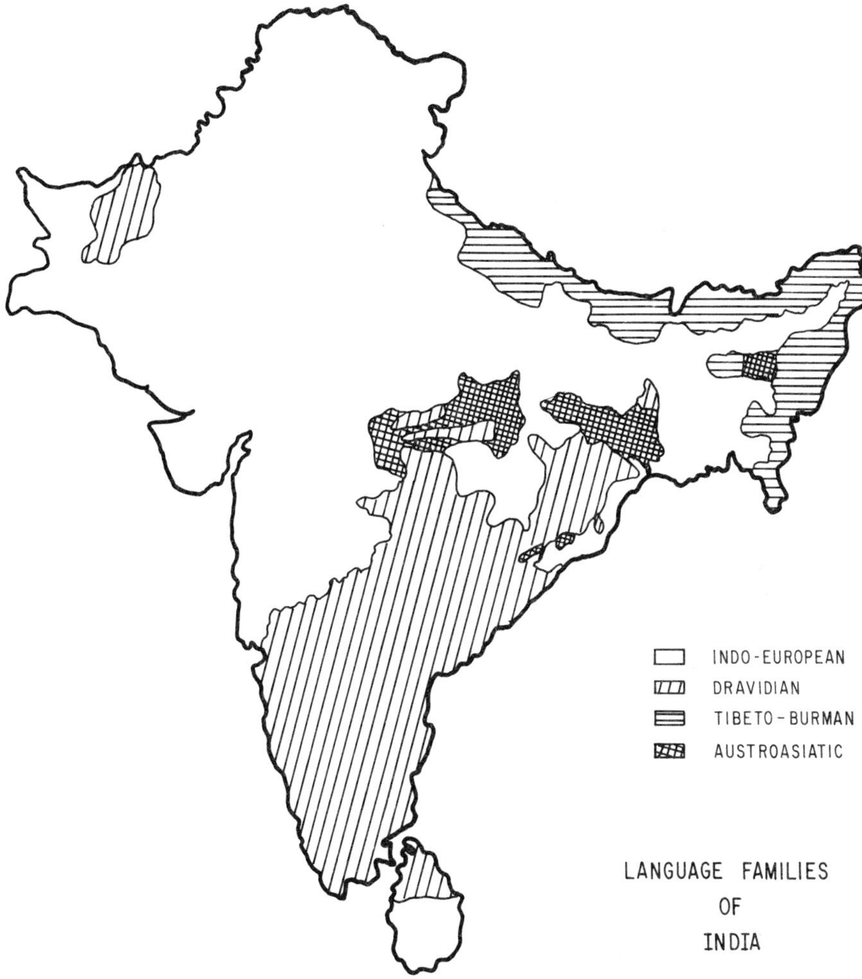
INDO-EUROPEAN
DRAVIDIAN
TIBETO-BURMAN
AUSTROASIATIC
LANGUAGE FAMILIES
OF
INDIA

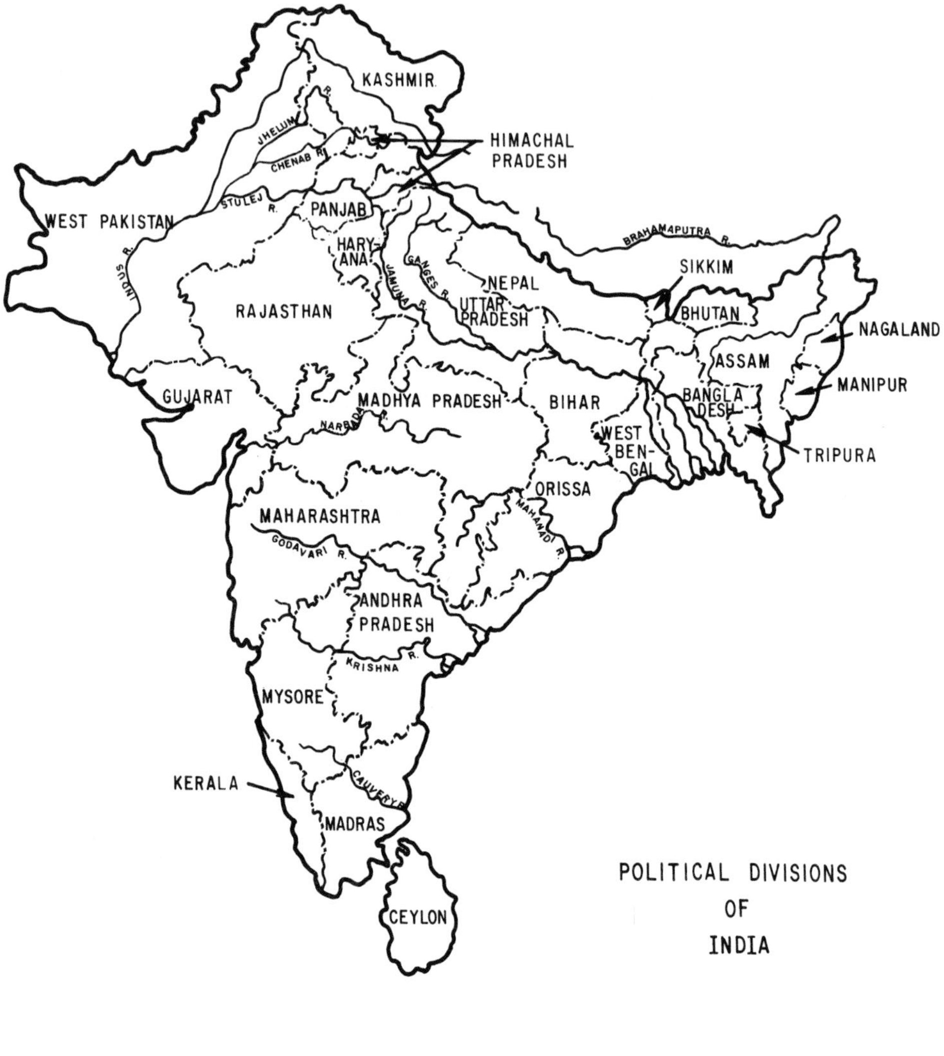

POLITICAL DIVISIONS
OF
INDIA

Appendix IV

BIBLIOGRAPHY

GENERAL BIBLIOGRAPHICAL NOTE

Items listed in the bibliography have either been used directly in this work or are cited as standard references for further reading. Many of these contain excellent bibliographies, but in addition there are several valuable bibliographic studies available to students of Indian culture, of which some of the more useful are listed below. For further information on Indian bibliography, see: Patrick Wilson, A survey of bibliographies on southern Asia, Journal of Asian Studies, 18 (1957); and, by the same author, Bibliography of Indian bibliographies, Berkeley: University of California Institute of International Studies (1957); and Maureen L. P. Patterson, Bibliographical control for South Asian studies, The Library Quarterly, 41:2, 83–105 (1971).

Bibliographic Studies

Fürer-Haimendorf, Elizabeth von
1958 An anthropological bibliography of South Asia. Paris: Mouton. Vol. 1, 1958; vol. 2, 1964; vol. 3, 1970.

India (Government) Anthropology (Department of)
1956 Cumulative index to current literature on anthropology and allied subjects. Calcutta: Government Press.

Journal of Asian Studies
Annual bibliography.

Kantikar, J. M., ed.
1960 A bibliography of Indology, Vol. 1, Indian Anthropology. Calcutta: National Library.

Spencer, Dorothy M.
1960 Indian fiction in English. Philadelphia: University of Pennsylvania Press.

Wilson, Patrick
1957 South Asia: a selected bibliography on India, Pakistan, and Ceylon. New York: Institute of Pacific Relations.

NOTES TO PART 1

There is little of a systematic nature on Indian personality formation, but see Carstairs (1957), Minturn (1963), and Steed (1955). On characteristic patterns of Indian thought, see Bharati (1966).

Although some of the material is dated, the standard work on Indian geography is still Spate (1967). Also useful but less detailed are Ginsburg (1958) and Spencer (1954). Geographic factors in archeological regions are discussed in Richards (1933) and Subbarao (1958).

The standard reference and bibliographic guide for Indian linguistics is Sebeok (1969).

NOTES TO PART 2

Indian archaeology is ably summarized by the Allchins (1968) and Wheeler (1968). Earlier but still useful are Gordon (1958) and Piggott (1950). Somewhat dated but popular is Wheeler (1959). On the Indus script, see Dani (1963) and Hunter (1934). For a thorough evaluation of recent "translations," see Zide and Zvelebil (1970).

The principal source for Vedic India is Keith (1925). See also Basham (1954, 28–43), and the relevant chapters in Majumdar (1951). For references to translations of the original Sanskrit texts, refer to the bibliographies in Basham and Majumdàr. One-volume selections from Sanskrit literature are useful; see, for example, Radhakrishnan and Moore (1957) and de Bary (1958). On the Asura myth, see Brown (1942).

For Buddhism, Conze (1951) is easily available and readable, but earlier works such as Eliot (1922) are still standard. See the bibliographies in these works and in Basham (1954) for translations of original sources. Stevenson (1915) is still a standard work on Jainism, but for an outstanding semantic analysis of Jainist categories, see Durbin (1970). Outlines of all the heterodox sects can be found in Basham (1954), Dās Gupta (1922–1955), and Renou (1958). On Tantrism, see Bharati (1965). In the latter study, note particularly the pattern of homologies between different traditions.

The six philosophical systems are summarized in various works. See, for example, Dās Gupta (1922–1955), Radhakrishnan (1923–1927), and Zimmer (1951). Translated selections are available in de Bary (1958) and Radhakrishnan and Moore (1957). From an anthropological point of view, the best account of Yoga is Eliade (1958).

The evolution of Hinduism is complex, but see the able discussion in Basham (1954, 297–345). In general, the best additional reading in this section is to be found in the available translations of the original sources.

All references to Upaniṣadic literature are to translations in Hume (1921).

NOTES TO PART 3

The best description of a hunting-and-gathering tribe is Fürer-Haimendorf's work on the Chenchus (1943). Of the many swidden agriculturalists, see the descriptions in Burling (1963), Grigson (1949), and Vidyarthi (1963). For descriptions of pastoralism, see Barth (1956), Fürer-Haimendorf (1964), and Rivers (1906).

There is no end of village studies. Among the more useful are the collections in Marriott (1955) and West Bengal Government Press (1955). On a regional basis, see Beals (1962), Epstein (1962), and Ishwaran (1966) for Mysore; Dube (1955) and Hiebert (1971) for Āndhra Pradesh; Béteille (1965) and Sivertsen (1963) for Madras; Orenstein (1965) for Mahārāshtra; Chauhan (1967) for Rājasthān; Eglar (1960) for the Panjāb; Lewis (1958) for Uttar Pradesh; Berreman (1963) for the Pahāri region; Leach (1961) and Ryan (1958) for Ceylon. Fukutake et al. (1964) cover Gujarāt and Bengāl.

On village Hinduism, see the relevant chapters in the village studies cited above. See also Whitehead (1916).

There is a vast and generally unimpressive literature on community development. Two of the better works are Dube (1958) and Mayer (1958).

An excellent account of Indian social organization is Mandelbaum (1970). Though it has many shortcomings, the basic source on Indian kinship is Karve (1953). Also useful are Kapadia (1966) and Prabhu (1954). One of the best monographs on Indian family organization is Madan (1965). Kolenda (1968) documents variability in the joint family while Ross (1961) gives a rather simplistic view of joint-family adaptations to an urban setting. Other important works containing information on family and kinship are Dumont (1957), Mayer (1960), and Yalman (1967).

The literature on caste is enormous, but the most important single interpretive study is Dumont (1970*a*). Dumont's work draws on two important earlier sources, Bouglé (1908) and Hocart (1950). Other useful works are Blunt (1931), Dutt (1931), Ghurye (1961), Hutton (1946), and Ryan (1953). On the jajmānī system, see Beidelman (1959) and Wiser (1936).

NOTES TO APPENDICES

The literature on Indian tribes and castes is beyond summary. The interested student is advised to steep himself in the various tribes and castes series—for example, Enthoven (1920–1922), Ibbetson (1916), Iyer (1928–1935), Russell and Hīra Lāl (1916), and Thurston (1909). This should be followed by selected monographs on individual tribes and castes. Here it is possible to mention only a few examples. Certainly no anthropologist should be ignorant of Rivers' work on the Todas (1906), the Seligmans' on the Veddas (1911), or of Fürer-Haimendorf's study of the Chenchus (1943). Bodding's *Santal Medicine* (1925) and *The Santals and Disease* (1925) are two of the best anthropological accounts of primitive concepts of disease and medicine. Though some accuse him of romanticism, none have surpassed Elwin's empathy and understanding of Indian tribals, and few have matched the detail of his *The Muria and Their Ghotul* (1947).

Brāhmaṇ social organization is treated in separate sections in most of the tribes and castes literature. See, for example, Thurston (1909, vol. I, pp. 267–393). Dated but still useful on sectarian differences is Bhattacharya (1896). Farquhar (1911) provides an essential outline of Hindu sects.

On asceticism the best account is Bharati (1961), but Ghurye (1953) is also useful.

BIBLIOGRAPHY

Allchin, Bridget, and Raymond Allchin
1968 The birth of Indian civilization. Harmondsworth, England: Penguin.

Andronov, M.
1964 On the typological similarity of new Indo-Aryan and Dravidian. Language, 25:119–126.

Barth, Fredrik
1956 Indus and Swat Kohistan: an ethnographic survey. Oslo: Forenede Trykkerier.

Basham, A. L.
1954 The wonder that was India. New York: Macmillan.

Beals, Alan R.
1962 Gojalpur. New York: Holt, Rinehart, and Winston.

Beals, Alan R., and Bernard J. Siegel
1966 Divisiveness and social conflict: an anthropological approach. Stanford, Calif.: Stanford Univ. Press.

Beidelman, Thomas O.
1959 A comparative analysis of the jajmani system. Monograph of the Association for Asian Studies, no. 8. Locust Valley, N. Y.: Augustin.

Berreman, Gerald D.
1963 Hindus of the Himalayas. Berkeley and Los Angeles: Univ. of California Press.

Béteille, André
1965 Caste, class and power. Berkeley and Los Angeles: Univ. of California Press.

Bharati, Agehananda
1961 The ochre robe. London: Allen and Unwin.
1965 The Tantric tradition. London: Rider.
1966 A functional analysis of Indian thought and its social margins. New York: Rider.

Bhattacharya, Jogendra Nath
1896 Hindu castes and sects. Calcutta: Thacker, Spink.

Blunt, E. A. H.
1931 The caste system of northern India. London: Oxford Univ. Press.

Bodding, P. O.
1925 Santal medicine. Memoirs of the Asiatic Society of Bengal, 10, 2:133–426.

1925 The Santals and disease. Memoirs of the Asiatic Society of Bengal, 10, 2:1–131.

Bouglé, Célestin
1908 Essais sur le régime des castes. Paris: Felix Alcan.

Brown, W. Norman
1942 The creation myth of the Rig Veda. Journal of the American Oriental Society, 62:85–98.

Burling, Robbins
1963 Rengsanggri: family and kinship in a Garo village. Philadelphia: Univ. of Pennsylvania Press.

Carstairs, G. Morris
1957 The twice born: a study of a community of high caste Hindus. London: Hogarth.

Chauhan, Brij Raj
1967 A Rajasthan village. New Delhi: Associated Publishing House.

Conze, Edward
1951 Buddhism: its essence and development. New York: Philosophical Library.

Dani, A. H.
1963 Indian palaeography. London: Oxford Univ. Press.

Dās Gupta, Surendra Nath
1922 A history of Indian philosophy. Cambridge: Cambridge Univ. Press. Vol. 1, 1922; vol. 2, 1932; vol. 3, 1940; vol. 4, 1949; vol. 5, 1955.

de Bary, William Theodore, et al.
1958 Sources of Indian tradition. New York: Columbia Univ. Press.

Dube, S. C.
1955 Indian village. Ithaca, N. Y.: Cornell Univ. Press
1958 India's changing villages. Ithaca, N. Y.: Cornell Univ. Press.

Dumont, Louis
1957 Une sous caste de L'Inde du sud. Paris: Mouton.
1970*a* Homo hierarchicus: an essay on the caste system. Trans. by Mark Saintsbury. Chicago: Univ. of Chicago Press.
1970*b* Religion, politics and history in India. Paris: Mouton.

Durbin, Mridula
1970 The transformational model of linguistics and its implications for an ethnology of religion: a case study of Jainism. American Anthropologist, 72:334–342.

Dutt, Nripendra Kumar
1931 Origin and growth of caste in India. London: Kegan Paul, Trench, Trübner.

Eglar, Zekiye
1960 A Punjabi village in Pakistan. New York: Columbia Univ. Press.

Eliade, Mircea
1958 Yoga: immortality and freedom. Trans. by Willard R. Trask. New York: Bollingen.

Eliot, Sir Charles Norton Edgecumbe
1922 Hinduism and Buddhism: an historical sketch. London: Arnold. 3 vols.

Elwin, Verrier
1947 The Muria and their ghotul. Bombay: Oxford Univ. Press.

Emeneau, Murray B.
1856 India as a linguistic area. Language, 32:3–16.

Enthoven, R. E.
1920 The tribes and castes of Bombay. Bombay: Government Central Press. 3 vols.

Epstein, T. Scarlett
1962 Economic development and social change in south India. Manchester: Manchester Univ. Press.

Farquhar, J. N.
1911 A primer of Hinduism. London: Christian Literature Society for India.

Fukutake, Tadashi, Tsutomu Ouchi, and Chie Nakane
1964 The socio-economic structure of the Indian village. Tokyo: Institute of Asian Economic Affairs.

Fürer-Haimendorf, Christoph von
1943 The Chenchus: jungle folk of the Deccan. London: Macmillan.
1964 The Sherpas of Nepal: Buddhist highlanders. London: John Murray.

Ghurye, G. S.
1953 Indian sadhus. Bombay: Popular Book Depot.
1961 Caste, class, and occupation. Bombay: Popular Book Depot.

Ginsburg, Norton (ed.)
1958 The pattern of Asia. Englewood Cliffs, N. J.: Prentice-Hall.

Gordon, D. H.
1958 The prehistoric background of Indian culture. Bombay: Popular Book Depot.

Gough, E. Kathleen
1959 Criteria of caste ranking in south India. Man in India, 39:115–126.

Grigson, W. V.
1949 The Maria Gonds of Bastar. London: Oxford Univ. Press.

Guha, B. S.
1938 Racial elements in the Indian population. Bombay: Oxford Univ. Press.

Gumperz, John J.
1969 Communication in multilingual societies. *In* Cognitive anthropology, Stephen A. Tyler (ed.),. New York: Holt, Rinehart, and Winston.

Haddon, A. C.
1927 The wandering of peoples. Cambridge: Cambridge Univ. Press.

Hiebert, Paul G.
1971 Konduru: structure and integration in a south Indian village. Minneapolis: Univ. of Minnesota Press.

Hocart, A. M.
1950 Caste, a comparative study. London: Methuen.

Hume, Robert E.
1921 The thirteen principal Upaniṣads. London: Oxford Univ. Press.

Hunter, G. R.
1934 The script of Harappa and Mohenjo-daro. London: Kegan Paul.

Hutton, J. H.
1935 Census of India, 1931. Report, vol. I, pt. 1. New Delhi: Government of India.
1946 Caste in India: its nature, function, and origins. Cambridge: Cambridge Univ. Press.

Ibbetson, Denzil
1916 Panjab castes. Lahore: Government Printing Press.

Ishwaran, K.
1966 Tradition and economy in village India. London: Routledge and Kegan Paul.

Iyer, L. K. Anantha Krishna
1928–1935 The Mysore tribes and castes. Bangalore: Mysore Government Press. 4 vols.

Kapadia, K. M.
1966 Marriage and family in India, 3rd ed. Bombay: Oxford Univ. Press.

Karve, Irawati
1953 Kinship organization in India. Poona, Deccan, College Monograph Series, No. 11. Poona: Deccan College.

Keith, A. B.
1925 The religion and philosophy of the Veda and Upanishads. Harvard Oriental Series, vols. 31, 32. Cambridge, Mass.: Harvard Univ. Press. 2 vols.

Kolenda, Pauline Mahar

1968 Region, caste, and family structure: a comparative study of the Indian "joint" family. *In* Structure and change in Indian society, M. Singer and B. S. Cohn (eds.). Chicago: Aldine.

Leach, E. R.

1961 Pul Eliya, a village in Ceylon: a study of land tenure and kinship. Cambridge: Cambridge Univ. Press.

1967 Caste, class and slavery: the taxonomic problem. *In* Caste and race: comparative approaches, A. de Reuck and J. Knight (eds.). London: Churchill.

Lévi-Strauss, Claude

1949 The elementary structures of kinship. Trans. by James H. Bell and J. R. von Sturmer. Boston: Beacon Press (1969).

1964 Mythologiques: Le cru et le cuit. Paris: Libraire Plon.

1966 The savage mind. (*Trans. of* La pensée sauvage. Paris: Libraire Plon, 1962.) Chicago: Univ. of Chicago Press.

Lewis, Oscar

1958 Village life in northern India: studies in a Delhi village. Urbana: Univ. of Illinois Press.

Lynch, Owen M.

1969 The politics of untouchability. New York: Columbia Univ. Press.

Madan, T. N.

1965 Family and kinship: a study of the Pandits of rural Kashmir. New York: Asia Publishing House.

Majumdar, D. N.

1943 Blood groups of the tribes and castes of U.P. Journal of the Asiatic Society of Bombay, 10:240–267.

1961 Races and cultures of India. New York: Asia Publishing House.

Majumdar, R. C.

1951 The Vedic age. Vol. 1 of The history and culture of the Indian people. London: Allen Unwin.

Mandelbaum, David G.

1970 Society in India. Berkeley and Los Angeles: Univ. of California Press. 2 vols.

Marriott, McKim (ed.)

1955 Village India. Chicago: Univ. of Chicago Press.

1959 Interactional and attributional theories of caste ranking. Man in India, 39:92–107.

Mayer, Adrian C.

1960 Caste and kinship in central India: a village and its region. Berkeley and Los Angeles: Univ. of California Press.

Mayer, Albert
1958 Pilot project, India: the story of rural development at Etawah, U.P. Berkeley and Los Angeles: Univ. of California Press.

Minturn, Leigh
1963 The Rājpūts of Khalapur, India. *In* Six cultures: studies of child rearing, B. B. Whiting (ed.). New York: Wiley.

Myrdal, Gunnar
1968 Asian drama: an inquiry into the poverty of nations. New York: Random House

Orenstein, Henry
1965 Gaon: conflict and cohesion in an Indian village. Princeton: Princeton Univ. Press.

Piggott, Stuart
1950 Prehistoric India. Harmondsworth, England: Penguin.

Prabhu, Pandhari Nath
1954 Hindu social organization. Bombay: Popular Book Depot.

Radhakrishnan, Sir Sarvepalli
1923 Indian Philosophy. London: Allen and Unwin. 2 vols.

Radhakrishnan, Sir Sarvepalli, and Charles A. Moore
1957 A source book in Indian philosophy. Princeton: Princeton Univ. Press.

Renou, Louis
1958 L'Hindouisme: les textes, les doctrines et l'histoire. Paris: Univ. de France.

Richards, F. J.
1933 The geographical factors in Indian archaeology. The Indian Antiquary, 62:235–243.

Risley, Herbert H.
1915 The people of India, 2nd ed. London: Thacker.

Rivers, W. H. R.
1906 The Todas. London: Macmillan.

Ross, Aileen D.
1961 The Hindu family in its urban setting. Toronto: Univ. of Toronto Press.

Rosser, Colin
1966 Social mobility in the Newar caste system. *In* Caste and kin in Nepal, India, and Ceylon, C. von Fürer-Haimendorf (ed.). New York: Asia Publishing House.

Russell, R. V., and Rai Bahadur Hīra Lāl
1916 The tribes and castes of the Central Provinces of India. London: Macmillan. 4 vols.

Ryan, Bryce

1953 Sinhalese village. Coral Gables, Fla.: Univ. of Miami Press.

Sebeok, Thomas A.

1969 Linguistics in South Asia. Vol. 5 of Current trends in linguistics. The Hague: Mouton.

Seligman, C. G., and Brenda Z. Seligman

1911 The Veddas. Cambridge: Cambridge Univ. Press.

Sivertsen, Dagfinn

1963 When caste barriers fall. New York: Humanities Press.

Spate, O. H. K.

1967 India and Pakistan: a general and regional geography, 3rd ed. London: Methuen.

Spencer, J. E.

1954 Asia east by south: a cultural geography. New York: Wiley.

Srinivas, M. N.

1956 A note on Sanskritization and Westernization. Far Eastern Quarterly, 15:481–496.

Steed, Gitel P.

1955 Notes on an approach to a study of personality formation in a Hindu village in Gujarat. *In* Village India, M. Marriott (ed.). Chicago: Univ. of Chicago Press.

Stevenson, Mrs. Sinclair T.

1915 The heart of Jainism. London: Oxford Univ. Press.

Subbarao, B.

1958 The personality of India. Baroda: Univ. of Baroda.

Thurston, Edgar

1909 Castes and tribes of southern India. Madras: Government Press. 7 vols.

Tyler, Stephen A. (ed.)

1969 Cognitive anthropology. New York: Holt, Rinehart, and Winston.

Vidyarthi, L. P.

1963 The Maler: a study in nature-man-spirit complex of a hill tribe. Calcutta: Bookland Private.

West Bengal Government Press

1955 India's villages. Calcutta: West Bengal Government Press.

Wheeler, Sir Mortimer

1959 Early India and Pakistan. New York: Praeger.

1968 The Indus civilization, 3rd ed. Cambridge: Cambridge Univ. Press.

Whitehead, Henry

1916 The village gods of south India. London: Oxford Univ. Press.

Wiser, William H.
1936 The Hindu jajmani system: a socio-economic system inter-relating members of a Hindu village community in service. Lucknow: Lucknow.

Yalman, Nur
1967 Under the bo tree: studies in caste, kinship and marriage in the interior of Ceylon. Berkeley and Los Angeles: Univ. of California Press.

Zide, A., and K. Zvelebil
1970 [Review of various published attempts to translate the Indus script.] Language, 46:952–968.

Zimmer, Heinrich
1951 Philosophies of India. New York: Bollingen.

INDEX